W9-CAZ-319

Best Resumes and CVs
for International Jobs

BEST RESUMES AND CVs

For International Jobs

Your Passport to the Global Job Market

Ronald L. Krannich, Ph.D.
Wendy S. Enelow, CPRW, JCTC, CCM

IMPACT PUBLICATIONS
Manassas Park, VA

BEST RESUMES AND CVs FOR INTERNATIONAL JOBS

Copyright © 2002 by Ronald L. Krannich and Wendy S. Enelow. All rights reserved. Printed in the United States of America. No part of this book may be used or reproduced in any manner whatsoever without written permission of the publisher: IMPACT PUBLICATIONS, 9104 Manassas Drive, Suite N, Manassas Park, VA 20111, Tel. 703-361-7300, Fax 703-335-9486, of e-mail: info@impactpublications.com.

Warning/Liability/Warranty: The authors and publisher have made every attempt to provide the reader with accurate, timely, and useful information. However, given the rapid changes taking place in today's job market, some information in this book, especially URLs of employment websites, may become obsolete. We regret any inconvenience such changes may have for your job search. The information presented here is for reference purposes only. The authors and publisher make no claims that using this information will guarantee the reader a job. The authors and publisher shall not be liable for any losses or damages incurred in the process of following the advice in this book.

Library of Congress Cataloguing-in-Publication Data

Krannich, Ronald L.
    Best resumes and CVs for international jobs: your passport to the global job market/
Ronald L. Krannich, Wendy S. Enelow
        p.   cm.
    Includes bibliographical references and index.
    ISBN 1-57023-183-4
    1. Resumes (Employment) I. Enelow, Wendy S. II. Title.

2002   2002107668

Publisher: For information on Impact Publications, including current and forthcoming publications, authors, press kits, online bookstores, catalogs, affiliate program, and submission requirements, visit our website: www.impactpublications.com.

Publicity/Rights: For information on publicity, author interviews, and rights, contact the Media Relations Department: Tel. 703-361-7300, Fax 703-335-9486, or info@impactpublications.com.

Sales/Distribution: All bookstore sales are handled through Impact's trade distributor: National Book Network, 15200 NBN Way, Blue Ridge Summit, PA 17214, Tel. 1-800-462-6420. All other sales and distribution inquiries should be directed to the publisher: Sales Department, IMPACT PUBLICATIONS, 9104 Manassas Drive, Suite N, Manassas Park, VA 20111-5211, Tel. 703-361-7300, Fax 703-335-9486, or e-mail: info@impactpublications.com.

Contents

5   Resume Examples By Special Populations 157

Best Resumes and CVs
for International Jobs

1

Global Resumes for International Jobs

L ANDING AN INTERNATIONAL JOB IS ALL ABOUT COMMUNICATING your qualifications to employers through the most efficient and effective method possible – the resume or curriculum vitae (CV). This career summary document, in turn, should grab the attention of employers so they will invite you to a job interview where you must then sell yourself for a job.

A Perfect Picture of Fitness

Above all, your resume or CV must be a picture-perfect presentation of your skills, abilities, and accomplishments. While it must avoid many common writing and presentation errors (see Chapter 2), including the lack of cross-cultural sensitivity, your resume or CV must focus on satisfying the expectations of hiring personnel who have a universal problem to solve that transcends national boundaries – finding and hiring someone who can *add value* to their organization or company. They want someone who will be the perfect fit for the job, however ill-defined and disorganized that job may be. Your challenge is to both meet and exceed their expectations with a job-winning resume that outclasses the competition. Best of all, you want to help the employer better define his needs and the job as requiring *your* particular expertise. You do this by creating a resume that clearly communicates to employers your most likely future success, based on a concise and powerful presentation of your past performance, skills, and accomplishments.

That's our task in the following pages – to make sure you are presenting your qualifications in the best manner possible by writing and delivering a resume that clearly communicates what you have done, can do, and will do for an employer. Within the space of one, two, or three pages, it must quickly grab the attention and sustain the interest of employers who will want to see the real you in person by inviting you to an interview. The very first impression it makes should be similar to a good ad or headline – it instantly focuses attention and motivates the reader to acquire the product. If professionally crafted and presented, your resume or CV should have an *"Aha"* effect on hiring officials: *"Aha! We must interview this candidate as soon as possible – before he or she gets away!"*

> *Hiring personnel have a universal problem to solve that transcends national boundaries – hire someone who can add value to their organization.*

This is not a task you should take lightly nor rush into without giving it your best professional effort. Like any compelling advertisement, you should take sufficient time and put lots of thoughtful effort into crafting your perfect resume or CV. As you will see from the many expertly crafted resumes and CVs presented in this book, our successful international job seekers produced first-class presentations which were well worth the time and money spent. Best of all, their resumes resulted in invitations to job interviews which, in turn, produced job offers and landed them the job.

Understanding a Process

Resumes and CVs are some of the most misunderstood, misused, and abused forms of job search communication. Many job seekers write dreadful documents that poorly reflect their goals and qualifications and thus quickly find their way into the trash cans of employers. Many such resumes are basically obituaries – excellent resources for writing about people who have passed away. If you don't want to be part of the living dead who get passed over for good jobs, you must avoid writing your obituary and sending it to employers who will literally treat your resume as "dead upon arrival."

Many resume problems relate to the lack of understanding of what a resume or CV is and what it should be designed to do for both job seekers and employers. Unfortunately, many job seekers still believe in the magical quality of resumes – they result in jobs. In fact, we have yet to meet an employer who hired someone based on their resume! Employers hire based on a combination of factors, but most of these factors follow sequential steps in the hiring process. The most important factor and step is the **job interview**. The resume helps employers screen which candidates they wish to invite to job interviews. This step-by-step process is very simple:

RESUME ➤ JOB INTERVIEW ➤ JOB OFFER ➤ HIRE

In other words, no resume, no job interview; no job interview, no job offer; no job offer, no job.

Defining Resumes Around Employers' Needs

So what exactly is a resume or CV? Once we answer this question, the tasks of writing and distributing a resume or CV become much easier and the focus of one's job search becomes much clearer. You'll avoid many mistakes (see Chapter 2) made by other international job seekers. Indeed, many job seekers believe a resume or CV is a summary of one's education and work history. Consequently, they try to include as much detailed information on what they have been doing during the past five, 10, or 20 years, as if employers really want to know everything about their educational background, previous employers, employment dates, duties, and responsibilities – perhaps even some personal history about their age, marital status, and hobbies.

While employers want to see information about your past work history, they aren't interested in hiring your past. They are only interested in your past as far as it may be a good indicator or predictor of future performance. They want to learn about your *pattern of accomplishments or performance* – what it is you have done in the past that is likely to recur in the future **for them**. Therefore, you need to present your past work history in such a manner that it clearly communicates what will most likely be your future performance should you work for this employer. Will you bring to this job the same recurring pattern of performance you demonstrated in your previous jobs? For example, if you reduced costs by 15 percent and increased productivity by 20 percent in your last two jobs, are you likely to do the same in this new job? Does your resume communicate this future quality to employers, or is it basically a historical compilation of who you worked for during the past five, 10, 20 years? Is your "pattern of performance" easy to grasp within 30 seconds of reading your resume, or does it require a great deal of interpretation and guessing on the part of employers who are not clear from reading your resume what you can really do for them? In other words, your resume or CV should be **employer-centered** and not self-centered. Rather than record your past work history, it should link your past performance to the hiring needs of the employer, who will then want to learn more about you by inviting you to an interview.

> *Employers are only interested in your past as far as it may be a good predictor of future performance.*

Resumes and CVs as Advertisements

You should have a very clear idea of what you are doing in terms of intended outcomes. Simply put, **your resume or CV should be an advertisement for a job interview**. You are advertising yourself to be invited for a job interview, be it an interview by e-mail, telephone, or a face-to-face meeting, or all three. Defined in this manner, your writing and distribution tasks should have a clear focus. Using the analogy of good advertising copy, you want your resume to provide just enough information to *generate interest* on the part of the recipient to motivate him or her to invite you to a job interview. Details about your work history are best left to the job interview, if an employer decides to ask questions about your previous employment. The job interview is where you sell yourself for a job offer. The fine details about your work history should not take up valuable space on what should essentially be a one- to two-page advertisement for a job interview – your resume or CV.

> *You want your resume to provide just enough information to generate interest to motivate the recipient to invite you to a job interview.*

Unfortunately, most job seekers fail to understand the defining purpose of a resume or CV and thus engage in a series of writing and distribution errors that have similar outcomes – few if any invitations to job interviews. Whatever you do, always keep in mind the central purpose of a resume or CV – to get a job interview. If you do this, you'll quickly know what to include or exclude on your resume. Better still, you'll understand why most resumes and CVs should be one or two pages in length, except in special circumstances as you'll see below and in our examples of longer resumes. Lengthy resumes and CVs often violate good principles of effective advertising – immediately grab attention and move the reader to take action with little hesitation!

Should You Use a Resume or CV?

Some people make a clear distinction between a resume and CV. You can make a distinction if you wish, but it's not really necessary and the distinction can lead to some very serious writing problems and misunderstandings about the job search. The more important question is this:

What type of resume or CV does an employer wish to see?

We do not make a clear distinction between resumes and CVs and for very good reasons. Resumes are what most American employers and multinational corporations wish to see. In the United Kingdom, Europe, and Asia, many employers refer to the resume as a CV or curriculum vitae, but they really mean the same thing. However, the CV often takes on a different definition when examined within American educational circles and among many European employers who follow the educational style. Such CVs are essentially compilations of credentials as defined by lists of degrees, titles, publications, activities, positions, awards, presentations, courses taught, evaluation comments, and other qualifying criteria normally associated with academia. In such professional settings, a long CV (five to 20 pages) may be much preferred to the efficient one- to two-page resume. Indeed, employers who are looking for such CVs are less concerned about future performance than with formal qualifications as defined by degrees, awards, and activities. Hiring individuals with such backgrounds adds to the overall prestige and reputation of the organization or institution. Therefore, they want to see all the professional details – the more the better – prior to inviting someone to an interview. If you are applying for a job with an organization that expects to receive a detailed CV and you send a one- to two-page resume, chances are you will be immediately rejected for having sent such a skimpy document that does not include the "details" of your professional background. Such recipients, for example, may be less impressed with the summary statement "published 20 articles in major professional journals over the past three years" than with the actual listing of the 20 articles by title, publication, date, and page length.

Are American-Style Resumes Acceptable?

We often hear complaints about so-called "American-style resumes" being used in applying for international jobs. It's a very curious complaint that goes something like this:

> American resumes are too aggressive; they often lack cultural sensitivity.

The truth of the matter is that there is no such thing as an "American resume." If there were, we and thousands of other career counselors and professional resume writers would have been out of business long ago. For us, there are good resumes and bad resumes, with most resumes tending to be bad to weak, regardless of their country of origin.

Indeed, our experience is that most American resumes, like most resumes written elsewhere in the world, tend to be poorly written by people you would think should know better since they are writing about themselves. That's exactly why the services of professional resume writers are increasingly sought after in the United States and abroad. Most individuals, regardless of their national backgrounds, have great difficulty in producing a well-crafted resume or CV

There's no such thing as an "American resume" – only good and bad resumes, the latter of which we see regardless of national origin!

that clearly communicates their qualifications to employers. This is in part due to their overall lack of focus on what's really important to employers and the hiring process.

The so-called aggressive and culturally insensitive American-style resumes are basically examples of bad resumes, whether written for employers inside or outside the United States. Many aggressive resumes tend to be written by individuals who are seeking jobs that require aggressive personalities and work styles – especially sales positions. Some of these resumes verge on the obnoxious. However, examples of bad resumes should not be equated with American-style resumes. If anything, resumes produced by Americans tend to be much better quality than resumes produced elsewhere in the world. One of the major reasons for this is because the fields of career planning and professional resume writing originated in the United States and now include thousands of credentialed professionals who work with job seekers in helping them organize their job search around their major strengths and the needs of employers.

During the past 30 years, this professional career planning movement has spread to Canada, Australia, and the United Kingdom. It also is making inroads into many countries in Europe and Asia. Today, hundreds of career planning and job search books are published each year in the United States on how to write resumes and letters, interview for jobs, negotiate compensation, assess skills, network, use Internet employment sites, and contact employers. Other career planning and job search books are written for particular population, occupational, and job assistance groups: students, minorities, women, military in transition, ex-offenders, non-profits, government, international, engineers, salespeople, $100,000+ executives, executive search firms, temporary employment, travel and hospitality, and computer and IT professionals. The list goes on and on. For a good overview of the breadth and depth of such career-related resources, including books, videos, and software, explore our publisher's online career bookstore: www.impactpublications.com. In addition, survey these websites of career professionals:

- **National Board of Certified Counselors, Inc.**   www.nbcc.org
- **National Career Development Association**   www.ncda.org
- **Certified Career Coaches**   www.certifiedcareercoaches.com
- **Career Planning and Adult Development Network**   www.careernetwork.org
- **Career Masters Institute**   www.cminstitute.com

If you need assistance in writing an international resume, we highly recommend contacting the professional resume writers listed in Appendix C (pages 216-220). As will become immediately apparent in Chapters 4 and 5, these 55 professionals, all members of the Career Masters Institute, generously contributed examples of job-winning resumes they developed with their international-oriented clients. Experienced in writing resumes for many different professionals in various occupational fields, they can be contacted by mail, phone, or e-mail. We consider this group of career professionals to be one of the most important resources you can use in conducting an international job search. Most of these professionals are located in the United States, Canada, and Australia but work with clients worldwide. Many have their own websites which include more examples of their work and services.

Career planning is a profession originating in and primarily based in the United States. It's becoming a global profession as it spreads throughout the world. A good indicator of this is the proliferation of regional and country employment websites. While nearly

100,000 employment-related websites are based in the United States, thousands of other employment websites are found in Canada, Australia, and the UK, as well as in such countries as China, Japan, India, France, Italy, Germany, South Africa, Singapore, Thailand, Vietnam, Mexico, Egypt, Israel, and Saudi Arabia.

Another good indicator of the international nature of career planning is the new website www.goin global.com which includes job search information on 23 countries – local websites, employment firms, headhunters, major employers, and professional services. As such, career planning has become a global rather than American profession which we see as increasingly improving the overall quality of the hiring process and individual careers. The focus of professional American resume writing expertise on communicating achievements and patterns of performance to employers has universal application.

> *The focus of professional American resume writing expertise on communicating achievements and patterns of performance to employers has universal application.*

Is Your Resume Culturally Insensitive?

There is some truth to the old cross-cultural rule of *"When in Rome, do as the Romans"* when writing a resume. While understanding culture is important in many situations, it also tends to be over-emphasized and unnecessarily constraining when looking for a job. In fact, many people do the silliest things in the name of cross-cultural communication. Yes, you should be sensitive to other people's greeting, meeting, and eating habits, but you may want to be less sensitive to their hiring and firing cultures. Indeed, you can go too native or "bush" and thereby lose your professional focus and values by succumbing to cultural peculiarities.

Not surprisingly, "culture" is often a double-edged sword. Take, for example, the fact that some European employers prefer handwritten resumes and letters. Why? Because they subject such communication to handwriting analysts who look for personality traits. While this is serious business for many European employers who truly believe in such analysis – professional handwriting analysts may be functionally equivalent to fortune tellers or shaman in other countries – for many Americans this is an example of cultural hocus-pocus, equivalent to doing a rain dance to improve the bottom-line of a company! In some countries employers want you to include your photo, age, weight, and marital status on your resume. But do you really want to work for an employer who hired you based on your handwriting, photo, age, weight, and marital status rather than evidence of your performance? You might wonder what else lies ahead for you on the job, especially if and when you will be subjected to a performance appraisal. Will it be based on an analysis of your spouse's behavior or some other bazarre cultural approach?

We assume you are interested in getting a good quality international job that reflects your professional values. In fact, in most international circles, Americans are well known for their organization, management, and technical capabilities, especially in business and government – less so in the non-profit sector. And one of the first problems many Americans encounter when working abroad is the lack of basic organization and management skills and technical expertise. Local performance problems are often excused on cross-cultural grounds – *"That's the way they do it in China, Italy, or Mexico."* Many local employers hire for all the wrong reasons – friends, relatives, college degrees, politeness, and hand-writing – and few can fire incompetent employees because of local labor laws, Byzantine politics, organizational ineptness, and a culture of acceptance and retribution. Many often face difficulties in hiring and retaining competent staff.

If you're looking for a good quality international job, you need to go beyond cultural nuances and look at employers from a professional global perspective. You have to ask hard questions about the employer, such as does he or she run a well-managed organization that values competent employees and rewards performance? Are you being hired for your special expertise or just as another employee who happens to come from abroad? We assume you probably want to work for someone who values your skills and abilities and rewards you for your performance. That's an important professional value that has universal application with many organizations around the globe. Such organizations welcome these values because they are trying to improve their position and profits in a highly competitive international economy.

> *Yes, you should be sensitive to other people's greeting, meeting, and eating habits, but you may want to be less sensitive to their hiring and firing cultures.*

If you are an American applying for a job abroad, you will most likely be held to a higher standard than others in the organization. Indeed, many international employers, even though based abroad, have high expectations for American applicants precisely because of their different educational backgrounds and organizational experiences. They hire Americans because they want them to behave like the best of business-oriented Americans in their organization. The last thing they want such an employee to do is to "go bush" in the name of cross-culture sensitivity. In fact, why else would they want to hire you? They know you come from a culture that values technology, skills, performance, and effectiveness – values which may be difficult to acquire from local hires. They expect American applicants to bring to the job special strengths associated with American business culture. Ironically, they want to hire your American skills and perspectives – not shed them in the name of cross-cultural adjustment! If you conform too much to the local employment culture, you lose the value such employers are looking for. Therefore, don't be afraid to write a resume that clearly expresses your global values and professional goals. To do less is to seriously misunderstand the role culture plays in the international employment process.

Key International Job Finding Resources

This book is all about writing and distributing job-winning international resumes. While we occasionally refer to other resources to help you land an international job, especially books and websites with international employment content, this is not a book about finding an international job. It's a book about how to better communicate your qualifications to international employers in order to get invited to job interviews. The processes of locating international job vacancies, using executive recruiters, and networking for information, advice, and referrals are outlined in several other resources. For more information on landing an international job, we recommend examining the following books:

The Directory of Websites for International Jobs (Ron and Caryl Krannich)

The International Job Finder (Daniel Lauber)

The Global Resume and CV Guide (Mary Anne Thompson)

International Jobs Directory (Ron and Caryl Krannich)

The Complete Guide to International Jobs and Careers (Ron and Caryl Krannich)

International Jobs (Eric Kocher with Nina Segal)

Work Abroad (Transitions Abroad)

Work Worldwide (Nancy Mueller)

Careers in International Affairs (Maria Pinto Carland and Michael Trucano, eds.)

Work Your Way Around the World (Susan Griffith, ed.)

Back Door Guide to Short-Time Job Adventures (Michael Landes)

How to Live Your Dream of Volunteering Overseas (Joseph Collins et al.)

Directory of International Internships (Dr. Charles Gliozzo and Vernicka Tyson)

Kennedy's Directory of International Recruiters (Kennedy Information)

Within the past five years, the Internet has become the international job seeker's best friend. Indeed, it's a wonderful medium for doing international employment research, networking for information and advice, exploring job postings around the world, putting your resume into online resume databases which are accessed by international employers, and communicating with recruiters and employers by e-mail. If you've not used the Internet for conducting an international job search, or if you're uncertain which sites are most useful, you might want to consult these gateway job search and international employment websites:

- **EscapeArtist**   www.escapeartist.com
- **AIRS**   www.airsdirectory.com/jobboards
- **The Riley Guide**   www.rileyguide.com/internal.html
- **Quintessential Careers**   www.quintcareers.com
- **International Job Links**   www.joblinks.f2Scom/index_eng.htm
- **About.com**   www.jobsearch.about.com/cs/
                                         internationaljobs1
- **Going Global**   www.goinglobal.com
- **University of Michigan**   umich.edu/~icenter/overseas/
  International Center   work/index.html
- **Transitions Abroad**   www.transitionsabroad.com
- **iAgora.com**   www.iagora.com
- **JobWeb**   www.jobweb.com/catapult/
                                         interntl.htm

For websites with lots of international content and job listings, be sure to visit the following sites:

- **Monster Work Abroad**   www.international.monster.com
- **OverseasJobs.com**   www.overseasjobs.com
- **PlanetRecruit**   www.planetrecruit.com
- **Global Career Center**   www.globalcareercenter.com
- **Job Pilot International**   www.jobsadverts.com
- **TopJobs.net**   www.topjobs.net
- **JobsAbroad.com**   www.jobsabroad.com
- **JobsBazaar.com**   www.jobsbazaar.com
- **Expatica**   www.expatica.com/jobs
- **Expat Exchange**   www.expatexchange.com
- **International Career Employment**
  Center   www.internationaljobs.org

Information on these and hundreds of other international employment websites are found in Ron and Caryl Krannich's *The Directory of Websites for International Jobs*.

For the world's largest collection of international-related employment resources, see the order form at the end of this book as well as visit Impact Publications' two websites:

- **Impact Publications**   www.impactpublications.com
- **iShopAroundTheWorld**   www.ishoparoundtheworld.com

You also can download the latest version of the popular ***Work, Study, and Travel Abroad*** catalog by going directly to this URL on Impact Publication's main website, which also includes several other downloadable career and travel catalogs in .pdf format:

www.impactpublications.com//index.php?SCREEN=impact_catalogs1&sid=VSluyg097jzhojQK

These catalogs and websites will keep you in touch with thousands of career-related resources that can assist you at every stage of your job search, whether at home or abroad!

2

Myths and Mistakes You Must Avoid

MUCH OF INTERNATIONAL JOB SEARCHING AND RESUME WRITING is centered in a series of myths and mistakes that take job seekers down a long and frustrating path where they encounter many failures and lost opportunities. Many of the myths and mistakes are generic to the job search process while others are peculiar to international job seekers who operate in a very different employment arena than their domestic cousins.

Myths and Realities

We've frequently encountered the following myths and realities with international job seekers who mean well but misunderstand how the job market operates:

MYTH 1: **The best way to find an international job is to submit a resume and cover letter in response to classified ads, respond to job postings on the Internet, post one's resume online, and use employment agencies specializing in international jobs.**

REALITY: Your chances of landing an international job using these traditional "application" methods are not very good. This is the advertised job market of high competition. Many of the jobs in this market are not so great and many may be nonexistent. While most job seekers spend a disproportionate amount of time exploring this market with resumes and letters, the results are usually very disappointing. In fact, you should not spend more than 20 percent of your time looking for a job using this approach. The international market is a highly personal job market where who you know is often more important to landing a job than what you know. The best way to land an international job is through the hidden job market of networking and recruiters which tend to maximize the highly personalized nature of this job market. Use your resume as a calling card for letting people you know – friends, colleagues, acquaintances, and cold-call contacts – that you are looking for a job. The single best approach will be networking by way of informational interviews. This method is spelled out in great deal in Ron and Caryl Krannich's *The Savvy Networker: Build Your Net for Success* and Bernard Haldane Associates' *Haldane's Best Answers to Tough Interview Questions* (both from Impact Publications). If you only learn one job search skill, make sure it's networking. It will be your lifeline into and around the international job market. This skill will serve you well throughout your international career.

MYTH 2:	**A good international resume will get me a good international job.**
REALITY:	Resumes don't get jobs – they advertise candidates for job interviews. Landing a job interview can be a function of several factors, including the quality of one's resume. Make sure you produce a first-class resume. After all, it is your calling card. It tells potential employers who you are and what you are likely to do for them. It may also become the basis for asking you questions during the job interview. But don't assign some magical quality to your resume. As noted for the reality of Myth #1, your networking activities in, conjunction with an outstanding resume, will most likely land you the job interview which hopefully will result in a job offer.
MYTH 3:	**The best qualified candidate will get the job.**
REALITY:	The candidate that impresses the employer the most will get the job. Many people with top-notch qualifications produce weak resumes that fail to communicate their major strengths. The so-called "best qualified" candidate is the one the employer likes the most. Above

all, you much communicate to the employer that you have the requisite skills, personality, and enthusiasm to produce expected outcomes. Once you get to the job interview, you must convince the employer that you have the necessary focus, personality, and enthusiasm to do the job better than other candidates.

MYTH 4: **Employers are in the driver's seat. They control the outcomes of the hiring process.**

REALITY: Many employers don't know what they really want and they often make bad hiring decisions. Many of them let candidates define their hiring needs by examining resumes and interviewing candidates. If you produce a first-class resume, chances are you may help such employers define their needs around the skills and capabilities outlined in your resume.

MYTH 5: **Most international employers want CVs which run several pages.**

REALITY: It depends on the employer and the position. A well-organized one- to two-page resume will suffice in many cases, especially if you are dealing with multinational corporations which prefer achievement-oriented resumes. In fact, you can achieve the best of both worlds – the American-style one- to two-page resume and the more detailed CV – by combining the two. Write a very powerful one- to two-page resume and then attach additional support pages that approximate the traditional CV. In so doing, your one- to two-page resume, in effect, serves as an "executive summary" for the more detailed information on your experience.

MYTH 6: **Most international employers want a photo and a great deal of personal information on a resume or CV.**

REALITY: It depends on the employer and country. You are well advised to ask about resume and CV requirements before submitting your resume or CV to an international employer. Unlike the United States where photos, age, gender, marital status, religion, weight, references, salary requirements, and other personal information are considered inappropriate to include on resumes, in many countries this information may be required or eagerly sought as part of the initial screening process. You'll have to decide if it's really worth pursuing a job that requires such personal information. Not including such information on your resume of CV could disqualify you from consideration.

MYTH 7:   **International employers don't like American-style resumes.**

REALITY: International employers you will most likely want to work for have no problems with excellent quality American-style chronological resumes. These resumes, which usually run one to two pages and are rich with action verbs and keywords, follow the principles outlined in this book. These resumes succinctly emphasize what you have done, can do, and will do for the employer. Like most employers, international employers don't want bad resumes that only describe in chronological order past duties and responsibilities which normally are assigned to a position. They want to know what you actually accomplished in the positions for previous employers. Ideally they would like to know about your predictable pattern of performance.

MYTH 8:   **You must understand the culture of other countries before you can write effective resumes for those countries.**

REALITY: It's not necessary to get hung up on culture when seeking an international job. The only thing you really need to understand is the particular needs of the employer which are more likely to center on the requirements of the position than on cross-cultural literacy. You acquire this understanding through your networking activities which center on the 5Rs of informational interviewing – **reveal** useful information and advice, **refer** you to others, **read** your resume, **revise** your resume, and **remember** you for future reference. You'll learn a great deal about what should or should not go on your resume by conducting informational interviews. If you think the employer has unique cultural requirements for resumes, you should be able to uncover these by asking questions about the particular style of resume required by the employer.

MYTH 9:   **It's not necessary to include a cover letter with a resume.**

REALITY: Cover letters are essential to the job search process. A letter should always accompany a resume. However, make sure your letter goes beyond just repeating the contents of the resume. The letter should help sell your resume and you by emphasizing your personality and enthusiasm – important hiring qualities that cannot be well expressed in a resume and that are usually the subjects of a job interview.

MYTH 10:   **It's best to broadcast your resume to as many international employers as possible.**

REALITY: Broadcasting your resume may make you feel like you are doing something to further your job search. However, this approach to resume distribution is largely a waste of time and money, unless you have an especially good mailing list that puts your resume into the hands of key employers or recruiters. Few employers ever interview someone who sends them an unsolicited resume. Employers have particular hiring needs. When needs arise, they start looking for candidates through a variety of sources, from personal contacts and recruiters to classified ads, Internet job postings, and searches of online research databases.

MYTH 11:   **Most of the job search can be conducted over the Internet.**

REALITY: The Internet is a very seductive job search tool which is frequently over-hyped by individuals who operate Internet employment sites. It's especially effective for employers who can inexpensively post job listings and search resume databases online. It's less effective for job seekers who often waste their time responding to online job postings which produce few if any results. In fact, fewer than 15 percent of job seekers in the United States get interviews based on their Internet job search efforts. Use the Internet wisely in your job search by focusing on research and networking activities and communicating by e-mail. Don't spend more than 20 percent of your job search time on the Internet. Interpersonal networking by using the phone or meeting face-to-face with contacts will prove to be your most effective job search method. Use your resume as a marketing tool for opening the doors of employers through networking. When it comes time to communicate directly with international employers, e-mail should play an important role, although faxes are still commonly used by many employers. You'll most likely use e-mail to transmit your resume and cover letter, answer questions, and engage in an online screening interview.

MYTH 12:   Once you send a resume, there's nothing much you can do other than wait to hear from the employer.

REALITY: Waiting seldom produces positive results. You need to take the initiative in following up on your correspondence. Give the employer four to five working days before you make a follow-up telephone call or send an e-mail or fax. In fact, rather than close your letter with the standard throwaway line *"I look forward to hearing from you,"* close it with an assertive follow-up statement that says *"I will contact you in on Thursday morning to see if you have any questions about my candidacy."* Be sure be make that critical follow-up contact. It can make a big difference between never hearing from the employer versus getting a job interview.

25 Resume Writing Mistakes You Should Avoid

Many resumes are literally "dead upon arrival" because the job seeker made serious writing errors. Employers frequently report the following resume writing mistakes job seekers make which often eliminates them from competition. Most of these mistakes center on issues of focus, organization, trustworthiness, intelligence, and competence. Reading between the lines, employers often draw conclusions about the individual's personality and competence based upon the number of errors found on the resume. If you make any of these errors, chances are your *credibility* will be called into question. Make sure your resume does not commit any of these writing errors:

1. Unrelated to the position in question.

2. Too long or too short.

3. Unattractive with a poorly designed format, small typestyle, and crowded copy.

4. Misspellings, poor grammar, wordiness, and redundancy.

5. Punctuation errors.

6. Lengthy phrases, long sentences, and awkward paragraphs.

7. Slick, amateurish, or "gimmicky" – appears over-produced.

8. Boastful, egocentric, and aggressive.

9. Dishonest, untrustworthy, or suspicious information.

10. Missing critical categories, such as experience, skills, and education.

11. Difficult to interpret because of poor organization and lack of focus. Uncertain what the person has done or can do.

12. Unexplained time gaps between jobs.

13. Too many jobs in a short period of time – a job hopper with little evidence of career advancement.

14. No evidence of past accomplishments or a pattern of performance from which to predict future performance. Primarily focuses on formal duties and responsibilities that came with previous jobs.

15. Lacks credibility and content – includes lots of fluff and "canned" resume language.

16. States a strange, unclear, or vague objective.

17. Appears over-qualified or under-qualified for the position.

18. Distracting personal information that does not enhance the resume nor candidacy.

19. Fails to include critical contact information (telephone number and e-mail address) and uses an anonymous address (P.O. Box number).

20. Uses jargon and abbreviations unfamiliar to the reader.

21. Embellishes name with formal titles, middle names, and nicknames which make him or her appear somewhat odd or strange.

22. Repeatedly refers to "I" and appears self-centered.

23. Includes obvious self-serving references that raise credibility questions.

24. Sloppy, with handwritten corrections – crosses out "married" and writes "single"!

25. Includes "red flag" information such as being fired, lawsuits or claims, health or performance problems, or starting salary figures, including salary requirements that may be too high or too low.

20 Production, Distribution, and Follow-Up Errors

Assume you have written a great resume, your next challenge is to make sure you don't make errors during the production, distribution, and follow-up stages of your resume. Here are some the most common such errors you must avoid:

1. Poorly typed and reproduced – hard to read.

2. Produced on odd-sized paper.

3. Printed on poor quality paper or on extremely thin or thick paper.

4. Soiled with coffee strains, fingerprints, or ink marks.

5. Sent to the wrong person or department.

6. Mailed, faxed, or e-mailed to "To Whom It May Concern" or "Dear Sir."

7. E-mailed as an attachment which could have a virus if opened.

8. Enclosed in a tiny envelope that requires the resume to be unfolded and flattened several times.

9. Arrives without proper postage – the employer gets to pay the extra!

10. Sends the resume and letter by the slowest postage rate possible.

11. Envelope is double-sealed with tape and is indestructible – nearly impossible to open by conventional means!

12. Back of envelope includes a handwritten note stating that something is missing on the resume, such as a telephone number, e-mail address, or new mailing address.

13. Resume is taped to the inside of the envelope, an old European habit practiced by paranoid letter writers. Need to destroy the envelope in order to extricate the resume.

14. Accompanied by extraneous or inappropriate enclosures which were not requested, such as copies of self-serving letters or recommendations, transcripts, or samples of work.

15. Arrives too late for consideration.

16. Comes without a cover letter.

17. Cover letter repeats what's on the resumes – does not command attention nor move the reader to action.

18. Sends the same or different versions of the resume to the same person as a seemingly clever follow-up method.

19. Follow-up call made too soon – before the resume and letter arrives!

20. Follow-up call is too aggressive or the candidate appears too "hungry" for the position – appears needy or greedy.

Whatever you do, make sure you write, produce, and distribute an error-free resume accompanied by a well-crafted cover letter. If you commit any of the errors outlined in this chapter, chances are you will be eliminated from consideration or your candidacy will be greatly diminished.

3

Principles of Outstanding Resumes

TAKEN TOGETHER, THE 45 MISTAKES OUTLINED IN THE PREVIOUS chapter are made by job seekers who do not understand the principles of good resume writing, production, and distribution. The following list of principles should help you avoid making such errors.

Writing

1. **Tailor the content of your resume to the hiring needs of the employer.** For example, what problems does he or she need to be solved? Does the content of your resume suggest you might be the person to solve those problems?

2. **Make sure your resume represents the real you in terms of your goals and major strengths.** It should never represent someone else's resume or canned resume language.

3. **Select an appropriate resume format** that best showcases your work history and achievements. In most cases this will be a chronological resume that stresses accomplishments for each position you held.

4. **Incorporate all essential categories on your resume.** This usually includes contact information, summary of qualifications, work history, and educational background.

5. **Avoid extraneous categories and information that do not enhance your candidacy.** This usually includes personal information, a photo, references, and salary information.

6. **Put the most important qualifying information first.** If education is the most important qualification for the position, put it first. If your last job is most important, put your experience first, working backwards from your current or most recent position (reverse chronological order).

7. **Attractively place your name and contact information at the top of the resume.** The very first thing a reader should see in your name, address, and contact numbers.

8. **Provide complete contact information.** If you have a fax number and e-mail address, include them. Unless you live in a very bad neighborhood, which would be obvious from a street address, you should generally avoid P.O. Box numbers.

9. **Consider including a job or career objective.** It should relate your skills to the employer's needs.

10. **Include a "Summary of Qualifications," "Career Profile," or "Keyword Summary" near the top of your resume.** This abbreviated section should highlight your most important skills and accomplishments. The "Experience" section will provide support for this statement.

11. **Incorporate in the "Experience" section your skills, abilities, and achievements.** This section provides *support* for your summary statements under "Summary of Qualifications." In addition to including the name and address of former employers and employment dates, it should include clear statements of your skills and accomplishments.

12. **Include action verbs and use the active voice when describing your experience.** Avoid the passive voice. For example, say "Increased profits by 22 percent" (active voice) rather than "Profits were increased by 22 percent" (passive voice).

13. **If you know your resume will be electronically scanned, use keywords throughout your resume and, if you want, include a "Keyword Summary"at the beginning of the resume.** Keywords are generally nouns that reflect the jargon of particular industries and employers. See pages 209-210 for examples of keywords for international job seekers.

14. **Avoid using the personal pronoun "I."** When you use the active voice, the reader assumes you are the one performing the action. For example, instead of saying "I expanded production by 26 percent," say "Expanded production by 26 percent." The use of "I" is awkward when outlining accomplishments. Worst of all, it tends to make you and your resume appear self-centered rather than employer-centered.

15. **Quantify whenever possible to provide support for your performance claims in the "Experience" section.** It's always more impressive to say "Annually increased sales by 30% during the past five years" than to say "Increased sales each year for five straight years."

16. **Account for any time gaps.** Most employers know how to "read between the lines" when interpreting resume content. If you have any time gaps, they may assume you are hiding something or may be a job hopper.

17. **Include all formal education degrees and academic highlights.** Incorporate any special skills and competencies related to your education.

18. **Mention any special training relevant to your objective and skills.** Such training may be more impressive to employers than your formal education degrees.

19. **Include professional affiliations that support your objective and skills.** Include those groups you played an active role in rather than just paid annual dues.

20. **Incorporate any special skills that support your objective.** This might include a relevant foreign language, computer expertise, or use of special equipment.

21. **Include any special awards or recognition that may enhance your candidacy.** Awards that demonstrate initiative, creativity, or leadership may be especially attractive for employers.

22. **Never include salary information on your resume.** Salary is something you discuss at the very end of a job interview – after you have had a chance to value the position (What's it really worth to you?) and after you have had a change to communicate your value to the employer (What do you appear to be worth to him or her?).

23. **Never include your references on your resume.** You want to control your references as much as possible. Your references should always be "Available Upon Request," although it's not even necessary to include that statement on your resume. It's understood.

24. **Incorporate the "language" of your profession when describing your experience and skills.** The language or jargon becomes "keywords" on your resume which increase your credibility.

25. **Make your language crisp, succinct, expressive, and direct.** Make your resume interesting reading and people will read it!

26. **Use appropriate highlighting and emphasizing techniques.** Try to incorporate no more than three alternative elements – **bold**, <u>underlining</u>, and bullets (■).

27. **Keep sentences and sections short and succinct.** Since most resume readers have limited time to scan resumes, the more user-friendly your resume, the more likely it will get read and reacted to.

28. **Keep your resume to one or two pages.** If CEOs making over $100,000 a year can get their resume into one or two pages, chances are you can also. You can ignore this principle if you are in education or health care.

Production

29. **Be sure to carefully proofread and produce two or three drafts of your resume.** Since your resume must be error-free, be sure to safeguard against any mistakes.

30. **Produce your resume on white, off-white, ivory, or light grey 20 to 50 lb. bond paper.** Paper color and texture make a difference in terms of the impression you make on employers. Be upscale and distinct!

31. **Print your resume on 8½" x 11" paper.** Avoid unusual size papers which may be difficult for others to print if you e-mail or fax your resume.

32. **Always print your resume on one side of the paper.** Avoid two-sided resumes, which are unprofessional.

Marketing and Distribution

33. **It's always best to target specific employers with your resume than to broadcast it to hundreds of employers or recruiters.** You want to get your resume in the hands of individuals who are in a hiring mode and who have an interest in your candidacy.

34. **Respond directly to the qualifying criteria outlined in classified ads and job postings.** Employers have specific skill and performance requirements. Make sure your resume and letter directly address those requirements.

35. **If you choose to broadcast your resume, the most efficient and cost effective way to do so is via e-mail and online resume databases.** While resume broadcasting is generally a waste of time and money, you may get lucky given your particular mix of skills. Several resume blasting companies can inexpensively broadcast your resume via e-mail to hundreds of recruiters in search of resumes. Putting your resume into an online resume database is another way to broadcast your resume. But, be realistic about your expectations.

36. **Make sure to always include a cover letter with your resume.** The cover letter should be designed to sell your resume. It's the sizzle that accompanies the ad.

37. **Avoid enclosing supporting materials with your resume,** such as letters of recommendation, transcripts, or samples of writing. Only include a cover letter with your resume. The other items either need to be requested or taken with you to the interview.

38. **Always address your resume to a specific person.** Avoid generic titles, such as "To Whom It May Concern" or "Dear Sir." If uncertain to whom to address your correspondence, make a phone call and ask for the proper name. You'll later need that name to do a proper follow-up.

39. **Send your resume and letter in a 9" x 12" envelope and affix first-class postage.** Flat resumes and letters stand out and are easier to handle than folded ones.

40. **Fax or e-mail your resume only if requested to do so.** Using someone's fax number or e-mail address to transmit your resume and letter without authorization to do so may be viewed as an unwarranted invasion of privacy. It may be held against you and thus becomes a negative. An exception to this rule is online resume blasting where pre-screened recipients – mainly recruiters but some employers – indicate they wish to receive such resumes by e-mail.

Follow-Up

41. **Follow up your resume and letter with a phone call within five days after the recipient receives it.** Timing is very important when conducting a follow-up. Try to follow up as soon as possible, within a few days after the recipient has had a chance to read it.

42. **Use the telephone to conduct a follow-up.** The telephone gives you immediate feedback and enables you to express your interest, personality, and enthusiasm.

43. **Follow up your follow-up with a nice thank-you letter.** Sending a thank-you letter is a thoughtful thing to do. Employers like thoughtful people and are usually impressed by such letters.

Resumes for Africa

27

Cyril DeParté Freeman
19 Seymour Avenue, Edison, NJ 08817
732-339-0777 ▪ cfreeman@hatmail.com

Accounting / Audit Professional

Highly motivated, disciplined accountant with 8 years' experience in major foreign banking institutions. Quick learner who readily accepts challenges. Skilled at tracking data and solving complex problems. BBA Degree in Accounting. Experienced in hands-on supervision and training. Expertise in:

✓ Accounts Receivable   ✓ Accounts Payable   ✓ Computerized Accounting
✓ General Ledgers / Journals   ✓ Bank Reconciliations   ✓ Financial Forecasts
✓ Credit / Collections   ✓ Financial Analysis / Reporting   ✓ Audit Preparations

Strong individual contributor and leader who performs at a high level of accuracy and productivity. Proven track record of mastering computerized accounting software and office systems applications.

Legal Alien – Unlimited Stay – Authorized to Work

PROFESSIONAL EXPERIENCE

NATIONAL BANK OF NIGERIA, Lagos, Nigeria   February 2000 – June 2001
Regulatory arm of the Republic of Nigeria created to protect depositors' funds following a chaotic civil war period. Turnaround situation. 175 employees. Annual revenues of $10 million - $100 million.

Manager – Accounts Division
Managed daily general accounting operations: A/R, A/P, general ledger, financial analyses, financial statement preparation, corporate banking services, corporate insurance accounting, reporting and documentation. Oversaw 12-member accounting staff including training, supervision and development.

- Reorganized the Accounts Division into 3 functional areas: Financial Accounting, Reconciliation, and Budgeting. Redesigned workflows and programs, realigned key accounting positions, consolidated similar functions, and established and enforced customer processing time limits. **Result:** Increased productivity, improved efficiency and upgraded quality of operations.

- Supervised monthly bank reconciliations performed by Reconciliation Officers, ensuring no errors. Analyzed and reconciled complex monthly financial statements: P&L statements, balance sheets ($150 million), and income ($100 million). Balanced fixed asset register and sub-ledgers to GL.

- Launched massive debt collection campaign as Acting Manager of Credit and Collections with responsibility for 25 borrowing accounts valued at $2 million. Improved credit portfolio bringing in $500K in one quarter. Earned President's "Top Performer Cash Award" for collections turnaround.

- Led initiative to uncover fictitious overtime, yielding 30% staff cost savings ($1.5 million annually).

- Key player in preparing and coordinating external audits, assuring accounts were free of any material misstatements prior to audit review. Served as liaison between management and auditors.

- Verified discrepancies, wrote financial reports and projections for multi-million dollar revenues, and presented findings to management. Chosen to prepare National Bank's $4 million annual budget.

- Successfully managed demanding workload. Completed projects accurately and on schedule.

Page 1 of 2

PROFESSIONAL EXPERIENCE

NIGERIAN DEVELOPMENT & INVESTMENT BANK (NDIB), Lagos, Nigeria   1998 – 2000
Privately owned financial institution engaged in a full range of investment and commercial banking services including commercial loans, savings and checking accounts, bond services, international and Western Union money transfers, foreign exchange trading, vault services and pre-export financing. 100 – 160 employees. Annual revenues of $2 million - $10 million.

Chief Accountant / Assistant Comptroller

- Pioneered the selection and introduction of a fully integrated accounting software application – Bank Manager – which accommodated both the retail ledger and the general ledger. Personally served as Systems Administrator assigning passwords and security access levels to users. **Result:** Significant improvement in the quality, accuracy and usefulness of financial data for daily operating management and long-range business planning.

- Updated policies and procedures for general accounting, financial reporting, cash management, and financial analysis. Implemented the flexibility required to respond to emerging growth needs.

- Chosen to coordinate external audits, ensuring that unaudited financial statements were prepared according to generally accepted accounting procedures and that the audits ran smoothly.

NIGERIAN MERIDIEN BANK LIMITED (NMBL), Lagos, Nigeria   1992 – 1996
Privately owned commercial bank with 180 employees and $10 million - $50 million annual revenues.

Chief Accountant, Washington Insurance Company – Division of NMBL (1995 – 1996)

- Promoted to serve on turnaround team to realign financial situation of 100% NMBL-owned company. Consistently met or exceeded corporate goals encompassing accounting, financial reporting and internal auditing. Annual revenues rose from $1 million to $5 million within 2 years.

- Designed and implemented a series of standards, policies and systems to more efficiently manage accounting / financial data collection, analysis and reporting.

Lending Officer / Assistant Manager – Credit & Marketing Dept. (1993 – 1995)
Management Trainee (1992 – 1993)

BANK AMERICA, N.A. / NIGERIAN MERIDIEN BANK LIMITED   1985 – 1991
Computer Operator / Systems Supervisor

EDUCATION & TRAINING
BBA Degree – Accounting, University of Nigeria, Lagos, Nigeria – 1991

Professional seminars and financial career development in:
✓ National Bank Accounting & Auditing (2000) .   ✓ Credit Analyses & Risk Evaluation (1994)

COMPUTER SKILLS

Windows NT	MS Office 2000	Bank Manager	Sage
Windows 98	MS Access 2000	Banker 80	BAS
MS Excel 2000	MS Word 2000	MIDAS	Internet / Email

Danny Sajid Vajpayee

237 Donelson Pike #305
Nashville, Tennessee 37214

Home (615) 367-4923
Work (615) 871-8600

FOOD & BEVERAGE MANAGEMENT

Qualified through professional training and experience to lead fast-paced, high-volume food and beverage operations within hotel, restaurant, and other food service environments. Strong qualifications in communication, team building, and team leadership. Effective motivator and trainer. Dedicated to continuous improvements in quality, productivity, efficiency, and customer service. Computer skills include Microsoft Meeting Matrix, Excel, and Word. Fluent in English and Zulu; conversational French. Key strengths include:

- Food & Beverage Operations
- Space Planning, Design, & Set-Up
- Customer Service

- Staffing, Training, & Scheduling
- Event Planning, Catering, & Banquets
- Inventory Management

Professional Training / Education

CERTIFIED HOSPITALITY SUPERVISOR – 2000
The Educational Institute of the American Hotel & Motel Association

POST-GRADUATE DIPLOMA – HOTEL MANAGEMENT – 1999
International College of Hospitality – Brig, Switzerland

BACHELOR OF ARTS – 1992 – University of Durban-Westville, South Africa

Food & Beverage Experience

NASHVILLE HOTEL & CONVENTION CENTER – Nashville, Tennessee   1999 – Present
Supervisor / Banquet Captain / Banquet Coordinator / Management Trainee

- Direct special event and banquet affairs for this facility with 2,883 guestrooms and over 600,000 sq. ft. of convention space. Currently completing 18-month Food and Beverage Division Training Program.
- Supervise and direct up to 300 temporary support staff to ensure adequate service coverage.
- Create and design detailed space and floor plans for banquets, dinners, receptions, and other special events using *MS Meeting Matrix* software.
- As on-site liaison with captains, catering managers, and banquet set-up managers, coordinate the planning, development, and delivery of customized service functions.
- Assist with floor management and catering for up to 6,000 persons/day on one floor.
- Provide ongoing support to management to determine server schedules (using *Excel* software) complete check entries, close out banquet office at night, and related areas.

Additional Experience

ARVIDA SECONDARY SCHOOL – Durban, South Africa   1996 – 1998
Head of Humanities Department / Senior Geography Teacher

UNIVERSITY OF DURBAN-WESTVILLE – Durban, South Africa   1993 – 1995
Coordinator & Tutor / Academic Program for Disadvantaged Communities

VARIOUS SECONDARY SCHOOLS – Durban, South Africa   1980 – 1993
Secondary School Teacher / Examinations Officer

Samuel Fuller Obidah, M.D.

203 Pinetree Drive, Lawrenceville, NJ 08648
(609) 771-1188 Home ▪ obidahsf@werldlink.net

OBJECTIVE: A position in the analytical, research and development area of a pharmaceutical / chemical company or related healthcare institution.

PROFESSIONAL SUMMARY

- Detail-oriented scientific professional and team member with more than six years' experience in research design and research project implementation.
- Knowledgeable of drug development and testing, including in-vitro and in-vivo studies, as well as pharmacodynamic and pharmacokinetic principles.
- Sound medical acumen with in-depth background in the pathophysiology of diseases, treatment strategies and applicability of drugs.
- Able to isolate and extract active ingredients from raw mixtures and assay their chemical activity using electrophoresis, chromatography and spectrophotometers.
- Work well independently and jointly to achieve meaningful goals within specific time frame.

EDUCATION

1998 **Advanced Trauma Life Support**, National College of Surgeons
Medical University Complex, Trinidad

1997 **Bachelor of Medicine and Bachelor of Surgery (M.D.)**
University of Liberia, Monrovia, Liberia

1989 **Master of Science, Applied Biochemistry (Biochemical Pharmacology)**
State University of Technology, Monrovia, Liberia

1985 **Higher National Diploma (Biological Sciences)**
Institute of Management & Technology, Monrovia, Liberia

PROFESSIONAL EXPERIENCE

1999 – 2001 **House Officer (**equivalent to **On-Staff Physician)**
National Hospital, San Christobel, Trinidad & Tobago

- Performed Emergency Room physician duties in a busy ER Center (200 – 360 patients weekly), developing a high level of skill in medical emergency techniques, including:
  - emergency room management of accident cases and acute illnesses.
  - examination, diagnosis and treatment of a variety of illnesses and diseases.

- Effectively adapted to changing circumstances in medical emergencies, setting priorities and constantly re-evaluating to optimize patient care.

1998 – 1999 **Lecturer I,** Health Sciences Division
Medical University of Science and Technology, Monrovia, Liberia

- Selected by Division Head to teach biochemical and pharmacological-based topics to pre-clinical medical students (2nd and 3rd year classes averaging 50 – 70 students per class).

- Designed and taught biochemistry practical lessons for 2nd and 3rd year students.

- Conducted research on acetylcholinesterases in heart and intestinal tissues. Research published in the <u>Bulletin of the Biotechnology Society of Liberia</u> and other journals.

(Continued)

32

PROFESSIONAL EXPERIENCE
continued

1997 – 1998   **Medical Intern,** University of Liberia Teaching Hospital, Monrovia, Liberia
- Acquired post-university medical training in major areas of medicine (internal medicine, pediatrics, surgery, obstetrics, gynecology) for independent medical practice.

1990 – 1996   **Lecturer II,** State University of Technology, Monrovia, Liberia
- Successfully taught biochemistry to four biochemistry classes each semester with 20 – 40 students per class. Designed and supervised all biochemistry practical lessons.
- Conducted research on drugs and chemical agents' effects on red blood cell integrity.

1988 – 1989   **Graduate Assistant,** State University of Technology, Monrovia, Liberia
- Performed laboratory demonstrations, organized tutorial sessions for four undergraduate classes, and assisted three professors in their research projects.

1984 – 1985   **National Youth Service,** Institute of Management & Technology, Liberia
- Conducted laboratory demonstrations for college-level general chemistry classes, emphasizing proper equipment use and scientific techniques.
- Established community outreach programs (e.g., demonstrations, lectures and small group discussions), educating the public on the role of medical services.

PUBLICATIONS & PRESENTATIONS

Obidah, S. F., and Brawah, D. O. (2001). Purification, Modulation and Molecular Properties of a Cholinesterase from the Heart of the African Giant Snail (*Achatina achatina*). Biochemistry and Medicine Journal. Accepted for publication in 2002.

Brawah, D. O., and Obidah, S. F. (2000). Lipid Modulation of Acetylcholinesterase Activity in the Gut of Aestivating African Giant Snail (*Achatina achatina*). African Conference of Medical Science and Biochemistry, Monrovia, Liberia. Proceedings and book of abstracts, pp. 6-11.

Obidah, S. F., and Brawah, D. O. (1998). Isolation and Purification of Acetylcholinesterase from the Giant African Snail (*Achatina achatina*). Bulletin of the Biochemistry Association of Liberia. Volume 8, pp. 1025-1029.

PROFESSIONAL ASSOCIATIONS
American Association for Medical Sciences
African National Institutes of Ethics & Medicine

Green Card – Authorized to Work – Unlimited Stay

Mohammed Amani

mohammed@amani.com

Egypt
PO Box 441, Cairo, Egypt
Phone: ++ 20-3-457-0907
Fax: ++ 20-3-459-7350

United States
47 Shady Lane, Dallas, TX 75229
Phone: 214-745-8940
Fax: 214-745-8941

International Business Development Executive
Start-Ups / Joint Ventures & Business Alliances / International Mergers & Acquisitions
Middle East , European & American Alliances

Professional Profile

Distinguished 20-year executive/management career creating and executing strategies for expansion and diversification in technology-intense industries. Strong record of developing successful ventures and business alliances with blue-chip corporations in U.S., Europe, and Middle East. Bilingual and bicultural; B.S. and graduate degrees from U.S. universities.

- Strategic Planning
- Trend Identification and Exploitation
- New Venture Start-up and Management
- Investment Strategy and Financial Analysis
- Administrative and Business Infrastructure
- Engineering, Construction and Technology Expertise

Professional Experience

PYRAMID INVESTMENTS, Cairo, Egypt   1998-Present
Privately owned venture capital firm active in real estate, construction, general trading, and manufacturing operations.

Business Development Advisor

Challenged to identify, qualify, evaluate, and recommend business development opportunities within the Middle East and globally, in alliance with international business partners. Assemble and manage project teams and lead projects from concept through exploration and conclusion, including market research, creation of financial plans and projections, business plan development, materials sourcing, partner development, and deal negotiation.

Evaluated and recommended the following projects currently under consideration or in implementation:

- Provision of Internet and Intranet services to the Middle East, through alliance with US-based multinational business partner.
- Launch of Video on Demand (VOD) in Egypt.
- Construction of power generation plants through BOT (build, operate, transfer) agreements.
- Construction of Egypt's largest shopping mall, a US$25 million project.
- Start-up of a global seaweed/food additive manufacturing operation.
- Establishment of a regional distribution system for MRO supplies and related information systems to a broad range of industrial, commercial, contractor, and institutional customers.
- Expansion into retail consumer goods; currently collaborating with US-based experts on trend identification, product selection, and marketing strategies.
- Establishment of a regional marine optical cable system, a US$500 million project.

CAIRO COMMUNICATIONS, Cairo, Egypt   1992-1998
US$80 million joint-stock company manufacturing cable and related communications equipment.

Senior Vice President, Business Development
General Manager, Tel-Com Division *(Telecommunications, Electronic Systems, Information Technology)*

Spearheaded business diversification initiative to expand cable company into new arenas — fiber optics, computer networking, and electronics manufacturing. Identified and developed business opportunities both independently and with international partners.

34

CAIRO COMMUNICATIONS, continued

Assumed General Manager position for newly created division for expanded technologies. Oversaw all operational aspects of the division, including strategic and business planning, sales and marketing, product development, manufacturing, finance, joint ventures, technology transfer, and administration.

- Predicted expansion of telecommunications infrastructure and launched Egypt's first optical cable manufacturing facilities; negotiated technology transfer through partnerships with **AT&T** (U.S.) and **Phillips** (Germany).
- Established an Information Network Integration Operation in alliance with **AT&T Network Integration, Inc.** (U.S.).
- Identified demographic and societal trends to support start-up of CD manufacturing and music distribution operation — another first in the region. Negotiated technology transfer with **Sony** (Japan). Plant successfully launched, profitably managed, and subsequently spun off as independent entity.

DEFENSE SUPPLIERS, INC., Rabat, Morocco   1989-1992
International consortium of 8 companies supplying defense products, services, and logistics support in Northern Africa.

President and CEO

Brought on board to shepherd the company from business plan to fully operational organization. Reported to multinational Board of Directors; developed and executed operational plans aligned with organizational goals and Board directives.

- Oversaw facility renovation and rapid manufacturing ramp-up; completed on budget in 4 months.
- Implemented key manufacturing technologies and ensured adherence to strict military service and maintenance data, methods, and procedures.
- Developed the first company-wide strategic plan and 5-year business plan. Established financial controls and reporting procedures.
- Exceeded goals for sales and contracts; established performance record that led to new government contracts.

EGYPTIAN INVESTOR GROUP, Cairo, Egypt   1989-1992
US$32 million consolidated holding company of Egyptian investors active in construction, project management, operation and maintenance of hi-tech and defense systems and structures.

Director of Business Development

As a member of the Executive Committee, participated in strategy development and operational guidance while also filling primary role in the identification and development of business opportunities. Served as liaison for a key offset investment with **Lockheed-Martin.**

PRIOR EXPERIENCE

Executive Director / Owner: Amani Industrial Engineering Consultants, Dallas and Cairo   1983-1989
Assistant Professor, Industrial Engineering: Texas A&M University, College Station   1980-1983

Education

M.S., 1979: Industrial Engineering   Texas A&M University, College Station, TX
B.S., 1977: Mathematics / Computer Science   University of Michigan, Ann Arbor, MI

Professional Affiliations

- American Institute of Industrial Engineers
- American Society of Civil Engineers
- Institute of Electrical and Electronic Engineers

Marc Chereau

APCD/The Gambia * Department of State – BANJUL * Washington, D.C. 20500-2400 Telephone: (220) 238560 or 281355 * Telex: 24356 GAMEX B * mchereau@waob.usd.gov

"There are no passengers on spaceship earth. We are all crew."
- Marshall McLuhan

INTERNATIONAL RESOURCE MANAGEMENT SPECIALIST
Agricultural Extension & Training / Rural Development
Natural Resource Management / Human Resource Development

PROFILE

Diversified international directorship and coordination background within multi-lingual, multi-cultural environments. Over 20 years of international consultancy, training, and management experience.

Success in planning and directing projects/operations for non-profit and for-profit organizations. Able to transcend cultural and language differences, bridging those diversities in creating strong working relationships. Focused and visionary hands-on professional. Excellent organizer and conflict manager.

- Fluent in English, French, Spanish, German, Arabic, West African Pidgin, and Wolof.
- Lived and traveled extensively in Africa. Lived on the West Bank (occupied Palestine) 1980 – 1981. **Travels:** Jordan, Egypt, Pakistan, Lebanon, Europe, Australia, China, Japan, and Russia.
- Spent formative years in international and domestic agricultural settings (parents worked as missionaries abroad, and later took over family crop and livestock farm in Minnesota).
- Wife is R.N. with domestic and international (U.S. Embassy) experience.
- Hold Private Pilot's license and Emergency Medical Technician (EMT) certification.

CAREER HIGHLIGHTS

INTERNATIONAL, INDEPENDENT AGRICULTURAL CONSULTANT   1988 – present
Detailed Addendum Listing of Consultancies Available Upon Request
- Advised and liaised closely with non-profit organizations, consulting firms, private companies, international and national development projects, and cooperatives.
  CLIENTS: World Bank; Tanzanian Ministry of Agriculture and Livestock Development; Zenni & Co., Consulting, Inc.; USAID; Government of Zaire; BANMA Corporation; Government of Haiti; Associate in Rural Development; Government of Kenya; Price-Waterhouse; Louis Dreger International; U.S. Peace Corps; Government of Mali, West Africa.

  SUCCESSES:
  - Developed training designs, guidelines and plans; conducted training needs assessment; coordinated, marketed and appraised post-harvest programs; developed multi-lingual training documentation; built prototype technology storage structures; evaluated existing agricultural infrastructures and presented recommendations/findings; evaluated human resource potential and agricultural and environmental fields.

PEACE CORPS – The Gambia, Africa   1991 – present
Associate Director
- Oversee volunteers in Natural Resource Management, Agriculture, and Rural Development.
- Manage community garden, soil and water conservation, and agroforestry extension projects.
- Design and implement training events; liaise with government, development and donor organizations; and develop operational agreements with various agencies.
- **Received commendation for Peace Corps management during the 1994 military coup.**

AMERICAN REFUGE TASK FORCE   1990 – 1991
Planning and Evaluation Coordinator (.5 position)
- Designed and implemented project/program evaluations. Supported relief projects in Sudan, Thailand and Malawi, as well as domestic programs.
- Trained domestic and international staff in project management systems and logframes; conducted evaluation workshop for field staff in Malawi.
- Developed a project proposal and budget for USAID-funded, public health-oriented rural development projects in Cambodia.

AGRICULTURAL PARTNERSHIP INTERNATIONAL   1987 – 1988
Director of International Training (1987 – 1988) **/ Vice President** (3 months, 1988)
- Designed, managed, and evaluated custom-designed human resource development training programs for this Washington DC-based consulting firm. Extensive overseas travel.
- Performed frequent needs assessment of host country institutions involved with Agricultural Production, Agribusiness, Cooperatives, and Rural Credit.
- Worked with Ivory Coast, Ghana, Guinea/Conakry, Mali, Thailand, Philippines, India, and Pakistan.
- Liaised closely with donor organizations, particularly ASID, as well as the Asian Development Bank, African Development Bank, and the World Bank.
- **Served as Vice President during last three months of tenure**; supervised ongoing projects in Uganda and Egypt; responsible for new project development in Chad and Swaziland.

USAID (Rwanda) / PEACE CORPS (Central African Republic)   1986
Training Specialist / Evaluator
- Evaluated the USAID-funded Agricultural Education and Extension project in Rwanda.
Program Consultant / Acting Associate Director
- Investigated and documented potential Peace Corps programs in the Central African Republic.

CARE – Congo / Brazzaville   1986
Extension Consultant
- Advised CARE on storage management and evaluated current situations.

ALLIANCE FOR SUSTAINABLE AGRICULTURE   1985 – 1986
Resource Guide Director
- Conducted research on pesticide issues relating to the Third World. Authored a resource guide on environmentally sound, technological appropriate agricultural practices worldwide.
- Developed questionnaires, supervised volunteers, and acted as organizational representative.

UNIVERSITY OF MINNESOTA – Minneapolis, MN   1982 – 1985; 1987
Research Assistant: College of Agriculture (1982 – 1985; 1987)
- Taught graduate level class, *Agricultural Extension Techniques*. Conducted research studies.
Resident Scientist: University of Minnesota and USAID (1983 – 1985)
- Conducted nationwide survey of Grain Storage Practices and Post Harvest Crop Loss Assessment in Rwanda. Designed training program and trained counterparts / technicians.
Peace Corps Recruiter (1982 – 1983)
- Managed campus recruitment activities. **Attained the highest campus projection in the country.**

PEACE CORPS – Cameroun, West Africa   1979 – 1980
Provincial Biologist / Extension Agent
- Advised regional office of Water, Forests, and Game on land-use planning and erosion control.
- Managed two game reserves, overseeing publicity, training, and programs.

MINNESOTA DEPARTMENT OF NATURAL RESOURCES   1978
Fire Control Foreman / Lake Survey Crew Chief / Field Biologist / Creel Clerk

EDUCATION

UNIVERSITY OF MINNESOTA – St. Paul, MN
Master of Science, Biosystems & Agricultural Engineering, 1984
- **Emphases: International Development, Vocational Training, and Agricultural Extension**
- **Thesis:** Post-Harvest Technology: Automatic Control of Crossflow Grain Dryers and Design of a Model-Predictive Controller.
Bachelor of Science in Biology with an emphasis in Natural Resources, 1978

LEADERSHIP ACTIVITIES

Eagle Scout Mentor ... Graduate of National Outdoor Leadership School

Resumes for Australia and New Zealand

Leanne Jones

58 Showdown Drive, Endeavour Hills, Victoria 3802
Telephone (03) 9706 8971 Mobile: 0425 698 712

Objective: **Flight Attendant**

CURRENT EMPLOYMENT

Customer Service September 2000 to Present
InterEmployment Services – Melbourne, Vic.
Contract work in customer service, secretarial support, and administration.
Customer liaison by telephone and in person to provide quality service.

PREVIOUS EMPLOYMENT

Waitress July 1997 – August 2000
Bartons Restaurant – Cairns, Qld.
Increased return business by 25% within six months through high standards of customer service. Effective resolution of customer complaints, serving food and beverages, and liaising with clientele. Interacted with staff and demonstrated sound interpersonal skills.

Sales Assistant June 1995 – June 1997
Orchid Place Newsagency – Cairns, Qld.
Liaised with public and meeting needs of customers, achieving 15% sales growth within 3 months. Supervised staff.

PART TIME

Waitress/Hostess February 1998 – August 1999
Tropical Endeavours – Cairns, Qld.
Award-achieving presentations of rare tropical fruit displays to passengers of all cruise liners docking in Cairns. Greeted passengers.

Personal Assistant June 1997 – February 1999
Motor Racing – Cairns, Qld.
Assisted athlete-organised travel arrangements and sponsorship deals. Toured throughout Australia, Switzerland, U.S.A., and Canada, interacting with people from different cultures.

Waitress February 1994 – April 1995
Pizza Place – Surfers Paradise, Qld.
Awarded Employee of the Month four months consecutively. Served food and beverages to customers. Assisted customers. Ordered stock, prepared food and ensured compliance with food handling regulations.

Sales Assistant February 1989 – January 1994
Orchid Newsagency – Cairns, Qld.
Responsible for customer service and monetary exchange transactions.

EDUCATION

Smithtown High School, Qld – 1993 *(Year 12) HSC*
Subjects: English, Math, Health, Accounting, Secretarial Studies
Member: Athletics team, Cross country team, Swim team
Homers University, Qld – January 1994 – May 1995 *Bachelor of Nursing*

Leanne Jones

58 Showdown Drive, Endeavour Hills, Victoria 3802
Telephone (03) 9706 8971 Mobile: 0425 698 712

COURSES	1999	**Senior First Aid Certificate (St Johns Ambulance)**
	1998	Basic French/French Vocabulary – Francois
	1997	Small Business Traineeship – Apprenticeship Services
	1994	Banquet Conquest – Conrad Casino

VOLUNTEER WORK

1997/1998	Cairns Mountain Bike Club – Teaching beginners riding skills/assisting with club days.
1994	Beach Nursing Home – Assisting elderly residents with daily living duties.
1995	Red Cross Door Knock Appeal – Collecting donations.
1992	Supported Reading Program – Teaching disadvantaged children to read and write.

TRAVEL EXPERIENCE

1997/1998 Business – Australia, U.S.A. Canada and Switzerland as a personal assistant. Pleasure – Australia, U.S.A., Hong Kong.

INTERESTS AND SPORTS

Music, travelling, and reading
Competitive mountain bike rider, swimmer, runner and hiking

PROFESSIONAL STRENGTHS

- Absolute commitment to customer service/culturally sensitive
- Compassionate/observant/assertive/high level of courtesy
- Good conflict resolution/team player/calm in crisis

SPECIAL SKILLS

Public relations, public speaking, hospitality and service industry, typing, computer literate, supervisory skills

REFEREES

Mrs Judy Conner	*Mr Michael King*	*Mr Paul Cross*
Tropical Advantage	Professional Athlete	Pizza Place
Ph: (07) 40 31 11 78	Ph: (07) 40 59 01 90	Ph (07) 40 41 21 22

WRITTEN REFERENCES

Available upon request

AVAILABILITY

Immediate

'*Beauty is hidden everywhere...revealing it is an art*'

44 Howard Crescent, Croydon 3136 Victoria • (03) 9777 5234 • Email: vincsar@hotmail.com

QUALIFIED BEAUTY THERAPIST • SALES REPRESENTATIVE

• SKINCARE SPECIALIST • PROFESSIONAL ADVISOR • RELAXATION/THERAPEUTIC TREATMENTS

Qualified beauty therapist and expert product sales professional. Acknowledged for talents in helping clients experience the ultimate in personal attention and relaxation, while simultaneously offering personalised product advice and skincare consultancy to boost salon revenues. Committed to high-quality customer service delivery. Key contributor to team efforts has been instrumental in consistently achieving sales growth and building a strong, loyal client base. **Professional strengths include:**

Skin Analysis	Comprehensive Product Knowledge	Staff Supervision
Skin Care	Facial Treatments	Decision Making
Beauty Advice	Manicures/Pedicures	Appointment Scheduling
Telephone Sales	Waxing	Customer Relations
Relaxation Treatments	Body Art Tattoos	Essential Oils

Computer Technology: Microsoft Word, Outlook, Internet and Email.

• Customer Focused • Personable • Energetic • Persuasive

EDUCATION & TRAINING

Diploma of Beauty Therapy (1999)
Melbourne University of Technology, Melbourne, Australia
Included 266 hours in field placements at 4 salons.

Certificate of Achievement: Body Glamour Art (2001)
Victorian Beauty & Nail Academy

Certificate of Credit: Bio Sculpture Gel Nail System (2001)

Other Training
Statement of Attainment: Lycon Product Knowledge
College Certificate: Demologica Product Knowledge

PROFESSIONAL EXPERIENCE

THE SUNSHINE BODY BEAUTY SALON, Melbourne ....Dec 99-Aug 01
Award-winning salon, with solid industry reputation and large clientele. Services include facials, waxing, manicures, pedicures and solarium sessions. Solid sales success promoting skin care, body products, cosmetics and essential oils.

Beauty Therapist
Reported to Store Manager

Successfully completed intensive beauty training and product knowledge sessions while concurrently committing to full-time salon employment. Quickly recognised by management, clients and other team members for natural leadership talents and strong product knowledge. Relieved manager in times of absence, directing daily salon operations, resolving problems, and negotiating with suppliers and sales representatives. Performed entire range of beauty treatments, advised on risks/procedures in safe use of solarium, and met all targets for value-added product sales.

JOHN JONES MENSLAND & HAPPY SURFWEAR, Melbourne 1997-2000
Prominent retailer specialising in men's apparel and male/female surf wear including bags, shoes and accessories.

Sales Assistant
Reported to Store Manager.

Achieved exceptional sales by applying influential selling techniques. Sourced out-of-stock items to "make the sale" and optimised service delivery via personalised communications. Designed displays for maximum customer impact. Rapidly gained recognition from management for assuming demanding tasks and meeting the challenges of peak sale periods with courtesy, speed and professionalism.

- Exploited sales potential; listened for unspoken clues to influence customers' buying decisions.

- Accomplished oustanding sales results by individualising each communication, recognising loyal/regular clients, and remembering pertinent facts from previous meetings.

PRIOR EMPLOYMENT

Various engagements as a Pharmacy Assistant throughout career, successfully established skills in sales and customer relations.

PERSONAL

Leisure interests include socialising with friends, personality profiling, skiing, scuba diving, and singing. Active participant in Youth Group Committees, coordinating social events and activities.

REFERENCES

Sharon Johnson, Manager
The Sunshine Body Beauty Salon
Telephone: (03) 9898 9898

Andrew Johns, Manager
John Jones Mensland
Telephone: (03) 9777 8787

Peter Friend, Pharmacist
(Ret'd)
Telephone: (03) 8871 0099

Employers above are willing to attest to professional capacity in influencing sales, forming relationships, and capably handing a diverse and busy workload.

FRANK ROBBINS

34 Peak Crescent
Byron Bay NSW 2456
• (02) 9898 7878
• pramul@bigpool.com

E-BUSINESS MANAGEMENT CONSULTING

BUSINESS DEVELOPMENT

TECHNOLOGY EXPANSION

- Financial Services
- Information Technology
- Telecommunications
- Government/Non Profit
- Health
- Retail & Wholesale

High-impact innovator. 6+ years experience consulting with global market leaders to develop business strategies, align management vision, and introduce cutting edge e-business technologies that deliver genuine results. Distinguished from contemporaries as possessing an intrinsic understanding of "what works" and the pragmatic realism that strategically translates plans into action.

CUSTOMER FOCUSED • COST CONSCIOUS • SOLUTION ORIENTED

KEY CREDENTIALS

- Alliance & Partnership Building
- Application & Product Development
- Project Management
- E-Business Consulting
- Strategy Development
- International & Domestic Market Expansion
- Budget Management/Resource Allocations
- Risk Assessments & Recommendations

- Board Presentations/Public Speaking
- Marketing Communications & Strategies
- E-Procurement/Supply Chains
- Intellectual Capital Development
- Consultative/Solution-Based Sales & Support
- E-Business Readiness Assessments
- Business Development/Market Expansion
- Benchmark & Goal Setting

SELECTED ACCOMPLISHMENTS

- Propelled unknown start-up company into an international player in the e-business market.
- Acknowledged e-business authority; trademarked and established e-business methodologies.
- Aggressively sought acceptance for recognition in the global business community; acclaimed by Open Market (USA) as the only non-US company competent in e-commerce implementations.
- Achieved first worldwide appointment by IBM Global Services to offer IBM's e-business readiness and opportunity assessment programs.
- Developed knowledge base adopted by universities and students for research and course unit study.
- Personally negotiated and secured IBM and Compuware as channel partners for e-business education services.
- Pioneered Asia-wide program for Unisys contributing $8M to top-line revenues.
- Spearheaded innovative "Go To Market" program for IBM, realizing 3.2% market share increase.
- Established a worldwide community forum for collaboration/problem solving and thought leadership on issues surrounding e-business, b2b e-commerce, and e-marketplaces.

CAREER SUMMARY

Business Consultant/Founder, *Multimedia Facts On-Line,* Australia, NY 1995-Present
Product Marketing Manager, *CloseNet,* Sydney Australia...1995
Marketing Manager – Asia, *HAL Asia-Pacific,* Hong Kong, New Zealand......................................1991-1993
Product Manager, *NTB,* Australia, New Zealand...1988-1991
Product Manager, *QWB,* New Zealand...1988-1989
Technical Sales Support, *Hotodo Computers,* New Zealand 1987-1988
Systems Executive, *Ballarat Industries,* India 1985-1987
Programmer/Sales Executive, *Hardtech,* India 1984-1985

QUALIFICATIONS

MBA, *Grand India University, India* (1984)

Business Consultant/Founder, *Multimedia Facts On-Line,* Australia, NY 1995-Present
Launched and grew to international recognition, fledging e-business practice, providing intellectual leadership to multimillion dollar companies worldwide. Consultancy has excelled in offering direction in strategy development, technological expansion, project management, and process reengineering services, delivering immediate and impressive revenue contributions and increased market share.

Over time have analyzed business performances, reengineered unproductive or unprofitable work practices, and positioned business strategically for each new growth phase. Expanded consultancy to offer e-business education, marketing and sales support services, and intellectual leadership.

<u>Selected Projects/Highlights/Results:</u>

Alliance & Partnership Building. *Clients: HAL; CloseMart (USA); ComputalAsia-Pacific.*
- Secured world's 1st e-business partner recognition for HAL E-Business Advisory Services.
- Gained recognition as an expert in CloseMart web-based e-commerce products.
- Negotiated successfully with HAL and Computal to offer recognized e-business education.

Application Development/Project Management. *Clients: CloseMart, First Bank, Telstra, John Smith Wines & Spirits, Internet Globe, World Federation of E-Finance.*
- Designed and developed e-commerce ready online prototype for marketing demonstrations and sales support (CloseMart USA).
- Established technical support documentation for First Bank's e-commerce hosting and payment enablement service.
- Launched e-companies: *Hotsport* and *Kid'sPlace;* project managed e-commerce implementation.
- Designed/developed Active X based website, recognized as one of top 50 ActiveX sites worldwide.

E-Business Planning & Strategy Consulting. *Clients: Seaset Telephone & Telegraph (Canada), Unitel, Austrade, BNQ Investments, Cable & Wireless Optus, Hallman.*
- Reviewed existing e-commerce strategies, assessed potential market opportunities, analyzed financials, conducted feasibility studies, recommended new models, and developed business cases for senior management acceptance.

E-Business Education. *Clients: ComputalAsia-Pacific, HAL Australia, Supertrade, DataP Systems, CFR & ComBit Conferences.*
- Delivered customized training courses and e-business education sessions throughout Australia, Singapore, Hong Kong, and Korea. Lectured and presented pre/post sales information, e-Sense methodologies training, and e-business strategy framework sessions to customers, employees, and senior executives.

E-Procurement, Supply Chain & Trading Partner Enablement Programs. *Clients: NETBiz (USA), City Sleuth (USA), HAL, BNQ General, DataP Systems, QNJ Insurance.*
- Developed and delivered program allowing buyer organizations to secure commitments from trading partners quickly – at low cost and low risk. Conceived business strategies for private b2b exchange, analyzed existing models, and produced reports on solutions and recommendations.

Marketing Strategy & Services. *Clients: CloseMart, ComputalAsia-Pacific, Chase Manhattan Bank, Telstra, AusPost, Department of Energy, ProMan Technology.*
- Provided services for prototype development, beta program development, brand enhancement, industry analysis, marketing research, and customer acquisition strategies.

Sales Support/Business Development. *Clients: HAL Australia, ComputalAsia-Pacific, FREE Group, Cable & Wireless Optus, Microfort Australia.*
- Offered sales support via lead generation programs. Qualified opportunities, developed solid relationships, and identified new prospects.

REFERENCES

Available Upon Request.

Paul Sorenski

234 Lorenmar Drive
Wellington 43324 New Zealand
Office: Phone: (04) 564 4692
E-mail: paul-sorenski44@hetmail.com

EXPERTISE: PROJECT MANAGEMENT / TEST or FIELD ENGINEERING

Top performer with over 10 years' progressively responsible experience in field engineering and directing large-scale projects worldwide. Combines effective technical, analytical and mechanical qualifications with a unique ability to handle multiple tasks expertly, while delivering projects on time and within budget. Track record of contributions to revenue gains, cost reductions and innovative enhancements. A solid leader, quick learner and problem solver with a strong commitment to bottom-line productivity.

EXPERIENCE

METRO HYDRAULICS LLC, York, Pennsylvania   10/95 to Present
(Global Hydro-Power Generation Manufacturer)
Site Manager/Field Commissioning Engineer (5/97 to Present)
Field Commissioning Engineer (10/95 to 5/97)

PROJECT MANAGEMENT

Site Manager
Promoted to manage the Automation and Remote Control (ARC) project for the Electricity Corporation of New Zealand's Waitaki Hydro Scheme, the largest automation project of its kind in the history of the hydroelectricity industry to date. Direct the activities of 5 subcontracting firms involved in the removal, development, installation and commissioning of 61 control systems. Maintain site accounts, source all electrical, mechanical, and hydraulic hardware not supplied by Voith Hydro, maintain testing and commissioning schedules, develop factory/site commissioning test reports and attend monthly project meetings.

✓ Successfully automated 8 power stations and a 58 km canal system consisting of 32 generators, 6 canal controls and an additional 23 ancillary controls, in record time (24 months). This allowed Voith Hydro to obtain $560,000 in bonuses and eliminate penalty fees.

TEST ENGINEERING

Field Commissioning Engineer
Concurrently assigned to complete the electrical, mechanical and hydraulic commissioning and final performance testing of 6 new hydroelectric generators and turbine control systems in Taiwan.

As Lead Commissioning Engineer, commissioned 25 hydroelectric turbine control systems and PLCs, performed factory equipment testing of 61 control cubicles and performed extensive factory testing on related Allen Bradley software, all within a 24-month period. Additionally responsible for designing mechanic hardware and hydraulic pressure systems, repairing station failures to 100% unit accuracy, and producing all factory acceptance and site commissioning test reports.

Continued...

45

✓ Developed customizable machine test report formats, which eliminated the need to produce new documents (up to 100 pages) for each test performed. These formats are currently being used for various Voith Hydro projects globally.

✓ Advised Voith Hydro to re-develop a more structured software format, which cut site commissioning and factory acceptance testing time by nearly 50% and improved customer satisfaction ratings.

A GOVERNOR COMPANY, Loveland, CO 7/88 to 10/95
Regional Sales Representative (9/94 to 10/95)
Field Service Representative (6/90 to 9/94)
Machinist (7/88 to 6/90)

Promoted through a series of increased responsibility as a result of excellent job performance ratings, persistence and contributions to productivity and quality enhancements.

PROJECT MANAGEMENT / TEST ENGINEERING

Field Service Representative

Selected from a competitive group of candidates to efficiently analyze any malfunctioning governor control system (e.g., 19th century mechanical equipment to current digital technology), utilize technical skills to perform service work and implement required program changes at hydroelectric power stations throughout the world. Trained customers' employees on-site in equipment maintenance and operation.

Concurrently assigned Site Manager for the supervision of a 2-month turnkey installation project, which involved the oversight of 2 subcontracting firms as they proceeded with the removal, installation and commissioning of 2 new turbine control systems. Ensured the performance of work according to schedule and within budget limitations. Successfully completed project ahead of schedule and under budget.

TEST ENGINEERING

Machinist

Manufactured various aircraft fuel control components utilized on commercial, private and U.S. defense aircraft systems. This was a very complex process, which required a very thorough inspection of the operation and components. Responsible for creating processes to increase productivity and reduce machine cycle time to manufacture each product.
✓ Successfully developed several set-up procedures, which produced more consistent products, increased productivity and shortened machine cycle time.

✓ Developed several employee-training videos for various machines that explained how to set up, manufacture and inspect various components throughout the machining process.

Prior: 1986 to 1988
Held positions as a Mechanic, Small Engine Chassis Repair Instructor and Sales/Service Manager.

EDUCATION

Stenspoint State Technical College, Stevens Point, Wisconsin
Small Engine Chassis Repair Degree

Rockwell Automation, York, Pennsylvania
Allen Bradley Programming

MARC R. HARRIS, MB BS (Hons) FRACS

Curriculum Vitae

Residence:
1456 East 1280 South ▪ Salt Lake City, Utah 84102
Phone: (801) 582-8862 ▪ Fax: (801) 583-8044
E-mail: marcharris@qwesz.net

Business:
University of Utah Health Science Center
50 N. Medical Drive, Salt Lake City, Utah 84132
Phone: (801) 585-5400 ▪ Pager: (801) 339-3934

SPECIALTY	**Otolaryngology**	
	Sub Specialties	
	▪ Otology	
	▪ Neuro-otology	
	▪ Disorders of the Facial Nerve	

EDUCATION

Post Graduate	Part 1 FRACS	March 1995	
	Part 2 FRACS	May 1999	
Tertiary	Sydney University		1986-92
	Bachelor of Medicine & Bachelor of Surgery		
	▪ Honours Class 1		
	▪ Awarded the Sir Edward Trenchard Scholarship		
Secondary	Sydney Grammar School		1980-85
	▪ Awarded Scholarship, 1980-85		
	▪ Dux of the Year, 1981-85		
	▪ Higher School Certificate Result: 490/500 (6th in State of New South Wales' Order of Merit)		
	▪ Awarded BHP Medal for Proficiency in Mathematics and Science, 1985		

MEDICAL TRAINING

Fellow	**Otology / Neuro-otology** University of Utah Health Science Center, Salt Lake City	7/00-6/01
Fellow	**Department of Otology / Neuro-otology** St. Vincent's Hospital, Sydney	1/00-6/00
Registrar	**Ear, Nose & Throat Surgery**	1996-99
	Royal Prince Alfred Hospital, 1999 Westmead Hospital (Adults & Children), 1998 Royal North Shore Hospital, 1997 Gosford Hospital, 1996	
Resident Medical Officer 2	Prince of Wales Hospital, Prince Henry Hospital	1995
Resident Medical Officer 1	Prince of Wales Hospital, Sydney Children's Hospital	1994
Intern	Prince of Wales Hospital, Prince Henry Hospital	1993

PUBLISHED WORKS

Thomas, B., Harris, M. "Obstructive Suprastomal Granulation Tissue After High Percutaneous Tracheotomy". *Anaesthesia and Intensive Care*. December 1999.

Thomas, B. "Endolaryngeal Surgery". *Mosby*. 1998. Acknowledged as 'an enthusiastic and accurate proof reader.'

Harris, M., Sherry, C., Williams, R., Gaston, C., Salazar, K., Barnes, H.R. "Facial Nerve Neuroma: Anatomical Locations and Radiologic Features". *Laryngoscope*. In press.

Gaston, C., Evans, C., Barnes, H.R., Harris, M., Ewing, J., Sherry, C. "High Resolution T2 MR Imaging of Cochlear Nerve Deficiency". *American Journal of Neuroradiology*. Submitted Feb 2001.

INTERNATIONAL PRESENTATIONS

"Cochlear Nerve Stimulation With a Novel Penetrating Electrode Array". To be presented to the Triological Society Meeting, Combined Otololaryngological Society Meeting. Desert Springs, California. May 2001. (See attached abstract)

"Facial Nerve Paralysis After Laser-Assisted Stapedectomy". Presented to the Facial Nerve Disorders Committee. American Academy of Otolaryngology, Head & Neck Surgery. Washington. September 2000.

"Medical Management of Meniere's Disease". Invited Speaker. Temporal Bone Course. Royal Prince Alfred Hospital. Sydney. May 1999.

"Intranasal Repair of Iatrogenic CSF Rhinorrhoea". Case presentation and literature search. Temporal Bone Course. Royal Prince Alfred Hospital. Sydney. May 1999.

RESEARCH IN PROGRESS

"A New Cochlear Nerve Implant Using the Utah Array".

A project involving implantation of the VIIIth nerve in cats using a newly developed array. The success of the array has now been proven. Current work involves mapping of the cat auditory cortex with the implanted array to prove the frequency specificity of each electrode. The next phase will comprise implanting the VIIIth nerve of patients undergoing labyrinthectomy for vertigo. (See above.)

"Superior Semi-Circular Canal Dehiscence".

A relatively new diagnosis, involving dehiscence of bone over the superior semi-circular canal causing a variety of symptoms including imbalance, the Tullio phenomenon and intracranial pressure-evoked nystagmus. Middle cranial fossa surgery to correct the defect has been performed in Utah over the past 18 months and Professor Shelton has now one of the largest series in the world. These cases, their follow-up and comparison to the controversial "spontaneous" perilymph fistula will be submitted to an international journal in March/April 2002.

REGISTRAR PRESENTATIONS & POST GRADUATE TEACHING

"What's New in Frontal Sinus Surgery". Presentation ENT CME Meeting. Sydney. August 1997.

"Obstructive Suprastomal Granulation Tissue After High Percutaneous Tracheotomy."
Winner Registrar's Paper Day. Registrar Meeting. Sydney. July 1998.

Presentations to Central Coast Area Health Service Resident's Meetings. 1996.
"Aboriginal Ear Disease". "Neck Lumps". "Acoustic Neuroma". "Middle Ear Infections".

Presentations to ENT Registrar's Meetings. 1996-98.
"Embryology of the Ear". "Nasal Obstruction". "Nasal Manifestations of Systemic Illness".
"Complications of Head and Neck Surgery". "Ototoxicity". "Otologic Manifestations of
Systemic Illness". "The Parapharyngeal Space; Anatomy and Pathology". "The Physiology
of the Auditory System". "Skull Base Neoplasms: Diagnosis and Treatment". "Surgical
Alternatives for Meniere's Disease".

Instructor, Temporal Bone Course, University of Utah, Salt Lake City (Current)
Invited Speaker, Otosclerosis and Laser-Assisted Stapedectomy. Salt Lake City. March 2001.

CONTINUING EDUCATION & INTERNATIONAL MEETINGS

St. Vincent's Temporal Bone Course, Sydney, November 1996
International Functional Endoscopic Sinus Surgery Course, Singapore, November 1997
Advanced Functional Endoscopic Sinus Surgery Course, Melbourne, October 1998
RPAH Temporal Bone Course, Sydney, May 1999
International Skull Base Surgery Course, Perth, May 2000
House Ear Institute Temporal Bone Course, Los Angeles, October 2000
American Academy of Otolaryngology, Head & Neck Surgery, Washington, September 2000
Intensive Interactive Head & Neck Imaging Course, Salt Lake City, September 2000
Combined Otolaryngological Society Meeting, Desert Springs, California, May 2001

PERSONAL DATA

Date of Birth: 8th April, 1968
Status: Married
Nationality: Australian
Languages: English, Hungarian

LICENSURE AND CERTIFICATION

New South Wales Medical Board, MPO 287126 (first registered 14/12/92)

Fellow of Royal Australasian College of Surgeons, Diploma No. 10181 (Admitted 25/2/00)

Certified, Early Management of Severe Trauma, October 1996

$\mathbf{C}$hristina
$\mathbf{C}$arroll
19 Bronwyn Street, Balwyn 3103 Melbourne Australia • (03) 9777 6543 • ccarroll@hotmail.com

> *It takes more than capital to swing business. You've got to have the A. I. D. degree to get by -- Advertising, Initiative, and Dynamics,* <u>Ren Mulford Jr</u>.

FOCUS: SPECIAL EVENTS • PUBLIC RELATIONS • ADVERTISING

In-depth understanding of high-impact corporate communications; committed to dramatically boost the profile of organisations, products and services by exploiting untapped opportunities for increased revenue growth.
Employment in hospitality, retail, public relations and advertising sectors ably support degree studies majoring in public relations.

Spirited, passionate, entrepreneurial and professional

CORE COMPETENCIES

- Promotions/Special Event Arrangements
- VIP Guest Communications
- Retail Management
- Public Relations
- Customer Relationship Building
- Staff Training & Development
- Dynamic Stock Merchandising
- Solutions-Based Sales
- Customer Needs Analysis
- Expert Mediation: "Getting to Yes"

- Market Research/Subject Interviews
- Statistical Compilation/Proposal Development
- Cooperative Advertising
- Corporate Identity Analysis
- Creative "Think Tank" Ideas/Brainstorming
- Crisis Communications
- Strategic Planning/Tactical Campaigning
- Issues Management
- Business Administration: Stock ordering, payroll, rostering

Computer literate: Word, Excel, PowerPoint, Publisher, Internet & Email.

QUALIFICATIONS & TRAINING

Bachelor of Arts (Public Relations), *Melbourne University,* Melbourne Australia..2000

Certificate of Hospitality, *William Angliss College* 1997

Victorian Certificate of Education, *Geelong Baptist Grammar School,* Melbourne Australia 1994
Roger Skeels Memorial Prize for Service to the School; School Prefect; Netball Captain; Swimming Captain; Softball Captain.

Training:
- First Aid Certificate, *St John Ambulance*
- Occupational Health & Safety Training
- Food & Beverage Hygiene

- Accounting (Basic Introduction)
- Certified/Registered Ski Technician
- Responsible Service of Alcohol

EXPERIENCE & ACCOMPLISHMENTS

MAJOR SPORTS, *Sales Consultant/Ski Technician,* Vail Colorado, USA.. Nov 00-Apr 01
Upmarket retail and rental outlet reputed for premium quality ski and snowboarding stock, and supported by a team of accomplished sales personnel contributing USD $160K weekly in peak season revenues.

Rapidly recognised for leadership qualities and subsequently entrusted to preside over several revenue impacting responsibilities. Front-line customer contact role expanded beyond product sales to counsel customers on "must-see" tourist sights and industry-related activities. Drove risk management strategies to minimise stock and revenue losses.

- Delivered significantly increased revenues through upselling techniques, superior product/technical knowledge and customer relationship building.

- Established streamlined ski and snowboard rental areas dramatically improving "at a glance" data available to staff, and maximising store layouts for ease of retrieval/storage.

- Circumvented potential stock shortages by establishing improved protocols for ordering food, drinks and retail items; facilitated all stock transfers and controlled all paperwork.

- Managed cash floats, reconciled daily takings and closed registers nightly.

ROLLS COMMUNICATIONS, *Intern* .... Dec 2000
Communications consultancy devising advertising, marketing and public relations solutions to the corporate sector.

Short-term contract supporting 45 consultants with administrative and marketing support services associated with major proposals for major clients. Conducted extensive market research for 2 major proposals:

- Established the research section for Nike's representation at the Sydney 2000 Olympics.

- Developed research protocols and conducted market research activities for the Australasian College of Surgeons. Successfully completed in-depth company and market profiles on schedule and to the client's approval.

VICTORIAN BRIGHTLIGHTS CINEMAS INTERNATIONAL, *Box Office/Gold Class Attendant* .... Nov 97-Jun 00
Premier cinema chain in Australia, with diverse media interests in FM radio, and leisure theme parks.

Rotated throughout box office, "Gold Class" cinema and Europa (art house) departments. Gained reputation for maintaining enthusiasm, motivation and a positive attitude despite the often hectic periods of one of the busiest cinemas within the chain, and outpaced other sales staff by utilising aggressive and persuasive upselling talents.

- Key contributor in "Think Tank" collaborations with management staff; devised ideas for special promotions, crowd handling, stock merchandising and improved service delivery.

- Exceeded customers' expectations when responding to questions on mainstream and art house cinema. Developed strong knowledge of film directors, synopsis, type and ratings.

- Virtually eliminated escalated customer complaints; dealt with issues swiftly, courteously and professionally without need for management's involvement.

- Supported special events and promotions team in devising and rolling out promotional strategies for new film releases.

- Maintained 100% accuracy in all cash handling and cash register reconciliations.

VICTORIA CASINO, *VIP Cocktail Attendant: VIP Mahogany Room,* Melbourne, Australia .... Nov 96-Jul 98
Delivered unobtrusive, professional customer service to VIP guests in the exclusive Mahogany Room gaming facility. Developed outstanding contacts among high-profile business people, celebrities and "premium high rollers" committing personal likes/dislikes in food, beverages, cigarettes and cigars to memory for superior personalised service.

OTHER EMPLOYMENT:

- Melbourne Park Hotel, *Bartender* (1997)

- The Cave Restaurant and Bar, *Food & Beverage Attendant* (1994-96)

- Victorian Arts Centre, *Cleaner* (1992-94)

- 345 FM Community Radio, *Marketing/Promotions Representative* (1993)

- Jane Johnson Model Management, *PR Representative*

TEAM BUILDING-LEADERSHIP ACTIVITIES

LADY DARYL CAMP 1994-1995
Traditional, highly respected camp involving physical and mental challenges that fast track skills in leadership, team building and team spirit.

PERSONAL

Excellent health. Current driver's license.
Leisure interests include gym work, netball, snowboarding, swimming, music and travel. (International travel includes Fiji, Hong Kong, US, UK, Turkey, Greece, Italy, Austria, Czech Republic, Germany, Belgium, Canada, Mexico and Noumea).

REFERENCES
Available Upon Request.

Peter Anderson

14 Bombay Court, Hallam Vic 3803 • (03) 8796 9856

Career Overview:

Design/Process Systems Engineer, possessing 15+ years hands-on experience and notable achievements within software and hardware environments. Demonstrated programming expertise, utilising a number of programming platforms, coupled with a sound understanding with the design and maintenance of hardware, achieving strict deadlines without compromising quality, and outstanding results receiving multiple Awards.

Other major successes achieved, by virtue of sound troubleshooting abilities, through envisioning solutions to technical dilemmas integrating latest resources and equipment, whilst embracing new technologies quickly and proficiently. Effective communicator with capabilities to lead as well as actively contribute within a team environment, including competencies in focusing and achieving results independently. Possess a sound logical and analytical approach, coupled with a high level of technical expertise in:

‣ C / C++	‣ Perl	‣ Pascal
‣ Source Safe	‣ DOOR	‣ Clear DDTS
‣ Solaris on Sun	‣ Linux on X86	‣ Win 32 (NT4/95)
‣ SQL/Informix	‣ Assembler	

Related Professional Experience:

FUJITSU   *1999 – Current*

Design Engineer (Printed Circuit Board Design)   *1995 – 1998*
Technical Lead (Software)   *1998 - Current*

Responsibilities as Technical Lead - Software:

- Headed a team of 2-3 engineers in the design and development of the Optus Environment Manager – completion three months ahead of deadline and 15% below expense budgets
  - ‣ *Optus Environment Manager is a Unix GUI application that monitors and manages controlled environment via an X.25 network throughout Australia. The CEV's contain the transmission equipment for the Optus CAN as well as battery, air conditioner and general systems. This application interacted with a large Informix database via ESQL*

- Trained two graduate engineers, providing an encouraging, learning environment, with ongoing supervision and support to ensure all company objectives were met

- Active team member (of four), responsible for the design and development of the FSX2000 FLEXR – building a solid rapport with fellow team members with a unified objective, which resulted in the project being completed six months prior to deadline
  - ‣ *FLEXR is a Win95 GUI application which acts as a local craft terminal for Fujitsu's 2000 subscriber line optical multiplexer*

Special Achievements:

‣ Award for overcoming mechanical obstacles and achieving tight deadline in completing a CE version of printed circuit boards 10% below expense budget for the European market.

Related Professional Experience – cont.

UPMARKET ELECTRONICS   *1992 – 1995*
Design Engineer
Responsibilities:

- Solid project design and development acumen, including:
  - "Paperless EEG system", a computer implementation of the traditional EEG chart recorder which acquires 24 analog channels, displays them and allows storage to a disk file. (Written in 'C' and running on a PC under a proprietary GUI)
  - DSP drivers (assembler) for EMG studies using a DSP-based, high-speed data acquisition system.
  - Single channel pH-controlled based on an 80C51 which communicated via an LCD panel locally and RS232 remote. (Firmware written in 'C')
  - Firmware for a remote-controlled, multi-channel biomedical preamplifier rack based on an 80C188. (Written in Assembler)
- Consulting Engineer to Hitachi, Uncle Bens, Albury Calibration & Engineering, Compumedics, Monash University, Harvest Bible College, ANKA Electronics and JR Electronics.

COMPUTERWIZZ PTY LTD   *1989 – 1992*
Design Engineer
Responsibilities:
- Design and development of:
  - DSP-based, high-speed data acquisition system, interfaced to a PC via the ISA bus. (DSP firmware; assembler, PC drivers; C++)
  - DSP co-processor which interfaced to a PC via the ISA bus. (DSP firmware; assembler, PC drivers; C++)
- Testing biomedical products for compliance with SEC AS3100 and FCC class B radiation limits

MONITURE PTY LTD   *1986 – 1989*
Design Engineer
Responsibilities:
- Spearheaded a digital video processing project from initial conception through to design and development, involving system design, electronic design, PCB design, prototype assembly and embedded controller programming.

Professional Development:

Graduate Certificate of Computing - *Deakin University*	*2000 – 2001*
Object Oriented Design Patterns Course – *Learning Education* **Advanced C++ Course** – *Learning Education*	*2001*
Object Oriented Analysis & Design with UML – *Learning Education*	*2000*
High Speed Printed Circuit Board & System Design – *Leading Edge*	*1999*

Referees available upon request

Resumes for Canada

NICOLA BRUNO, B.Comm.

150 Armstrong Way, Toronto, Ontario, M7H 1H3, Canada

Home: 416.999.6000 E mail: nbruno@fistar.ca

ACCOUNTING

Dedicated and resourceful professional with a broad perspective in general accounting. Detail oriented, accurate and industrious, able to extract pertinent information, patterns and trends from a mass of data and present concise summaries. Reliable and optimistic; works well independently and as a key player in a team environment. Fosters positive relationships with peers, suppliers and management. Persistent, multi-tasker, proactive, innovative and tactful communicator. Experience includes:

* General Ledger
* Expense Accounts
* Accounts Payable

* Accounts Receivable
* Integrating Technology
* Data Entry

* Payroll
* Regulatory Compliance
* Office Administration

Motivated, flexible, thrives on a challenge, results oriented and solutions focused. Strong proponent of implementing and utilizing technology to facilitate productivity and more defined reporting and efficiency.

PROFESSIONAL EXPERIENCE

Seagate Transportation Inc., Vancouver, British Columbia   1999 - 2001

Trucking company with 150 employees, primarily on contract to lumber industry. Held following position prior to relocation:

ASSISTANT TO CONTROLLER

Accomplishments:

■ Played the key and leading role in the transfer of the ADP system from a third-party company to an in-house operation.

Process involved: Initiating and handling negotiations with KPMG and presenting comprehensive case for benefits and the $20,000 purchase to senior management. Oversaw system installation; developed the 110 payroll deduction codes and chart of accounts; worked with union stewards to facilitate their requirements and deductions. Informed all employees through print and in-person communications. Supervised 5-month transition between the general ledger and the new system.

Result: Monthly payroll processing costs dropped from $700 to $100, productivity improved by 4 full days per month, and fiscal reporting was error free, more defined and more expedient. Project completed within budget and schedule, on time for new fiscal year.

Responsibilities:

■ Generated the working papers for year end, reconciled accounts, and worked towards audit.

■ Compared, analysed and provided the Controller with business and discrepancy reports.

■ Administered union contract relevant to wage changes, long-term disability and indemnities.

■ Controlled payroll processing including payroll spreadsheets, holiday pay accruals, benefit calculations and deductions.

■ Acted as company intermediator between insurance company and employees. Maintained staff records, administered pensions, extended health benefits, and reported ROE and WCB claims.

■ Consistently met stringent monthly deadlines for large volume of accounting, human resource and other administrative work.

■ Prepared and administered PST/GST and Receiver General submissions.

■ Asked by management to train replacement prior to leaving company.

Bank of Nova Scotia, Richmond, British Columbia   1997 - 1999
PERSONAL BANKING OFFICER
- Provided personalized, quality service to individual clients, processed payments and reconciled customers' accounts.
- Patiently and methodically worked to amicably resolve customer complaints.
- Recognized for taking a leadership role to organize and implement sales initiatives and programmes. Earned a reputation for conceiving and designing unique displays and print marketing material.
- Accomplished a 75% success rate in debt recovery from accounts in arrears.
- Led the RESP program introduction in branch. Organized and facilitated seminars and training; motivated colleagues to sell the product.
- Selected by management to undertake a 5-month assignment to manage the lending department at the Kitimat branch.
- Assisted customers in selecting appropriate investments and bank accounts to obtain maximum yields to achieve objectives. Tracked investment portfolios with clients' input.
- Actively marketed and sold an array of financial products including mutual funds, RSPs, GICs and RIFs.

Seagate Transportation Inc., Prince George, British Columbia   1994 - 1997
PAYROLL CLERK (Part time while attending university)
- Oversaw the verification, analysis, data entry and processing for the 150-employee bi-weekly payroll.
- Handled employee inquiries regarding pay.
- Acted as General Office Assistant, filing and maintaining staff and company records.

EDUCATION

University of British Columbia, Vancouver, British Columbia   1997
BACHELOR OF COMMERCE
Major - **Accounting**

CERTIFIED GENERAL ACCOUNTANT   Student pending Spring 2002

CONTINUING EDUCATION

Strong proponent of continuous learning. Relevant courses have included:

Company Contracts/Benefits	CONIFER	2000
Understanding Life Insurance Policies/Accidental Death	CONIFER	2000
Administration of Medical Benefits	Government of B.C.	2000
Conflict in the Workplace - Dealing with Difficult People	Skill Path	1999
Relationship Negotiation	Bank of Nova Scotia	1999

COMPUTER SKILLS

Computer literate in the following software programs:

ACCPAC, Simply Accounting, Adagio Ledger, Adagio Payables, ADP Canada Payroll, MS Office Suite.

John McCleary Josephson
176 Woodhaven Drive, Eatontown, NJ 07724
732-927-5555 Home ▪ jmjoseph@hetmail.com

OBJECTIVE

Entry-level Mechanical Engineering position utilizing my experience and knowledge in engineering science process improvement and technical support.

PROFILE

- ☑ Mechanical Engineering Technology Diploma. Diverse technical, analytical, and problem-solving skills and experience including field work.
- ☑ Proven leadership abilities and a "make it happen" attitude that leads to the achievement of team and individual goals.
- ☑ **Computer Skills:** ArcView GIS V3.1, Vocarta, GW basic, Quattro, Lotus, Fortran 77, Pascal, Alice Pascal, Win 98, Office 2000, WordPerfect, DOS.
- ☑ **Technical Skills:** GIS mapping, GPS systems, AutoCAD, MSDS, WHMIS.
- ☑ **Qualifications Training:** Radiation protection (Orange Badge, AECB).

EDUCATION

Diploma in Mechanical Engineering Technology   1998
Yorktown University, Yorktown, Ontario, CANADA

Specific Mechanical Technology Program coursework included:
Fundamentals of Statics, Dynamics, Mechanics of Materials, Fluid Mechanics, Heat Transfer, Thermodynamics, and Machine Design.

RELEVANT EMPLOYMENT

Field Technician, Applied Engineering, Ltd. (*civil engineering*) 1999 – 2000
Madison, Ontario, CANADA

- Conducted pavement management study of 14,000 kilometers within Canada, New Jersey, New York, Virginia and Nevada. Performed semi-automated collection of pavement data utilizing ultrasonic and laser sensors, as well as video logging, and submitted improvement reports.

- Mapped all concrete and signage in Reno County, Nevada using voice-to-data technology in GIS mapping interfacing with GPS systems.

Water Lancing Crew, Corley & Davids, Inc. (*energy services*)   1998
Yorktown, Ontario, CANADA

- Worked in teams of 2 managing computer-assisted robotic steam generator cleansing (low volume, high pressure) of the Yorktown Nuclear Generating Station, increasing efficiency of heat transfer pipes.

Facilities Technician, The Hunter Group (*chemicals manufacturing*)   1997
Blackstone, Ontario, CANADA

- Provided facilities support for this chemical purification plant, assisting in the pumping, bottling and warehousing of organic solvent upgrades.

RECENT EMPLOYMENT

Data Coordinator, Eatontown Urology (*healthcare services*)   2000 – present
Eatontown, NJ

- Track urology patient data for long-term clinical research drug studies. Accurately input information from 3 nurses, utilizing proprietary database.

- Routinely manage information from 4 drug studies simultaneously (10+ patients per study), interfacing daily with physicians, drug companies and monitors. Transmit patient information via the Internet, ensuring security.

Willing to travel or re-locate within the tri-state area.

THÉODORE JODOUIN

54 Émile Avenue
Brockville, ON F1J-7Y9
CANADA

Home: (519) 555-0987   Work: (519) 454-6682

GLOBAL BUSINESS DEVELOPMENT
New Ventures / Project Management / International Relations

Dynamic project management career with over 11 years within international arenas. Expert legal strategist promoting growth, funding, support, and implementation of proposals within developed and emerging nations. Persuasive and skilled negotiator possessing superb communication abilities in English, French, Italian, Portuguese, and Mandarin Chinese. Strong proficiencies in:

- Business Strategy & Strategic Planning
- Financial Management
- International Business Relations
- Multi-Site Project Management

- Multicultural Team Building & Leadership
- Capital & Operating Budgets
- Executive Negotiations & Presentations
- Corporate & International Law

Lawyer and member of Law Society of Upper Canada.

KEY INTERNATIONAL PROJECTS

- Spearheaded planning and inception as **National Office Director** of a CN$3M, high-profile **housing project in West Bank/Gaza**. Led consultations between all stakeholders including: World Bank (WB), International Financial Corporation (IFC), and National Mortgage and Housing Corporation (NMHC).

- Directed **international negotiations** with Chinese authorities (Ministry of Construction and Shanghai's Sanshi District Government) in conjunction with Canadian Department of Foreign Affairs, Industry, and Trade in order to secure **Canada-China housing demonstration project in Shanghai**.

- Assumed **implementation and direction** of housing finance **project in Gabon**, including establishment of liaisons between Canadian Embassy, Gabonese Officials, and BBEK Construction (Canadian Firm).

- Worked in **co-ordination with CIDA** to establish **Slovakia National Housing Agency Project.**

- **Negotiated contractual arrangement** with "Développement International Millére (DIM)" and NMHC to **ensure completion of Housing Finance project in Bali**.

PROFESSIONAL EXPERIENCE

NATIONAL MORTGAGE AND HOUSING CORPORATION , Toronto, ON   1998- present
(Ambassador of Canadian Expertise helping Canadian companies export their building prowess within international arenas)

HOUSING EXPORT DEPARTMENT
Project Manager – International Projects (1999 – present)

High-profile leadership position participating on special task force launching new international department. Utilized superior analysis abilities to accomplish advisory services as well as hands-on involvement in strategic, operating, organizational and financial affairs. Demonstrated diplomatic decorum by operating at senior official level as Canadian envoy for newly created department.

Co-ordinated and supervised all highly technical procedures while maintaining liaisons with appropriate stakeholders. Responsible for extensive negotiations, maintaining keen awareness of cultural diversity and international relations issues.

- Instrumental in launching NMHC's first national tender call, screening qualified Canadian builders for large international project. Responsibilities included drafting of TOR's, leading selection committee, organizing trade mission, and advising stakeholders regarding defining issues (legal, business, political, and cultural).
- Extensive experience negotiating and partnering with international organizations including World Bank (WB), International Financial Corporation (IFC), and Canadian International Development Agency (CIDA).

HOUSING EXPORT DEPARTMENT
Project Manager – International Projects (Cont.)

♦ As National Office Project Director, successfully negotiated CIDA contracts totaling in excess of CN$3M for inception and implementation phases of international housing project, including financial management and HR allocation.
♦ Organized and co-ordinated management-level orientation training and briefing sessions within international milieus.
♦ Orchestrated international trade missions to establish feasibility studies and research utilized in formulating final proposals and contractual agreements.
♦ Solely responsible for project management duties including building of financial projections, writing of TOR's/Statements of Work/ MOU's/ financial reports, drafting of clauses for consultants and subcontractors, and negotiating funding agreements from foreign officials, Ministry of Housing, and the Ministry of Finance.

LAND MANAGEMENT DIVISION
Research Officer – Business and International Development (1998)

Researched international business, drafting series of powerful documents utilized to transition organization into becoming advocate for exportation of Canadian housing industry. Papers included:
♦ Risk Management in International Contracts ♦ Chinese Organizations Dealing with Foreign Investments ♦ Doing Business in China (Information Package) ♦ Joint Venturing in China ♦ Summary of Federal & Financing & Assistance Programs for Exporters

EARLY LEGAL EXPERIENCE

Progression through series of positions building on litigation and corporate law expertise. Responsibilities hinged on multi-party contract negotiations involving legal due diligence while ensuring optimum client relationship management. Early exposure to international scene through work with Canadian government's highest legal arenas. Employers included:

Geoffrey Miller Law Offices, Gloucester, ON (1997)

Shawn Micheal Law Firm, Ottawa, ON (1993-1997)

Supreme Court of Canada, Ottawa, ON (1990-1992)

House of Commons, Ottawa, ON (1989 – summer intern)

EDUCATION / PROFESSIONAL DEVELOPMENT

Bachelor of Education (Cum Laude), University of Carleton, Ottawa, ON	1995
Baccalaureate of Laws (LLB), University of London, London, ON	1991
Bar Admission Exams, Law Society of Upper Canada	1993
Bachelor of Arts (Political Science), St Thomas University, Fredericton, NB	1990

(Major: International Relations)

♦ **Project Management**, McGwir International Executive Institute (2000) ♦ **Mortgage Lending for Residential Housing**, Real Estate Institute of Canada (1998) ♦ **International Housing Finance**, Wharton Real Estate Centre, University of North Bay (1997) ♦ **Mandarin Chinese**, University of Toronto (1995)

COMPUTER EXPERTISE

♦ AmiPro I & II ♦ Lotus 1-2-3 ♦ Freelance ♦ Liaison
♦ Microsoft Project Management ♦ MS Word ♦ MS Excel ♦ Internet

Extensive References Available Upon Request

TIMOTHY FIELDS

PO Box 556
Porcupine, Ontario–Canada P0N1C0
Home: 705/266-5432, Work: 705/987-5543
tfields6@heetmail.com

EXPERTISE: OFFICE MANAGEMENT

Experienced in strategic planning, staff motivation and management. Track record in streamlining and upgrading operational procedures to improve production and reduce costs. Rapidly promoted throughout career to increasingly responsible positions based on consistent contributions to productivity, quality and efficiency improvements. Effective combination of analytical and interpersonal skills. Advanced PC skills including leading office applications. Familiar with French.

PROFESSIONAL EXPERIENCE

Staffing Management
- As Project Geologist, direct staffing and contractor functions including recruitment, hiring, training, scheduling and performance appraisal. Evaluate current and long-range staffing requirements, including contract negotiations. Manage a staff of 16 geologists, support personnel and contractors. Fostered a positive working environment among team, which led to improved efficiency ratings.
- As Teaching/Research Assistant, supervised research activities of 4 graduate and undergraduate students.
- As Associate Geologist, directed geological mapping activities of 9 crew members and contractors. Outlined production goals, motivated and trained team to achieve peak performance, which resulted in the completion of tasks ahead of schedule.
- As Senior Field Geologist, managed exploration activities of 5 junior geologists and contractors.

Budget Administration & Cost Control
- As Project Geologist, retain accountability for all exploration activities while managing exploration budgets of up to $2 million Canadian dollars. Streamlined exploration activities, which led to a 15% savings and productivity improvement.
- As Teaching Assistant, led team responsible for budget oversight and administration, resulting in additional annual funding.

Quality Control & Improvement
- As Project Geologist, developed innovative database storage and retrieval systems, which realized significant productivity improvements.

General Business Management
- As Project Geologist, formed industry alliances which helped to identify and capitalize upon new business opportunities to dominate markets and drive long-term asset / revenue gains.

Project Management
- As Project Geologist, led the successful development of new exploration programs, resulting in the discovery of 4 new nickel sulfide occurrences and nickel metal sources. Reported directly to the President and District Exploration Manager.
- As Presidential Volunteer, devised educational programs for area schools which fostered improved relations with local industry and the community.
- As Associate Geologist, proposed and directed exploration programs that led to the discovery of a nickel sulfide deposit and copper zinc occurrence.

Regulatory Compliance
- As Project Geologist, Senior Field Geologist and Associate Geologist, prepared reports, correspondence and documentation for government affairs and reporting procedures.

60

PROFESSIONAL HISTORY

LOTOTUMPH MINES INC., Timmins, Ontario–Canada 1994 to Present
Project Geologist (1/95 to Present)
Exploration Geologist (5/94 to 12/94)

UNIVERSITY OF COLORADO, Denver, CO 1992 to 1994
Teaching/Research Assistant (8/92 to 4/94)
Volunteer President of Honors Society (12/92 to 4/94)

HUMBRIDGE LIMITED, Timmins, Ontario–Canada 1989 to 1992
Associate Geologist

TTY–RETER MINES LTD., Toronto, Ontario–Canada 1988 to 1989
Senior Field Geologist (6/87 to 3/89)
Junior Field Geologist (6/87)

EDUCATION / PROFESSIONAL DEVELOPMENT

MS/ECONOMIC GEOLOGY   1998
University of Alabama, Tuscaloosa, Alabama
GPA 4.0

BSc/GEOLOGY   1988
University of Western Ontario, London, Ontario–Canada

MANAGEMENT TRAINING COURSES:

OK JUNIOR 1998
Course in Finland with focus on organization management and corporate strategies.

COMPETENCY DEVELOPMENT 1997 to 1998
Lototumph-sponsored course with focus on applying corporate competencies to executive and managerial positions.

TOTAL PERFORMANCE MANAGEMENT 1991
Falconbridge-sponsored course with focus on management techniques.

COMPUTER SOFTWARE SKILLS

MS DOS, Windows 95, MS Office Applications, AutoCAD, Lotus Smart Suite, Adobe Illustrator

REFERENCES

Excellent references and letters of recommendation furnished upon request.

Jarad Winslow, M.D., F.R.C.P. (C)

PSYCHIATRY

681 Babble Brook
Belton, WA 98006, USA
telephone (600) 515-777-0321
FAX (600) 515-777-0322

Curriculum Vitae

Personal Data

Birthdate: June 10, 1932
Birthplace: Jamesboro, Victoria, Canada
Marital Status: Married, four children
Wife: Alana
Social Insurance Number: 555 555 555
Citizenship: Canadian and American

Education

University of Western Ontario, London, Ontario, Canada

1949–1951; Pre-Medicine
1955–M.D., with Honors

Postgraduate Training

Rotating Internship, General Hospital, Calgary, Alberta, Canada
    July 1955–June 1956

Psychiatric Residency (Adult, Adolescent and Child),
University of Michigan Medical School (Neuropsychiatric Institute),
July 1960–June 1964

Faculty Positions Held

Instructor of Child Psychiatry and Paediatrics,
University of Washington, July 1, 1964

Clinical Instructor, idem. (1/4 time) 1966–1967

Clinical Assistant Professor, idem. 1967–1971

Clinical Associate Professor, idem. 1971–1979

Clinical Professor, July 1979–November 1992

Hospital Positions

Attending Staff, Children's Orthopaedic Hospital,
Seattle, Washington, 1966–November 1992

Board Certification

Fellowship, Royal College of Physicians & Surgeons of Canada
(Specialty in Psychiatry, by examination) January 1973

Current Practice

Consultant, Child and Youth Psychiatry:

    British Columbia Ministry for Children & Families

    Adolescent Crisis Response Program, Surrey

    Mental Health Evaluation and Clinical Consultation Unit,
    University of British Columbia

Licensure Practice

Medical Council of Canada (Ontario), June 1955

Basic Sciences License, Minnesota, June 1963

Michigan State Board of Registration, by examination (Medicine),
June 1963

Washington State Board of Medicine–current

College of Physicians & Surgeons of B.C.

December 19, 1990, #13333

Organizations	Canadian Psychiatric Association
	Fellow, American Psychiatric Association
	B.C. Psychiatric Association
	B.C. Medical Association

Prior Special Local Responsibilities

Governmental Relations Committee

Washington State Psychiatric Association

Past President, Seattle Chapter of the Washington State
Psychiatric Association

Former Chairman, Peer Review Committee–Washington State
Psychiatric Association

Former Chairman, Child Psychiatry Committee,
B.C. Psychiatric Association

Prior Consultation Experience & Clinical Activities

1956–1960	Royal Canadian Army Medical Corps
1964–1977	Paediatric Adolescent Clinic, University of Washington Medical Centre
1966–1977	Haematology-Oncology Service, Children's Hospital, Seattle, Washington
1966–1986	Fircrest School, Seattle, Washington, State Residential Program for Developmentally Disabled
1976–1981	Eastside Mental Health Centre, Bellevue, Washington: Children & Adults
1977–1989	American Psychiatric Association Peer Review Program
1979–1981	Ryther Child Centre; Out-Patient Staff Consultation
1981–1986	Valley Cities Mental Health Centre, Auburn, Washington, Pre-school Children Day Treatment and Out-Patients
1986–1992	Region X, U.S. Social Security, Administration
1960–1992	Washington State Department of Social & Health Services
1966–1992	Private practice, Adult, Adolescent & Child Psychiatry, Seattle, Washington
1993–Present	Private practice, New Westminster, B.C.

Special Interest and Expertise

In addition to general child and adult psychiatry, I have acquired significant experience in <u>Consultation</u>. Originally I was a full-time in Psychiatry at the University of Washington Medical Centre, jointly appointed to paediatrics for consultation-liaison activities as well as teaching. This continued when I entered private practice and I was able to consult in a wide variety of clinical situations as well as continue to teach consultation, adolescent development, and child psychiatry. The consultation was both patient-centered and provider-centered, and included development of some program-centered consultation as well. Consultation to the State Department of Social & Health Services involved evaluation of adults, adolescents, and children in situations of abuse and neglect, and this led to <u>Forensic Work</u>: Reports to the Court, testimony concerning children's best interests, parental fitness, and treatment needs.

In 1975, I was nominated to the Washington State Psychiatric Association's Peer Review Committee to participate in the American Psychiatric Association Peer Review Program. This involved reviewing out-patient and in-patient treatment for the contracted review program to OCHAMPUS, the military dependents' benefits overseer. This led to being asked to do site visits to "problem providers" and a wider variety of reviews, eventually for Blue Cross of Washington-Alaska, where I was employed 10 hours per week, consulting to nurse reviewers and directly with physician providers concerning length of stay and treatment planning.

The consultation to the Social Security Administration, a Federal Agency, was quality assurance work, overseeing the State Disability Determination Service's accuracy in making psychiatric disability determinations in both adults and children.

Bibliography   Social Class, Schizophrenia and the Psychiatrist in Am. J. Psychiat; 120:149, August 1963, with R.A. Moore, M.D., and E.P. Benedek, M.D.

A Family Mourning Process (with G.D. Jensen, M.D.) in Family Process, Vol. 6, #1 March 1967.

I have been qualified as an expert witness in British Columbia, as well as eight Washington counties in matters related to emotional and mental disorders.

PETER BERNARD

#404 – 921 Hapner Street ◻ Vancouver, BC V9B 7W7 ◻ Tel / Fax: 604-449-5622 ◻
pbernard@novus-tele.net

PROFILE

Expert technical solutions professional offering a unique combination of IT talent and a flair for business building and management. Solid track record of achievement applying computer programming skills to solve business operational issues, with a consistent focus on positively impacting the bottom line. Broad-based talents encompassing product development, project management, strategic marketing, virtual marketing and new business development on an international scale.

TECHNICAL SUMMARY

Programming Tools:	MS Visual Studio 6, C++, PHP, GTK+, PHP-GTK, ASM, Perl, HTML
Databases:	MYSQL, SQL 7, Access, FoxPro
Platforms:	Windows 95, 98, 2000, ME, NT, LINUX, UNIX
Network Essentials:	MS BackOffice Server 4.5, MS SQL Server, MS Proxy Server, MS Exchange Server
Linux / Unix Software:	CPAN, RedHat, Apache, Perl Modules
Applications:	MS Project 2000, MS Visio 2000, MS Office 2000, MS FrontPage 2000, Adobe PhotoShop, Web Position Gold

EXPERIENCE

KNOWLEDGE, INC.   Portland, OR

Web Based Consultant Manager – December 2000 to Present

Designed, built and launched OnlySearch.com, an Internet search engine, using C++, MYSQL and PHP. Formulated and executed a lucrative marketing strategy and affiliate program which generated consistently increasing revenue and strongly positioned the company for its ultimate quick sale.

Achievements:

- Maximized advertising revenue, which increased from $400 each month to $30K from 2,000 customers each month at peak.
- Guided the search engine's growth from zero to more than one million visitors monthly within only eight months.

NETBAND, INC.   Vancouver, BC

Business and Product Development Specialist – 1998 to 2000

Established business structure and best practices for PeopleRealm.com, in addition to leading web-based product development. Opened the U.K. office, which ultimately accounted for approximately 25% of total business revenue. Expanded and strengthened core business, developed new business channels and secured major contracts for services such as web hosting and data centers, all of which generated about 20% of the bottom line. Directed partner, client and supplier communications, and administered legal documentation and contracts.

Achievements:

- Managed several product development projects, most notably, conceptualized, researched and prepared a business plan and P&L analysis for Easy Design, an application providing users with minimal technical expertise the ability to design a functional, effective web site. The product accounted for approximately 10% of all business revenue.

Continued on Page 2

65

- Led a year-long project to revitalize the reseller program to provide automation and structure for increased, sustained profitability that accounted for approximately 15% of total business revenue, whereas previously it had been operating at a loss.
- Initiated, designed and marketed the channel partner development program to provide Internet services through notable firms such as Linknet and Smarts.com.

Marketing Manager – 1998

Oversaw all marketing and media buying which integrally involved planning and scheduling Internet marketing strategies, cost monitoring, expense management and contract negotiation with online and offline media firms. Raised the level of communication between sales and marketing to ensure a concerted effort in reaching the target customer. Provided reports directly to the company president.

Achievements:

- Reduced advertising expenses 60%, while simultaneously increasing revenue 30% over the course of twelve months, by leading renegotiations on all the online and offline media contracts.
- Envisioned and established a corporate identity, complete with a unified and highly identifiable slogan and logo on all marketing materials.

NORTH UNION BEVERAGE   **Manchester, UK**

Computer Operator – 1996 to 1998

Managed an IBM AS400 Sub system that supported several thousand users across the country. Loaded and backed up stock control data at periodic intervals and resolved technical issues to minimize downtime. Performed data management, accessed records and generated reports.

EDUCATION & TRAINING

HND, COMPUTER SCIENCE **Northern England College**	1991 **Birmingham, UK**
COMPUTER PROGRAMMING STUDIES **The College of Technology**	1990 **Barnsley, UK**

- Cobol
- C
- Database Management

- Data Communications & Networking
- Information System Design
- Information Systems Management

John Taylor

Tel: (613) 239-1552 ← john_taylor@heetmail.com

PRODUCT DEVELOPMENT SPECIALIST
Telecommunications Networks & Systems

Six years experience in developing voice/data/signaling network products for a global leader in telecom solutions. Solid experience in product cycle--from conception through design, testing, sales, marketing, customer relations, and operations. Specialist in product/solutions issues. Integral team member on end-to-end design for voice, data, and multimedia networks. European experience.

Education: BSc, Computer Engineering.

PRODUCT/SOLUTION EXPERIENCE

TECHNICAL LEAD - Network Engineer, Network Architecture & Validation Team
NorthbayNetworks, Ottawa 11/99 - present

The Network Architecture and Validation Team works with other NorthbayNetworks lines of business and external partners to ensure the reliability of new products and ensure end-to-end system delivery, including network interoperability. *Challenge*: Northbay was developing a Passport Voice Gateway (PVG)-UE 600 Integrated Voice/Data Solution but it was failing tests and slipping on its availability date. *Role:* Worked closely with and influenced NorthbayNetworks development, product line management and sales organizations by highlighting product/solution quality of service, voice/data physical transport, performance, and network capacity issues. *Result*: The project result was a two-month slip in the general availability date of the solution with over 50 issues generated. In the end, this avoided customer outages/complaints with a quality network solution. *Demonstrated Quality:* Ability to explain technology from the outside in perceptively thereby alleviating customer miscommunications.

PRODUCT DEVELOPMENT ACHIEVEMENTS

SENIOR DESIGN ENGINEER - Signalling Solutions Group
NorthbayNetworks, Ottawa, ON 8/98 - 11/99

Challenge: To provide all the functionality necessary to augment the ANSI protocol stack centric BroadBand STP with an ITU-TS compliant protocol stack necessary for European adaptation of the Broadband STP product. *Role:* Lead Developer on the Broadband STP (Signaling Transfer Point) product. Trained the Ottawa STP organization (30 engineers) and helped build a close working relationship between Morrisville, North Carolina and Ottawa, Ontario sites. *Results:* Documented, designed, implemented, and tested the ITU Message Transfer Part (MTP) and Gateway Screening SS7 routing protocol provisioning and real-time database modifications which allowed the product to be introduced into the European market. • Produced a proof of concept Broadband STP product demonstration for the CeBit 99 European trade show which provided the Broadband STP with European market visibility. • Solely responsible for the implementation of an STP interworking feature, which allowed a single, STP to route SS7 traffic to other networks, configured with different network indicators (NI). • Authored the Requirement Matrix and the Feature Description documents for the ITU 14-bit Integration project. These documents defined the requirements, requirement compliancy, and high-level description of the entire project. *Demonstrated Quality:* Ability to adopt the content and technology to the customer audience for both present and future demands through strong communication skills at all levels.

DESIGN ENGINEER - Signaling Server Group
Northbay Networks, Morrisville, NC   6/96 - 8/98

Challenge: To develop a measurement subsystem.   *Role*: Architected, documented, implemented and tested the Operational Measurement (OM) Subsystem for the BroadBand STP, which totalled 22k lines of real-time C++ code. The OM Subsystem provided a means of collecting and viewing OM data at specific time intervals. Typically, OMs were counters that were incremented when a particular event took place. OMs were organized into a format and used by Telephone Operating Companies and designers to assess the system's performance and health.   *Result*: Met all deadlines, was error free and above reliability expectations. Also, developed trust with colleagues through a close working relationship. Consequently, became a specialist in this product, which resulted in critical assignments. *Demonstrated Quality:* Enjoys working with challenging situations in multi-task, pressure environments.

PRODUCT DEVELOPER - ServiceBuilder™Product Development
Bell Northern Research, Research Triangle Park, NC   5/94 - 8/95

• Developed the *ServiceBuilder™End-To-End Product Delivery Process* that documented the process by which software is created, stored, and delivered from the Northbay development environment to installation and propagation at a customer site. • Architect of the *ServiceBuilder™Software Update System* that provided a mechanism to track software, update, and install software loads on supported ServiceBuilder customer nodes. • Assisted in the high-level design of a new switch-based application that would produce logs and operational measurements. *Demonstrated Quality*: Possesses great conceptual orientation, specializing in "thinking outside the box".

EDUCATION

BSc, Computer Engineering, North Carolina State University, Raleigh, NC, 1996

CITIZENSHIP

U.S. Citizen with Canadian work visa.

ACTIVITIES

• Music *(Play tenor and bari saxophones)* • Individual Sports *(Cycle)* • Team Sports *(Sailing)* •
• Scuba • Hiking • Camping •

References available on request.

Resumes for Eastern Europe

Gregor Woczinski

32 Andrews Street, Livingston, NJ 07039
(973) 740-5555 Home ▪ (973) 206-7777 Mobile ▪ wocz1228@hotmail.com

QUALIFICATIONS

- ☑ **Commercial pilot** qualified by a combination of flight time experience, augmented by undergraduate level studies and enhanced by specialized professional training.
- ☑ Competent and knowledgeable in the field of aviation with specific expertise in multi-engine airplanes as well as gliders. Proven flight and safety record.
- ☑ Capable, physically fit pilot requiring minimal instruction or supervision.
- ☑ Present a positive, professional image and attitude. Experienced team player.
- ☑ Green Card – Authorized to Work – Unlimited Travel.

LICENSES & RATINGS

- Commercial license 3248799 (FAA regulations)
- Commercial license III-2122 (ICAO regulations)
- Glider license S7332
- Ratings include: IFR and multi-engine airplanes (FAA and ICAO regulations)

FLIGHT TIME

Flight Hours
Total Hours: 830
Pilot in Command: 525 Hours
Glider: 350
IFR: 340
Multiengine: 106

Aircraft Types
PZL-110
ZLIN 142
PZL-104
TB-9 Socata
Cessna 150/Cessna 172
Cessna 172 RG

EDUCATION

1999 – 2000   Graduate – Commercial, Instrument & Multi-Engine Certification Courses
International Aviation Institute, Atlanta, GA

1993 – 1998   Graduate – Aviation specialization, Major in Pilotage (GPA 3.5)
Institute of Technology, Rzeszow, Poland

EMPLOYMENT

1999 – 2001   Hilton Hotel & Conference Center, Atlanta, GA
Front Desk Clerk
- Facilitated reservations, check-ins and customer service for busy 300-room hotel catering to high-end corporate clients and tourists. Delivered quality service efficiently and responsibly.
- Quickly gained communication and project management skills interfacing with 500-600 clients weekly, meeting their expectations courteously and professionally.

SPECIAL SKILLS

Computer: Windows 98, MS Word 2000, Excel 2000, reservations database, Internet Explorer
Languages: Polish, Russian, German and Slovak

Willing to relocate

DMITRY ASMONOV

6503 Wendwest Drive
Charlotte, NC 27854

(503) 884-0130 Home
DMITRY.ASMONOV@ayl.com

CAREER PROFILE

Senior Research Chemist   **Organic/Synthesis Chemist**   **Project Manager**   **Professor/Lecturer**

Internationally recognized scientist in academic, pharmaceutical and industrial chemistry. Hands-on and theoretical expertise in organic chemistry and synthesis, organophosphorus chemistry, organic nitro-compounds and methods of analysis. Lecturer/Instructor in multi-cultural environments in Africa, England, Western Europe and Russia. Experienced in multi-nuclei NMR, FT-IR, UV/Vis, MS and Chromotography; ISO9001, OSHA and HazMat environments. Fluent in Russian and English.

EDUCATION   Belgorod State Pedagogical Institute, Belgorod, USSR
Ph.D., Organic Chemistry
M.S., Chemistry
B.S., Chemistry and English

RESEARCH PROJECTS and INTERESTS

"Study of wide range of organic compounds possessing the Element-H bonds in the reactions with phosphoric anhydride and polyphosphoric acid"
– Leistershire University

"Design, synthesis and study of organophosphorus compounds with pronounced pharmaceutical potential"
"Target orientated systhesis of AgHal crystal growth modifiers"
– St. Matthews Technical University

"Synthesis and study of Phenybut and its analogues possessing mild tranquilizing, anaesthetic and other effects"
"Synthesis, structure and chemistry of nitrated phosphorus containing heterocycles"
–   Belgorod State Pedagogical University

LECTURING EXPERIENCE

Organic Chemistry, General Physical Chemistry, 1996-1997, 1981-1992
General Organic Chemistry, Mechanisms of Organic Reactions, Technology of Organic Products, Chromatography (short course), 1992-1996

COMPUTER KNOWLEDGE

Windows 95 – MS Word, Excel, Access, Outlook
Molecular Modeling Software   Corel Draw   Internet Research

PROFESSIONAL AFFILIATION

American Chemical Society, since 1997

PROFESSIONAL EXPERIENCE

BORLANTIC CHEMICAL COMPANY, Charlotte, North Carolina   1997 – 2001
Research and Development Synthetic Chemist
- Shifted the orientation of a textile chemical company to a premier developer of high-tech chemistry products for industries including metal working, machinery, fire protection and others.
- Designed, synthesized and developed a number of compounds for industrial production including surfactants, detergents, emulsifiers, lubricants, corrosion inhibitors, flame retardants and softeners.
- Coordinated chemical product development and production, and communicated with departments throughout the process to ensure quality.
- Wrote Standard ISO Operating and Manufacturing Procedures and monitored documentation.
- Troubleshot and formulated product samples and pilot batches to meet requirements of customers and conventional standards.

ST. MATTHEWS TECHNICAL UNIVERSITY, St. Petersburg, Russia   1996 – 1997
Associate Professor/Research Group Leader
- Supervised the research of 5 scientists, Ph.D. and Master's candidates in organic synthesis and organophosphorus chemistry.
- Implemented new technologies at chemical industrial enterprises producing photosensitive materials and pharmaceuticals.

LEISTERSHIRE UNIVERSITY, Stokes-on-Trent, UK   1992 - 1996
Honorary Researcher/Lecturer/Conference Presenter
- Supervised research of graduate students in organic and organophosphorus chemistry.
- Lectured at University on organic chemistry, technology of organic compounds, computer modeling, and made presentations at International Conferences.
- Collaborated and consulted with various pharmaceutical companies and performed research in collaboration with Ilford, U.K. (International Paper).
- Coordinated the collaboration of Staffordshire University with four St. Leistershire universities and scientific enterprises; was interpreter and negotiator at interuniversity meetings.

ST. MATTHEWS TECHNICAL UNIVERSITY, St. Petersburg, Russia   1981 – 1992
Associate Professor/Deputy Head of Chemistry Faculty/Research Group Leader
- Supervised a group of 7 Ph.D. and M.S. researchers, lecturing organic and physical chemistry.
- Presentations at International Scientific Conferences.

BYERSKY STATE PEDAGOGICAL UNIVERSITY, Belgrade, Yugoslavia   1977 – 1981
Senior Researcher
- Design, synthesis, structural studies and structure – pharmaceutical activity analysis of drug candidates.

DEPARTMENT OF EDUCATION, Lusaka, Zambia   1971 – 1973
Chemistry and Physics Teacher – High School

PUBLICATIONS   Seventy-seven (77) since 1976

Books: *Nitroalkenes* (with V.V. Karapalin, E.S. Lipina and V.M. Veresvitskaya), John
                       Wiley & Sons, 1994.
                       Phosphoric Anhydride: Structure, Chemistry and Applications (with P.M.
                       Gughlin and J.C. Tebby), John Wiley & Sons, 1999.

Representative Articles:

"Pospholenes Nitration by Dinitrogen Tetroxide," (with M.R. Veresvitskaya and V.V. Karapalin)
Zh. Organ. Khim. 1976. Vol. 12. No 4. P. 912-913.
"Synthetic Approach to Nitrophospholene Oximes," (with M.R. Veresvitskaya and V.V. Karapalin)
Zh. Obsch. Khim. 1979. Vol. 49. No. 10. P. 2390-2391.
"Stereochemistry of 1-oxo-1-alkoxy(hydroxy)-3,4-dimethyl-3,4-dinitrophospholanes" (with G.A.
Berkova, M.R. Veresvitskaya, V.V. Karapalin and V.I. Zakharov) Zh. Obsch. Khim. 1980. Vol. 50.
No. 12. P. 2680-2688.
"Synthesis and Structure of Nitrophosphole Oximes," (with M.R. Veresvitskaya, GA. Gerkova and
V.V. Karapalin) Zh. Obsch. Khim. 1981. Vol. 51. No. 11. P. 2418-2425.
"Synthesis of Cyanoketene," (with P.M. Gughlin) Zh. Obsch. Khim. 1988. Vol. 58. No. 10. P. 2403-
2404.
"Molecular and Crystalline Structure of 1-methoxy- and 1-(2-chloroethoxy)-2-oximino-3-methyl-4-
nitro-3-pholene-1-oxides," (with V.V. Tkachiov, L.O. Atovmian and M.R. Veresvitskaya) Zh.
Struct. Khim. 1988. Vol. 29. No. 2. P. 112-117.
"Phosphorylation of Azoles by Phosphoric Anhydride," (with P.M. Gughlin and A.V. Gugkaev) Zh.
Obsch. Khim. 1990. Vol. 60. No. 5. P. 1182-1183.
*"Interaction of Phosphoric Anhydride with CH-, NH-, PH-, SH-Acids," (with P.M. Gughlin)
Phosphorus Sulfur. 1990. Vol. 49/50. Part 1. P. 247-250.
"Cyclotrimerization of Ketenes as the Synthetic Approach to Floroglucene Derivatives," (with P.M.
Gughlin and N.S. Essentseva) Zh. Obsch. Khim. 1991. Vol. 61. No. 5. P. 1269-1270.
"The Target Orientated Synthesis of AgHal Microcrystals Modifiers," (with P.M. Gughlin) Zh.
Nauchn. Prikl. Photogr. 1992. No. 2. P. 128-132.
"Phosphorylation of Cyclic Derivatives of Urea by Phosphoric Anhydride," (with P.M. Gughlin and
A.L. Govorkov) Zh. Obsch. Khim. 1992. Vol. 62. No. 1. P. 220-221.
*"Interaction Between Phosphoric Anhydride and Organic Compounds with Prototropic Properties,"
(with J.C. Tebby and P.M. Gughlin) Phosphorus Sulfur. 1996. Vols. 109-110. P. 465-468.

Complete list of publications upon request

*Publications in English

SERGEY P. VOLOSHINOV

1500 N. Lombard Street
Ellensburg, Washington 98926
(509) 963-0967
spvol@cps.com

Expertise

Demonstrated proficiency in the development of unique circus arts techniques as well as educational program design, development and management.

Technical Skills

International circus arts performer adept in:
juggling,
balancing,
hat manipulation,
acrobatics,
aerial acrobatics,
trapeze,
wire walking,
teeterboard,
rolling globe,
unicycle,
clowning and
magic.

Education

School for Ballet and Circus Arts,
Volgograd, Russia

Completed degree program in Classical Ballet, specializing in Acrobatic Skills

Affiliations

Actors Guild of Variety Artists

Citizenship

United States
Russia

Language Fluency

English
Russian
French
Spanish

INTERNATIONAL CIRCUS ARTS DIRECTOR

Creator, instructor and director of circus arts programs in educational institutions and corporate environments worldwide.

- Innovator of teaching methodology to maximize students' potential, strengths and self-confidence.
- Talented trainer and coach who has developed students of all ages.
- Award-winning member of the Volzhskiy Troupe performing worldwide with Ringling Brothers Barnum and Bailey Circus.
- Invited as guest instructor and consultant at the renowned Ringling Brothers Clown College to train future performers.

ACCOMPLISHMENTS

- **Initiated and expanded circus arts education program at Central Washington University that doubled revenues in just 2 years.**
- **Designed workshops, trained staff and coordinated circus arts program for major corporations throughout the world.**
- **Instructed and developed numerous students who achieved success as celebrated performers in international circus programs.**
- **Created and performed peerless juggling acts including "Unsupported Ladder" and Musical Drum Juggling, with internationally acclaimed Volzhskiy Troupe.**
- **Directed development of the successful Big Top circus program, an annual event for the past 15 years.**
- **Multiple award winner for "Best Performing Act" in the European World Circus Competition and Cirque Atarré.**

PROFESSIONAL EXPERIENCE

Central Washington University • Ellensburg, Washington • 1989-present
Director of Circus Arts Program

Design and direct all aspects of circus arts instructional program at the university. Recruit, supervise and train instructors, building department from a staff of 3 to 10. Plan and manage program's operating budget. Coordinate instruction schedule and related activities; maintain and purchase equipment. Initiated design and implementation of effective safety standards for program.

New York School for Circus Arts • New York, New York • 1985-1989
School for Ballet and Circus Arts • Volgograd, Russia • 1980-1985
Circus Instructor

Created and instructed circus arts program for students ranging from 7 to 18 years old. Developed and advanced the careers of numerous students who subsequently performed internationally.

CONSULTING EXPERIENCE: As consultant, provide expertise in the design and presentation of circus arts workshops. Develop in-house trainers in creating circus productions to develop individual skills and promote teamwork (1989-present).

PRIOR PERFORMING EXPERIENCE: International circus arts performer with the Volzhskiy Troupe, specializing in unique acrobatic/juggling acts.

VENIC TRYSTOLOVIC

21203 Teaston Circle
New York, New York 01123
(212) 232-9088
vtrystolovic2@intlnet.com

INTERNATIONAL CONSULTING / PROJECT MANAGEMENT
Growth Oriented Company Focus

Proven ability to train, lead teams and manage advanced civil engineering projects with extensive expertise in, but not limited to, the design of reinforced concrete, prestressed concrete, composite and steel structures. Able to interact and communicate effectively with all levels of management, including external clients.

SUMMARY OF QUALIFICATIONS

- *Familiar with engineering and team management principles that guide one-of-a-kind, advanced-technologies structural projects. Project leader, innovative project developer and communicator with outstanding technical development achievements. Developer of innovative structural solutions utilizing a variety of design, software and integrated material-structural engineering techniques. In all projects utilize strong foundation in mechanics, structural and materials engineering. Transferable skills in research, writing, engineering and innovations with transferable consulting skills that guide advanced-technologies structural projects.*
- *Able to act as liaison to clients to understand and define their specific, high-tech needs while delivering those solutions through the management of small, research-and-development focused engineering teams. Present complex engineering problems in clear, appealing and technical writing format to various audiences and customers without high-tech engineering skills or background. Outstanding overall balance of highly technical skills along with the ability to focus multiple internal entities and external customers on product requirements and product solutions.*
- *Technical reviewer for various engineering organizations including National Science Foundation, American Concrete Institute, American Society of Civil Engineers, Japan Concrete Institute.*
- *Citizenship: United States Citizen. OPS 83, LISP, Pascal, Fortran 77, Basic. Fluent in Italian, Croatian, German. Certified Scuba-Diver, Trained in Mountaineering and Repelling Techniques.*

SKILLS SUMMARY

- *Damage Assessment/Analysis*
- *Non-Destructive Testing*
- *Seismic/Non-Seismic Repair/Retrofit*
- *Procedure Design & Analysis*
- *Bridge/Building Design and Analysis*
- *Structural System Analysis*
- *Solid Mechanics, Fracture Mechanics and Micro-Mechanics of Cementitious Composites*
- *New Technology Development/Implementation*

- *Product Development*
- *Technology Transfer*
- *Computer Programming/Modeling*
- *Auto-Adaptive Structures*
- *Project Management*
- *Technology Evaluation*
- *Procedure Development & Optimization*

EDUCATION

1987   UNIVERSITY OF LONDON, England, *Master of Science, (DIC)*
1986   UNIVERSITY OF BELGRADE, Yugoslavia: *Master of Civil Engineering (Specialization in Steel and Concrete Design)*

1995-Present	**Assistant Professor** *of Civil Engineering, University of London*
	Director of Scale Structural Testing Laboratory *(Constructed Facilities Laboratory - Engineering Graduate Research Center, London Common University)*
1992 - 95	**Assistant Professor** *of Civil Engineering, University of London, London, England*
1991 - 92	**Visiting Assistant Professor** *of Civil and Env. Eng., English Technology Institute, Manchester, England.*
1987 - 91	**Research Assistant,** *Rutgers University and University of London (European Campus, Belgrade Yugoslavia)*
Summer 1988	**Structural Engineer,** *GAI Consultants Inc., Monroeville, PA.*
1986 - 87	**Research Assistant,** *Imperial College of Sci. and Tech., London, England.*

DESIGN HONORS, AWARDS AND RECOGNITIONS

- **Gyebi Kufuor Memorial Prize** for excellence in Concrete Structures and Technology, Imperial College Award (1987).
- **Stojadinovic Concrete Bridge Design Award** - annual industry award, Yugoslavia (1986).
- **Oak Ridge Associated Universities Junior Faculty Enhancement Award** (1997).
- Featured on numerous national and international television and radio interviews and shows including *CNNfn (financial) network, CNN Headline News, CNN Airport Network, CNN International Network, CNN Science and Technology Week, FOX TV, National Public Radio (91.5 FM – WUNC), Voice of America, Associated Press, KCBS San Francisco, CNN Radio, KNX Radio - Los Angeles, WPTF, Howard Stern Radio Show, Inside Science, WRAL -5, CBS, FOX 50.*
- Featured in popular press articles in ASCE *News, Concrete Construction, UnisSci - Daily University Science News* (nisci.com), University of London's *Londoner & Bulletin.*

DEVELOPMENTAL AWARDS & TRAINING AND TEAM-MANAGEMENT

- Recruited, developed, trained and managed R&D-focused engineering teams that included a total of 111 Research Engineers, 42 Research Associates, 21 Research Scientists and one Visiting Research Scientist from *Polish Academy of Sciences.* Developed and taught numerous undergraduate and graduate courses on Reinforced Concrete Design, Prestressed Concrete Design, Statics, Structural Mechanics, Construction Materials, Concrete Materials, Statistics and Probability.
- Won and managed, as the main investigator, a total of $3 million in federal (International Science Foundation), national and industrial research and development projects on various aspects of assessment of non-seismically designed reinforced concrete frame buildings, development of improved seismic retrofit techniques and design guidelines for bridges and buildings, and development of multiaxial plasticity models for high-performance fiber composites.

COMMUNICATION SKILLS

Presented and published in numerous national and international journals, conferences and meetings on issues related to development of design guidelines for flexural and shear retrofit of reinforced concrete (R.C.) members, seismic retrofit R.C. buildings, punching shear failure of reinforced concrete slabs, reinforcing bar bond behavior, bridge deck overlays, auto-adaptive and "smart" structures, non-destructive testing of concrete structures, mechanisms of concrete cracking, and development and behavior of high-performance concretes and fiber composites.

- Published 14 <u>peer-reviewed papers</u> in national and international journals (e.g., American Concrete Institute *International Materials Journal, US and European Structural Journal,* and *Journal of Cement and Concrete Composites*) and two book chapters. Presented 39 invited-lectures. (*Presentations to select audiences by personal invitation only. These do not include invitations to conference presentations.*)
- Published 24 conference and workshop papers. Presented 43 conference and international meeting papers.

TECHNOLOGY TRANSFER *(Invention Disclosures)*
PSRSMA – 1999
US/England Cementitious Composite – published by the New York University Press

PROFESSIONAL AFFILIATIONS

- American Concrete Institute (ACI). Full member of ACI Committees: 325 - Concrete Pavements, 348 - Structural Safety, 446 - Fracture Mechanics, and 544 - Fiber Reinforced Concrete. Associate member of ACI Committee 440 - FRP Bar and Tendon Reinforcement. American Society of Civil Engineers (ASCE). Earthquake Engineering Research Institute (EERI). International Association of Bridge and Structural Engineering (IABSE). Materials Research Society (MRS). Society for Experimental Mechanics (SEM).

Reference, report, seminar and publication information available upon request.

LIUBA WOHLFON

301 North Byron, Suite 53-111 • Raleigh, NC 28755 • (910) 578-7110

OBJECTIVE: An entry-level professional position applying knowledge of international business practices and language skills.

EDUCATION : M.B.A., Finance/Investments, University of Southern Mississippi, 1996
B.A., Foreign Languages, Rostov State University, Rostov-on-Don, Russia, 1992

KEY SKILLS & AREAS OF EXPERIENCE

♦ **Linguistic Ability:** Fluent (verbal and written word) in Russian, German, and English. Conversant in French and Spanish. Possess a well-developed, multicultural understanding of many countries, including Spain (traveled to Seville, Granada, Cordoba), Sweden (Stockholm) and Germany (Dusseldorf). Resided near Dusseldorf for one year.

♦ **Communication/Presentation:** Prepared and delivered presentation, an industry and competitive analysis of Pillsbury, for graduate-school project. Applied Porter's S.W.O.T. principles. Worked as member of five-person team. Also conducted an assessment, using S.W.O.T. analytical procedures, to assist in developing a marketing strategy for Percy Quinn State Park.

♦ **Instruction/Translation:** Instructed U.S. Marines (Special Forces) in Russian at Jimmy Carter Warfare Center, Fort Sumter, South Carolina.

♦ **Financial Analysis:** Performed discounted cash flow analysis, net present value (NPV) analysis and internal rate of return (IRR) for capital budgeting projects, using Excel spreadsheet. Identified and selected five mutual funds -- from 300 -- to establish an optimal mutual fund portfolio, using mathematical models.

♦ **Financial Instruments:** Extensive knowledge of various financial instruments such as options (calls and puts), futures and other derivatives. Used Black-Schole's Option Pricing Model to calculate the value of an option.

♦ **Scholarship/Award:** Selected as one of 10 candidates (from 100) to participate in an international business seminar series held in New Orleans. Seminar covered international finance, export/import of goods, letters of credit documentation and the cultural aspects of global business practices.

WORK HISTORY: Magna Carta Funding Corporation — Cornelius, N.C. (7/98-Present)
- Financial Analyst

Northview Junior High School — Hopedale, Va. (1/94-6/94)
- Teacher, French and Spanish

Jimmy Carter Warfare Center — Fort Sumter, S.C. (2/92-12/93)
- Teacher, Russian

SuperValue, Inc. (formerly Wetterau, Inc.) — Minneapolis, Minn. (6/92-8/92)
- Interpreter for president of international sales force for this grocery distributor.

COMPUTER SKILLS: Microsoft Office (Word, PowerPoint, Excel)

THOMAS C. GRAMMENOU

37, Astigos Street 26222, Thessaloniki, Greece • Tel: 0030-61-426666 • Mobile: 0030-64-426984
Fax: 0040-48-425555 • Email: grammenou@ggg.net

SENIOR EXECUTIVE PROFILE
VICE PRESIDENT / GLOBAL DIRECTOR / SENIOR OPERATING MANAGEMENT
**Pharmaceutical - Medical - Consumer with emphasis in Process Reengineering
and International Business Development**
Start-up, Turnaround and High Growth Organizations

DYNAMIC EXECUTIVE with vision-driven management career combining 12 years' experience propelling and leading international business initiatives worldwide. Superior motivation with a powerful drive to succeed; thrive on challenge but seek first to discover unique opportunities. Positive intellectual with exceptional capacity to segment, converge, analyze and ultimately integrate innovative ideas and concepts into effective solutions.

EXPERTISE IN INTERNATIONAL OPERATIONS with comprehensive knowledge of European, American and German culture, business practices and methodologies. Broad travel throughout Europe, US and Germany with powerful cross-cultural and educational experiences. Demonstrated ability to productively conceive tactical strategies, execute business plans and implement innovative processes to deliver results while expanding international markets. Aggressively seek profitable growth utilizing innovation as fundamental motivator.

EXCEPTIONAL LEADERSHIP capacity combined with excellent communication and interpersonal skills. Compelling ability to clearly communicate ideas into multiple cultures and positions of responsibility simultaneously, creating an indispensable advantage in the international economy. Recognized for matchless ability to grasp the relationship between bottom-line profitability while mentoring and motivating team members.

ADVANCED ANALYTICAL SKILLS AND INNOVATIVE APPROACH TO PROBLEM ANALYSIS AND RESOLUTION delivering continuous cost-effective solutions. Keen analysis of market dynamics, competition and macroeconomic demographics. Persuasive negotiation skills that generate win-win situations. Expert skill in leveraging cross-franchise and cross-functional efforts to decrease operating expenses.

Fluent in Greek and English with basic knowledge of German. Willing to relocate internationally. PC literate.

CORE EXECUTIVE COMPETENCIES

• **Operations Management**	• **General Management**	• **Recruiting / Mentoring**
• **Strategic Planning & Development**	• **Qualitative Assessment**	• **Organizational Development**
• **Sales / Marketing**	• **Market Development**	• **Training and Development**
• **Crisis Management**	• **P & L Forecasting**	• **Negotiations / Presentations**
• **Recruiting**	• **Logistics**	• **Credit Control / Finance**

SELECTED ACHIEVEMENTS

- **Ignited sales 299%** over four-year period (1994–1998) by implementing innovative strategies and tactical plans, resulting in doubling net income.
- **Achieved Outstanding Sales Performance Award** (1997) by DePuy-PAROS for increasing international sales market by 53% in only one year.
- Delivered dramatic **97% sales increase**, (1992–1994, PAROS Franchise).
- Significantly **increased sales by 71%,** improving gross profits by 16% and doubling net income.

NOTABLE PROJECTS / VENTURES

BUSINESS CONSULTING   1998 – present
Business Development Project:
Currently leading development of several small retailers (Medical–devices, disposable, equipment, instruments, Pharmaceutical–OTC pharmaceutical, vitamins, natural health products, and Consumer–cosmetics, toiletries, fragrances and personal products) to consolidate organizations. Conceive, develop and coordinate all aspects of business plan, analyzing existing potential as well as stratagem for future expansion. Harmonize and consolidate existing logistic systems to develop a superior centralized process.

(Business Consulting – continued)

SIGNIFICANT CONTRIBUTIONS

- Projected value of newly formed company is expected to reach $140 million.
- Spearheaded recruitment process and assessed potential employers to select appropriate management personnel and sales force as well as design innovative incentive program.
- Conceived and developed major promotional plan to execute strategies to achieve 5-year business plan.
- Prepared and instituted negotiation stratagem to facilitate procurement of products from multinational companies.

Military Medical Service Project:

Recruited to assess quality of products and pricing provided by medical/pharmaceutical/consumer companies to military hospitals in Greece. Monitor and assess companies' service and performance levels, proposing alternative solutions as necessary.

PROFESSIONAL CAREER HISTORY

Metsovo – Medical Products, Athens, Greece   1986–1998
(Originally division of Metsovo Consumer Product until becoming a separate entity in 1991.)

—Fast track promotion through increasingly responsible engineering, project management and operating management positions. Recruited to each successive position based on consistent contributions to productivity, quality, efficiency improvement and cost reductions. Key player in building company from ground zero to a functional, effective and highly profitable growing entity.

QUALITY DIRECTOR (1996–1998)
Managed and directed all aspects of evaluations and continued improvement of Total Business Control and Assessment Processes. Orchestrated in-house research, organization and implementation of quality control programs. Spearheaded negotiations between local Metsovo Medical Company, the International Companies and governing members regarding current state of Qualitative Assessment of Business Processes.

SIGNIFICANT CONTRIBUTIONS

- Created and effected innovative employee training seminars.
- Implemented initiatives to drive successful achievement of ISO 9002 Quality Assurance level.

FRANCHISE DIRECTOR – DePuy-PAROS Division (1992–1996)
—Total sales achieving $12 million, 1/3 total revenue of Metsovo -Medical Products. Managed operating budget of $2.6 million.

Conceptualized and implemented all aspects of total business plan encompassing development and execution of innovative marketing strategies. Evaluated viability of business opportunities, and initiated and presented winning business proposals. Full accountability for profit and loss. Oversaw and directed staff of 18 sales and marketing team members and support services team, delivering all aspects of successful team leadership to include incentives, motivational training and enhanced measures to increase productivity. Led all facets of public relations including interaction with global corporate leaders.

SIGNIFICANT CONTRIBUTIONS

- Developed and established an expanded network of dealers.
- **Championed #1 ranking for Paros** in knee replacement market and #6 for hip replacements.
- Established an outstanding sales and marketing team; achieved zero headcount turnover.

BUSINESS MANAGER – PAROS Franchise (1991–1992)
—Division specializing in neurosurgical implants and instruments and spinal surgical instruments.

Wrote and implemented Business Plan with full accountability for profit and loss including financial review of each division, analyzing budget and allocation. Full responsibility for sales and marketing team and support services team comprised of 10 staff members. Oversaw Franchise's human resources including staffing and operations management. Directed research to interpret data regarding market trends and company objectives.

(Professional Experience PAROS Franchise – continued)

SIGNIFICANT CONTRIBUTIONS
- Promoted MEDOS (shunts) achieving #1 position in the market with 54% market share for PAROS in Greece.
- Achieved zero headcount turnovers.

BUSINESS MANAGER – Medical Franchise & Dental Franchise (1990–1991)
— *Division specializing in infection control products, hemostats and advanced wound care products.*

(See job description for PAROS Franchise)

SIGNIFICANT CONTRIBUTIONS
- Successfully reduced inventory to less than 80 days from 266 days in one year.
- Accelerated time frame for receivables from 205 days to 132, by implementing more effective business practices in the dental sector.
- Radically expanded the emergent dental business by 275% in one year, resulting in exorbitant profits.

PRODUCT MANAGER – Ethicon Sutures & Iolab Franchises (1988–1990)
—*Division of wound management products and ophthalmologic products.*

Managed and directed sales and marketing team of five and support services team of three. Trained sales staff and company employees on product history, characteristics and marketing targets. Initiated sales objectives and forecasted market fluctuations, while controlling inventory and maintaining competitive pricing. Prepared manuals with technical specifications, and offered user training to customers. Trained sales staff and company employees on product history, characteristics and marketing targets.

SIGNIFICANT CONTRIBUTIONS
- Created innovative sales strategy to achieve **sales growth of 88%** in four years.
- Implemented strong product management initiatives to establish exponential growth in the ophthalmic suture market.
- Captured 65% of market share by 1992 for synthetic absorbable sutures.
- Pioneered successful launch of laparoscopic business into Greek market, establishing a reference point for other launches.

ASSISTANT PRODUCT MANAGER – Ethicon Sutures (1986–1988)

EDUCATION

Master of Science (Mechanical Engineering: Materials/Biomedical), Harvard University – 1987
Bachelor of Science (Mechanical Engineering), Boston University – 1983
Bachelor of Engineering Technology (Mechanical Engineering), Boston University – 1983

PROFESSIONAL CAREER DEVELOPMENT

The Leadership Challenge– Metsovo, Greece – 1997
Advanced Management Program – International Institute for Management Development, Switzerland – 1992
Effective Divisional Management – Metsovo, Greece – 1989

Keywords: *Vice President of Sales & Marketing, Vice President of Global Sales & Marketing, Regional Vice President of Sales & Marketing, Managing Global Director, Global Quality Director, Sales, Marketing, Business Development, Total Business Management, Logistics*

OGANOV G. VERGEY

1085 SUMMIT ◆ WARD CITY, MISSOURI 64106
PHONE: 816-741-0557 ◆ WIRELESS: 816-532-1018
EMAIL: MULTICOUNTRITRADING@AOL.COM

INTERNATIONAL TRADE AND BUSINESS DEVELOPMENT

- ❖ EXPERTISE IN INTERNATIONAL TRADE, IMPORT/EXPORT BUSINESS INITIATIVES AND POTENTIAL, AND NEW PRODUCT DEVELOPMENT TO MAXIMIZE PROFIT POTENTIAL.
- ❖ KNOWLEDGE OF EUROPEAN CULTURE AND CUSTOMS; SKILLED IN CONSULTATIVE SALES AND EFFECTIVE NEGOTIATIONS.
- ❖ INSIGHT TO IDENTIFY MARKET NEEDS; CONDUCT RESEARCH ON MARKET PENETRATION IN COMPETITIVE FIELDS.
- ❖ COORDINATE MARKETING, LABELING, AND DISTRIBUTION OF PRODUCTS.
- ❖ LANGUAGES: ENGLISH, RUSSIAN, ARMENIAN, TURKISH, SLOVIC.

BACKGROUND AND EXPERIENCE

MULTI COUNTRY TRADING CO., LTD.   1994 - PRESENT
WARD CITY, MISSOURI

DEPUTY TRADE REPRESENTATIVE
BROKER OF INTERNATIONAL TRADE PRODUCTS (MEAT, CONFECTIONERY, BEVERAGES, LIQUOR, FOOD, OIL, LUMBER). DIRECT NEW BUSINESS DEVELOPMENT, MARKETING OF PRODUCTS, NEGOTIATING WITH CLIENTS AND PREPARING FEASIBILITY STUDIES AND BUSINESS PLANS.
- ➢ Representative Markets: Russia, Austria, Sweden, Denmark, Poland, Germany, Kazahstan, Uzbekestan
- ➢ Contracted with a major political party of Russia to import and distribute used U.S. farm equipment. (450 units/$11 million annually)
- ➢ Established a market for a select line of doors/windows utilizing Russian lumber, manufactured in Sweden, and imported to the United States. ($1.2 million)
- ➢ Established a market for a chemical industry unit of natural gas re-manufacturing for residential utilization in a former Russia republic. ($3.5 million)

EXPERIENCE IN RUSSIA

CREATOR TRADING COMPANY   1992 - 1993

PRESIDENT/CO-OWNER
INITIATED/STARTED AN IMPORTED/EXPORT BUSINESS SPECIALIZING IN RETAILED BEVERAGES, CONFECTIONERIES, AND AUTOMOBILES. PRIMARY AFFILIATIONS WITH POLAND AND GERMANY. OPERATED FIVE RETAIL FACILITIES.

OTECHESTVO PRINTING AND PUBLISHING   1990 - 1992

GENERAL MANAGER
MANAGED OPERATIONS SPECIALIZING IN PUBLICATION OF BOOKS AND NEWSPAPERS.
- ➢ MEMBER: BOARD OF DIRECTORS

OGANOV G. VERGEY

EDUCATIONAL BACKGROUND

UNION UNIVERSITY OF RUSSIA
MOSCOW, RUSSIA

MASTER OF BUSINESS ADMINISTRATION - 1992
EMPHASIS: INTERNATIONAL HOSPITALITY

RUSSIA PRINTING ACADEMY
MOSCOW, RUSSIA

BACHELOR OF TECHNOLOGICAL ENGINEER - 1990
MAJOR: PRINTING

CONTINUED PROFESSIONAL DEVELOPMENT
PENN VALLEY COMMUNITY COLLEGE
- ENGLISH

1993

CONFERENCES/SEMINARS:
INTERNATIONAL FOOD TRADE SHOW, MOSCOW, RUSSIA   1997
UNITED STATES MEAT FEDERATION CONFERENCE, VAIL, COLORADO   1996

OTHER SIGNIFICANT ENDEAVORS

MEMBER

UNITED NATIONS CLUB
FOUNDING KANSAS CITY, MO LOCAL CHAPTER
NOVGOROD, RUSSIA TO BE SISTER CITY

1997

PERSONAL DATA

MILITARY: SPECIAL FORCES; COMMANDER OF PLATOON; 1988-1989

Resumes for the Far East

83

Charles Gresham

Apartment B205, 6-19-11 Rinami Rzabe
Rinato-ku, Tokyo 203, Japan

voice ● (8l-3) 5555-5555
e-mail ● cgresham@aol.com

Global Aviation Program Management ● Airline Management ● Consulting

Career Profile

Experienced global aviation professional with over fifteen years of technical and managerial background in profitable oversight of multimillion-dollar domestic and international airline programs, teams, and engineering support. Director/North Asia for Boeing and previous experience with Eastern Airlines. Hold M.B.A. in International Business.

Constantly utilize knowledge gained from positions as major aviation supplier *and* airline customer. Enhance program and airline management through experience as airline manager, commercial pilot, aviation instructor, airframe / powerplant mechanic, and aviation sales / marketing professional.

Key Areas of Expertise

- Aviation Program Management
- On-Site Consulting
- Off-Site Team Management
- Jet Engine & Aviation Services
- Aviation Education
- Labor Relations

- Airline Engine Shop Management
- Heavy Maintenance
- Aviation Safety
- Maintenance Planning & Management
- Airframe & Powerplant Mechanic
- FAA Regulatory Compliance

- GE Six Sigma Tools
- Cost-Per-Hour Programs
- Expense Reduction
- Airline Transport Pilot
- Cross-Cultural Business
- French Language Proficiency

Global Aviation Program Management Qualifications

Consistently drive results in a rapidly changing industry, within global cultural environments.
Frequently receive corporate recognition for excellence in program management, leadership, and sales. Produce multi-million-dollar achievements in leading-edge project management, team administration, and project troubleshooting.

Use business abilities, interpersonal skills, technical expertise, and a quick grasp of issues, to influence parties to reach win-win solutions from a position of mutual respect.
Met airline fleet production schedules and spare engine requirements while manager of an Eastern Airlines 250-employee jet engine shop. Maintained labor relations and employee productivity in a difficult union environment.

Led domestic and international on-site aviation program support teams for Boeing customers including Japan Airlines, Air France, Douglas Aircraft, and Grumman.
Managed multi-million-dollar projects including high-value, cost-per-hour sales and support proposals at Japan Airlines and other Asian customers. Helped Boeing minimize costs, meet delivery, and achieve contract schedule commitments on a major engine program by coordination of innovative design approaches.

3,000 flight hours with Flight Instructor, Commuter Airline, and Corporate Pilot experience. Licensed Airframe and Powerplant Mechanic.
As a flight instructor, trained 23 student pilots for FAA certificates, achieving a 91% first-attempt passing rate for FAA pilot certificate examinations. Instructed students for FAA airframe / powerplant mechanic written exam.

Work effectively within Japanese and Asian business and societal cultures.
To do business in Japan is to become like water dripping on a rock: adaptable, tremendously patient, diplomatically persistent, controlled, listening more than talking, and considerate of Asian preferences for personal contact and written correspondence.

Easily absorb and practice the nuances of multi-cultural business practices and social values.
Lived five years in Japan, five years in Paris, and additional years in the Middle East and Europe. World traveled, and experienced with sales and service support for multi-cultural business units.

Recent Career Development and Accomplishments

BOEING AIRCRAFT ENGINES, JAPAN AND USA

1988 to present

Director – North Asia
BOEING Engine Services, Tokyo, Japan

(1999 to present)

- **Challenges**

Build corporate relationships and sell high-value jet engine maintenance programs to Asian airlines including Japan Airlines, Japan Air Systems, Asiana, and Korean Air. Surpass annual sales goal of $15 to $20 million in products and programs including US-based MCPH, overhaul services, and component repair. Accomplish this in a competitive yet conventional corporate environment that has been historically reluctant to outsource.

- **Action Steps**

Developed extensive customer contact and education. Pursued direct involvement with marketing, business development, and product support teams. Promoted joint venture concepts within parameters of Japanese business practices. Acted on declining Japanese economy as opportunity to increase conservative Japanese executives' awareness of offshore maintenance programs as viable cost-reducing options. Applied GE Six Sigma Tools in daily activities.

- **Results**

In first year, generated $350 million in new business proposals and penetrated new markets. Increased sales over 30%. Recognized as consistent top performer.

Manager – Commercial Engine Support Programs
Assignment: Japan Airlines, Tokyo, Japan
(1997 to 1999)

- **Challenges**

As on-site program manager, assure Japan Airlines' (one of Boeing's most demanding customers) satisfaction with Boeing jet engine programs. Increase sales and provide leadership to seven-member service team in Japan and Korea. Oversee $2.1 million administration budget. Complete a GE Six Sigma Project for customer response time improvement.

- **Action Steps**

Provided solid business and technical support on Boeing jet engines with effective leadership of technical, program, and product support team for CF6-80C2 and CFM56 engines. Coordinated with marketing to increase sales. Maintained frequent VP-level contact and contributed guidance in engineering, business, and contract matters.

- **Results**

Recognized by Boeing as a sustained high performer. Established relationships of trust with all levels of Japan Airlines' management including Senior VP levels. Completed a GE Six Sigma Project that improved customer technical response time and enhanced customer satisfaction. Sold high-value jet engine upgrade / modification / spare part programs.

Senior Propulsion Representative – Commercial Engine Programs Operation
Assignment: Douglas Aircraft, Long Beach, CA

(1996 to 1997)

- **Challenges**

Provide on-site engineering, business, product, upgrade, and flight operations support as well as re-engining studies to Douglas Aircraft Corporation (a major airframer) on high-value commercial engine programs for MD-11, DC-10, and KC-10 aircraft and CF6 engines.

- **Action Steps**

Resolved technical and business matters and facilitated customer acceptance / delivery of these high-value products. Coordinated resolution of contract and financial matters.

- **Results**

Recognized by Boeing for a major contribution to customer satisfaction in the introduction of a high-value product to service - the Boeing CF6-80C2 engine on the Douglas MD-11 aircraft.

Early Technical Experience and Accomplishments

BOEING (continued)

Airline Representative – Field Service Operation
Assignment: Air France, Paris, France, and MD-11 Flight Test, Yuma, AZ (1993 to 1996)

Contributed CF6 technical support to shop, hangar, flight line, test cell, and flight operations as well as to the introduction of the CF6-80C2 at Air France.

Senior Representative – Business Planning and Market Development
Assignment: Grumman Aircraft, Bethpage, NY (1990 to 1993)

Controlled Boeing's costs by direct participation in Grumman's U.S. Navy F-14 re-engining program. Coordinated design concepts and resolved business / contractual matters for this $70M+ military engine development program.

Regional Sales Manager – Boeing Engine Services / Strother
San Diego, CA (1988 to 1990)

Using technical background, increased sales of high-value jet engine services by 35%, growing to $2 million (in 1982 dollars). Prepared proposals, market forecasts, and negotiated contracts for 170 Boeing business aircraft.

EASTERN AIRLINES, SAN DIEGO, CA **1987 to 1988**
Manager of Rolls Royce Engines, Jet Engine Overhaul Shop Foreman, Production Planner

Supervised 250 employees on Rolls Royce RB-211 jet engine overhaul / repair. Managed Lockheed L-1011 fleet jet engine program. Handled complex labor relations, promoting union-member inclusion, motivation, and performance.

BOEING AIRCRAFT ENGINES, FRANCE AND SAUDI ARABIA **1984 to 1987**
Field Service Representative – Paris, Europe, Middle East. Aviation Instructor – Dhahran

Provided customer support in Europe, the Middle East, and Africa. Provided technical support to engine overhaul shops. Conducted formal aviation technical training in Saudi Arabia and supervised foreign nationals.

Hands-on Aeronautical Background

3,000 pilot-hours and 1,000 flight-instructor hours (bi-annual refresher training) with commuter airline and corporate pilot experience Broad knowledge of **commercial / business aircraft and military aviation** with **jet engine emphasis. Recruited / trained instructors** for New England Aeronautical Institute and prepared students in Spain and England for **FAA airframe / powerplant mechanic written exam.** Experienced **airframe and powerplant mechanic and jet engine shop foreman.**

Technical Training: Flight Instructor Refresher Training – 1997, MD-11 Performance Engineers Course – 1992, MD-11 Cockpit Familiarization – 1992.

FAA Certificates: Flight Instructor - Airplane / Instrument, Ground Instructor - Advanced and Instrument, Airline Transport Pilot - Multi-Engine, Airframe and Powerplant Mechanic

Education and Management Development Courses

M.B.A. in International Business, Columbia University, New York, NY 1983
B.A. in Aviation Maintenance Management, Ardell University, Naperville, IL 1981
FAA Airframe and Powerplant Mechanic, Yeager Aeronautical University, San Diego, CA 1977

Boeing Professional Education: Services Growth course, Six Sigma "Greenbelt" training, Engine Services sales seminar, Advanced Marketing Management seminar, Negotiations Skills workshop. **State University of New York Course:** Four-week management training. **McDonnell Douglas Course:** Market Development

William B. McGuire

billmcguire@aol.com

Beijing, China
Tel.: 86-47-7423-8960
Fax: 86-47-7423-0045

General Management / Operations Executive

Start-up, Turnaround, and Rapid-Growth Companies / Building Presence for U.S. Corporations in China

Areas of Expertise

- Strategic Planning and Executive Decision-Making
- Product Positioning, Packaging and Launch
- Sales and Marketing Strategy and Execution
- Market Penetration — New Business Development

- Multicultural Business Operations
- Strategic Alliances and Partnerships
- Customer Service and Relationship Building
- Team Leadership / Motivation / Development

Career Highlights

- Achieved rapid speed-to-market in successful product introduction in Chinese market through hands-on leadership of strategic planning, product development, packaging, marketing, and distribution.

- Established substantial market presence for U.S. corporation in China — increased sales exponentially to multi-million dollar level in first year of aggressive launch of new sales operation.

- Consistently delivered strong sales results, innovative sales programs, and creative team / partnership initiatives.

- Demonstrated ability to rapidly acclimate and develop strong business relationships in multicultural environments.

- Achieved business functional Chinese language level.

Professional Experience

ASIAFOOD, INC., Beijing, China, 1999-Present
Publicly traded US food processor involved in start-up joint-venture in China, marketing and distributing branded food products through affiliation with Nickelodeon
—Chief Operating Officer: China (2001-Present)
—Vice President Sales and Marketing (2000)
—Sales Director / National Sales Manager (1999)

Advanced rapidly from Sales Director to COO position… assumed responsibility for organization in transition and struggling to gain market share.

Successfully introduced in Chinese market a line of 5 snack-food products, all branded with Nickelodeon characters. Within one year, led the organization from concept through packaging, distribution, and successful launch, in an invigorating environment of teamwork, joint problem-solving, and common commitment to goal achievement.

- Instrumental in strategic planning and crisis management to resolve differences with Chinese joint venture partner… took a leadership role in dismantling the joint venture relationship (through extensive Chinese government red tape) and reengineering the company for independent operations. Recruited a talented cross-functional management team for the new organization.

- Initiated the development of a B2B e-commerce platform to interface between US companies and China-based retailers. This platform was a critical component to demonstrating a viable marketing strategy and retaining our investment funding.

- Investigated co-packing partners and established relationship with Chinese branch of Kool Karton, one of the world's largest packaging companies. Directed product packaging redesign involving native Chinese designer and extensive consumer test-marketing, resulting in packaging that was preferred by Chinese children 4 to 1 over original US-created design. Identified and contracted with local distribution partner.

- Launched snack products and spearheaded sales and marketing initiatives within a challenging retail environment. Secured distribution with large multinationals and local supermarket chains.

- Managed all facets of product launch and marketing on an extremely tight budget through effective negotiation and creative partnerships with packaging and distribution companies.

87

Professional Experience, continued

POULTRY FARMERS OF AMERICA, Annapolis, Maryland, 1989-1999
Poultry processor with worldwide sales of US$5 billion

—Director of Sales and Marketing and Chief Representative in China — Beijing, China (1997-1999)

Developed business strategy and directed all sales activities to drive poultry sales in China. Prepared budgets and forecasts; managed staff and operations; coordinated sales activities with US-based support functions. Negotiated pricing, shipping, delivery, and other critical details of perishable-goods supply.

- Recruited to launch PFA's Beijing office to increase market presence, capture market share, and develop business opportunities in the vast Chinese market. Built operation from start-up: located, renovated, and equipped office; recruited, hired, and trained multinational staff; created and implemented business policies and procedures.
- Delivered immediate and impressive sales results: **2000% increase over prior year** in 1998; **432% increase** in 1999.
- Secured preferred position for PFA's top-quality products in the best hotels in Beijing and Shanghai (Holiday Inn, Westin, and Hilton) by identifying and supporting key distributors.
- Captured 20 new accounts for non-food products related to poultry processing.

—Manager, Poultry Products Sales, Annapolis, Maryland (1992-1997)

Managed international and domestic sales, positioning, and pricing for 1.25 million tons of poultry products with annual sales of US$150 million

Developed corporate strategies and marketing programs with complete proforma P&L accountability. Oversaw new product development and marketing. Personally managed all international customers and sales initiatives.

- Built internal alliances to ensure integrated and coordinated sales and delivery efforts.
- Trained and mentored sales associates; successfully developed a high percentage for increased responsibility.
- Developed long-term key supplier arrangements with Procter & Gamble, Colgate Palmolive, and Lever Brothers.

—Sales Representative, Annapolis, Maryland (1989-1992)

- Delivered significant cost efficiencies at two bulk terminals exporting product to the Far East and Europe.
- Created and successfully implemented innovative program to increase profitability by eliminating middleman.

WEDDLE'S FEED & SEED, Iowa City, Iowa, 1987-1989 — *Family-owned feed ingredient merchandiser*
—Feed Ingredient Merchandiser

AGRARIAN INDUSTRIES, INC., Kansas City, Missouri, 1983-1987 —*Regional supply cooperative*
—Regional Procurement Coordinator (1985-1987)
—Feed Ingredient Merchandiser (1983-1985)

Education and Professional Development

B.S. Agronomy, Agribusiness Emphasis, 1977
University of Kansas — Lawrence, Kansas

Zenger-Miller and Frontline Management Training

SUE L. CHENG
telephone: 3399-7744

6E Tower, Hillsdale Bay
Taipo, NT, Hong Kong
e-mail: slcheng@hongxkong.net

■ **OBJECTIVE**

To apply skills and knowledge of e-business, e-government and telecom markets in the Asian-Pacific Region, project management and cross-cultural communications (Western and Asian) acquired through experience in diverse business environments.

■ **EDUCATION**

M.B.A. with a concentration in Management of Global Information Technology and e-Commerce Marketing, May 2001
AMERICAN UNIVERSITY SCHOOL OF BUSINESS, Washington, DC

Selected Management Consulting Projects:

- **Redman, Brotter & Williams Communications, Washington, DC** – Conducted comprehensive assessment of the business practices of the Washington DC-based public relations firm. Designed a detailed e-business plan focusing on process improvement and communication strategies, integrating order fulfillment, service delivery and customer relationship management, resulting in significant reduction in daily operating costs.

- **ADI Management Institute, Alexandria, VA** – Performed an on-site analysis of the organization's management information systems requirements and designed procurement system that integrated contracting, accounting and receiving processes, resulting in more responsive, user-friendly system with real-time trackable data.

- **PacSystems Inc., Arlington, VA** – Analyzed existing business model and global expansion opportunities for a B2B e-marketplace serving the U.S. packaging industry. Conducted extensive research of major international packaging markets in Asia and Europe. Designed and presented to senior executives the region-specific sales/marketing for effective market positioning and entry. Commended on research depth and dynamic presentation style.

Awards:

- Case competition winner out of 10 teams in the Managers in International Economy class on Steinway's entry strategy to the China market. Professor's comment: *"You made the best presentation on that case ever; no one else was even close."*

B.S. in Communications, graduated summa cum laude, 1992-1996
UNIVERSITY OF RICHMOND, Richmond, VA

■ **INTERNSHIPS**

FORSTERI INTERNATIONAL, Washington, DC	2000-2001
CAPITAL CORPORATION, Washington, DC	2000-2001

Intern – During MBA program, completed internships related to business outreach, e-commerce marketing and e-business/e-government analysis. Engagement projects included:

Capital Corporation – Conducted market risk analysis on telecom, Internet and e-commerce development throughout the Greater China Region (China, Hong Kong and Taiwan) and identified global market trends, growth areas and investment opportunities for Aster Technologies, a client of the international investment and consulting firm. Results were published for senior decision makers on Aster's Intranet.

■ INTERNSHIPS
continued...

Forsteri International – Assessed e-business policy/leadership and e-government readiness in the China market for the global technology and policy consulting firm and clients, including Dunston-Patterson, Jones Smythe and Hamden. Contributed research and analysis to company publication, *"Risk E-Business: Seizing the Opportunity of Global E-Readiness."* Utilized contacts in China and acted as liaison between firm and Chinese Ministry of Information Industry that regulates Internet and telecom development.

■ EMPLOYMENT

AMERICAN UNIVERSITY, Washington, DC   1996 - 1999
Project Manager – Multicultural Affairs

Initiated, created and marketed cultural training initiatives, special events and educational programs; conducted workshops on cross-cultural issues. Designed department's website and served as webmaster. Coordinated, authored and produced all office publications. Accomplishments:

- Revamped, secured funding and successfully promoted the academic training program. Results: increased participation rate 30% and achieved the highest retention rate organization-wide (34% above national average). Served as consultant to other organizations to establish similar programs.

- Appointed by President to direct the cross-functional strategic planning efforts that resulted in the development of the effective Leadership Training Institute.

- Chosen as internal consultant for the human resources practice in staff recruitment and retention to improve the university's diversity progress.

■ TECHNICAL SKILLS

Microsoft Office Suite, Lotus Notes, SQL, HTML, SPSS, Datatel, Netscape Communicator, NJStar (Chinese Language Software), Compass Marketing Software and PageMaker.

■ LANGUAGES

Fluent in Chinese (Mandarin and Shanghai Dialect) and English

■ REFERENCES

Available on request

WALTER deLEON
65-42829272

24 Parkway Road, Singapore 288408
wdeleon@email.net

INTERNATIONAL BUSINESS EXECUTIVE – SOUTHEAST ASIA
Mergers & Acquisitions ... Strategic Planning ... International Business Development
Diplomatic Protocol ... Foreign Investments ... Cross-Cultural Relationship Management

Top-flight senior-level executive with more than 18 years' experience leading corporations through complex start-up, turnaround, and high-growth cycles to meet financial and quality objectives. Strong qualifications in P&L management, IT, and project management. Fluent in English, Mandarin, and Cantonese. B.S. in MIS.

Negotiations ... Successful in structuring and negotiating favorable private financings, expansions, mergers, and acquisitions.

Operations ... Expert in analyzing existing operations and sophisticated technologies and creating effective strategies to streamline processes and improve performance.

Risk Management ... Extensive experience in creating strategic risk financing strategies and management plans, which effectively reduce exposure and limit liability.

Consulting ... Senior-level advisor to international executive financial, operating, and management teams.

Notable Accomplishments and Expertise:

Challenge: Expand company operations and diversify income streams for a retail brokerage company. *Action:* Led the organization's first-ever entry into institutional sales and corporate finance activities. *Result: Solidified the company's economic position by creating higher revenues from new sources, improving cash flow, and mitigating the risks of single-source income.*

Challenge: Champion a new business opportunity for the fastest growing bank in Indonesia. *Action:* Launched a successful structured finance department for Collateralized Bond Obligation (CBO) activities. *Result: Positioned the organization as a top-notch investment bank in the Asian market, generating $4.7 million (US) in profit within the first 8 months of operation.*

Challenge: Pioneer risk management controls to reduce extremely high-embedded risks. *Action:* Executed internal policies and procedures. *Result: Strengthened the organization's internal procedures and eliminated the risk of losing more than $10 million (US).*

Challenge: Assess the integrity and viability of one of the world's leading professional services organization's trading systems prior to global market expansion. *Action:* Created foreign equities and margin trading systems; developed accounting and settlement procedures meeting generally acceptable risk management standards; and analyzed existing supporting software applications to ensure viability. *Result: Identified and eliminated a potentially devastating flaw in the design and logic of the system and procedure pre-expansion.*

PROFESSIONAL EXPERIENCE

WORLDWIDE, INC., Singapore – since 1998
Director
   Provide financial, business, technology, and e-commerce consulting solutions to executives and major corporations. Recruited as Special Matter Expert for Ernst & Young for Asian Pacific region.

INTERNATIONAL BANK, Indonesia – 1995 to 1998
Advisor
   Promoted to serve as advisor to one of Indonesia's fastest growing private banks. Launched the organization's first-ever structured finance department.

Managing Director
   Recruited for management experience, international expertise, credit and risk management knowledge, marketing and negotiating skills to lead the organization's first entry into the corporate arena.

GLOBAL SECURITIES, Singapore – 1993 to 1995
Institutional Dealer
   Managed Singapore and Malaysian equities for Fortune 500 and asset management companies.

MERRILL LYNCH, Singapore – 1991 to 1993
Investment Advisor
   Promoted U.S. equities and treasury products for this diversified global investment firm.

TAYLOR & BROWN, United States – 1984 to 1991
Director – Lleondy Co., Ltd.
General Manager – Goal Win Co., Ltd.
   Recruited to manage 27 retail stores, 2000 employees, and 3 wholesale lines in New York and San Francisco. Promoted to start-up the Lleondy garment manufacturing facility in Los Angeles, creating a successful wholesale line for J.C. Penney, Target, and Woolworth.

EDUCATION

Bachelor of Science in MIS
University of North Carolina, Chapel Hill, North Carolina

SAM LAPAGE

5-33-332 Hashimoto-cho, Chikusa-ku
Nagoya, Japan 464-0035
Email: slp@onenet.net
+81.52.888.3288 (home), +81.52.888.2222 (fax), 555.555.5555 (US voicemail)

HIGHLIGHTS

Master's degree from highly-regarded Japanese university.

Multilingual project manager with international experience in marketing, market research, and consulting, along with practical experience in computer technology and telecommunications.

Extensive experience with start-up businesses, retail franchises, and OEMs. Significant experience assisting companies enter foreign markets.

Highly effective customer relationship manager in international environments.

Build team environments and foster open communication.

Flexible and willing to travel extensively and relocate nationally or internationally.

SUMMARY / ACHIEVEMENTS

INTERNATIONAL BUSINESS MANAGEMENT. Strong finance and accounting background. Used international experiences of language and cultural knowledge to negotiate new contracts, discover new product lines, and create new business. Effectively developed and managed international start-ups.

Spearheaded and established new niche market retail chain with exclusive contracts between head office in Japan and manufacturing companies in New York and Munich that generated over $1 million in revenue within 1 year.

Proven success in reducing costs; producing substantial profits, even in declining and competitive markets; developing new procedures; problem solving; negotiating; communicating; and motivating employees.

ENTREPRENEURIAL MINDED. Led start-up company to successfully achieve online retail sales of $1.5 million within 3 years. Aptitude and interest in Internet businesses. Innovative problem solver and effective communicator with out-of-the box mentality who develops quality management, marketing, and sales teams. Selectively delegate responsibility to lead personnel.

SALES / CUSTOMER SERVICE TRAINING. Trained sales team of 20 employees on newly designed computer software usage and customer application.
Supervised and trained new customer service staff in sales, cashiering, problem solving, and inventory control.

Oversaw retail sales and customer service procedures for processing sales in excess of $4 million annually for 2 stores producing substantial profits.

MULTI-LINGUAL/CULTURAL. Advanced business level Spanish and Japanese. Traveled on business worldwide.

EMPLOYMENT

Overseas Exchange, Inc. Japan, Nagoya, Japan
President / Owner, 1998 – Present
International corporation established in Japan in 1997 with American management and delivery / shipping branch. Startup with online retail sales of ice/roller hockey equipment with annual sales of $1.5 million. Ranked #1 ice hockey Internet site in Japan from 1998 – 2000.

Oversee P&L and prepare monthly/annual financial reports in Japan and US. Prepare financial analysis including cash flow, income statements, and balance sheets.

In charge of website development, marketing and advertising, sales, communications, and customer service.

Attend all overseas sporting goods and footwear trade shows in search of new products.

Recruit, train, and develop sales force in call center.

Research and locate new business opportunities in ever-changing global economy.

VOLUNTEER/ AWARDS/ ASSOCIATIONS

Member, American Chamber of Commerce in Japan (ACCJ), 1997 – Present.

Founder and Coach, Youth In-line Hockey League, Nagoya, Japan, 1997 – Present

Member, American Business Community in Nagoya (ABCN), 1996 – Present.

Japanese Ministry of Education Fellowship (Monbusho) 1995 – 1997. *Equivalent to US Fulbright.*

Group Leader / Counselor, Experiment for International Living, Brattleboro, VT. (Mexico 1991 and Australia 1992).

COMPUTER SKILLS

MS PowerPoint, Publisher, FrontPage, Outlook, Excel, Word. Corel Office, Word-Perfect, Photoshop, Illustrator, Intuit Kobanto (Japan), and Quicken.

✗ Established start-up business as foreigner in Japan. Obtained 99% of stock share in company (very unusual for foreigners).

✗ Brought company from debt to profit within 11 months by analyzing and implementing effective sales and accounting systems.

✗ Attained stable annual sales of $1.5 million within first 3 years.

Midway's Company, Ltd., Hiroshima, Japan
International Director/New Business Consultant, June 2000 – May 2001
Senior Management Consultant for start-up manufacturer of niche-oriented consumer products. Midway's employs over 100 in 21 stores in Tokyo, Osaka, Nagoya, and Hiroshima with annual sales of over $100 million. Company sells "extreme" sporting goods: surf-, skate-, snow-, and windboards and are ranked in top 5% in industry.

Reported to President/CEO and supervised and trained 50 employees in software usage, direct sales, and footwear specialties.

Formulated strategies and negotiated with manufacturers on key issues relating to pricing, delivery quantities, and business expansion. Oversaw retail sales and customer service procedures for processing sales of $1+ million annually.

Directed training and management of retail sales and distribution of computerized foot pressure measurement system.

Attended international manufacturing conventions to acquire new products and negotiate exclusive distribution contracts.

Acted as translator and new business development advisor.

✗ Instrumental in acquisition of 9 new stores. Increased annual sales from $53 million to $100 million in 1 year.

✗ Opened 2 new stores with annual revenues of $4 million. Secured 2 exclusive distribution contracts with German and American manufacturers.

✗ Increased footwear annual sales by 75% in 1 year.

Iniha Inc., Nagoya, Japan
Translator/Import Specialist, April 1997 – March 1998
Architectural firm/construction company with 250 employees and $500 million in annual sales. Managed 10 import specialists. Taught cost reduction methods for packing, shipping, and distribution of materials. Accountable for receiving over $150 million worth of materials.

✗ Developed methods for reducing import duties by 45%. Reduced inventory losses from 9.5% to 3%.

EDUCATION

Nagoya University Graduate School of International Development, Nagoya, Japan
M.A. International Cooperation, 1997
GPA: 3.95. Graduated in top 1% of class.
Extra Curricular Activities: **Treasurer** of Aichi Foreign Student Association, 1996-1997.

CERTIFICATIONS

Intensive Japanese, YWCA Language School, Nagoya, Japan 1995
Intensive Spanish, Instituto de Relaciones Culturales, Mexico City, 1989

RICHMOND T. CARTER
32 Sanjing West Road ▫ Changzhou, Kiangsu, China
Residence 8852 2017 3919 ▫ Business/Mobile 0852 4701 9442

richcarter@ghuan.cz.js.cn

WORLD CLASS MANUFACTURING
Supply Chain & Distribution Management / Manufacturing Engineering
Business Process Reengineering / Purchasing & Materials Management

Highest-ranking country executive in large global manufacturing operations throughout Europe and Asia. Expert in hi-tech, high-volume manufacturing environments in the US and abroad with full P&L, capital expenditure and executive staffing accountability. Extensive distribution network with major OEMs in the computer hardware and electronic component market, with high-profile achievements including building manufacturing plants and installing operations for 4 of the largest disk drive manufacturers in the world.

Multinational Boards of Directors
Renowned International Conference Speaker

PROFESSIONAL EXPERIENCE

Exilor Peripherals; Irvine, CA   1996 – 2000
Billion-Dollar Multinational Disk Drive Manufacturer

President, Asia Operations
    Challenge: Redesign all manufacturing processes to include robotics assembly, cell concept and Kan Ban manufacturing methods. Chartered to transition the culture and operations into "Six Sigma" disciplines and restructure to a batch-mode manufacturing process.

    Achievements
- Directed multi-site plant operations for high-volume manufacturing facilities in Singapore, South Korea, Malaysia and the Peoples Republic of China. Combined revenues exceeded $1 billion, with 13 executive reports and 5,000 employees. Improved output volume from 300,000 per month to over 1,000,000 per month in one year. Accelerated production from under 385,000 units per quarter to over 4 million, increasing gross margins 300%.

Southern Digital Corp; San Diego, CA   1990 – 1996
Billion-Dollar Multinational Disk Drive Manufacturer

Vice President, Asian Operations (1990-1996)
    Challenge: Charged with the organizational redesign and implementation of sophisticated Western manufacturing strategies to position country operations for aggressive growth and expansion initiatives.

    Achievements
- Introduced JIT methodology, substantially increasing inventory turns and saving $250 million the first year. Reduced scrap $23 million in less than 24 months and ultimately reduced scrap levels to .65%. Designed and implemented "End-of-Life" strategies for disposition of obsolete materials.

- One of only two Western executives assigned to the Singapore National Productivity Board designed to set-up training grants and programs for various Asian businesses and industry. Negotiated tax incentives for new and existing US companies with local Asian governments. Negotiated a 23-year tax-free status for three multinational companies and saved Southern Digital $50 million in annual tax obligations.

Professional Experience continued...

Landview Corporation; Denver, CO   **1983 – 1989**
Billion-Dollar Multinational Disk Drive Manufacturer

Vice President Singapore Operations (1985-1989)
Challenge: Lead multinational cross-functional team through research, design and execution strategies to expand into the Asian market.

Achievements

- Established communications with government officials to define permitting, zoning, code requirements and labor standards. Under strict government monitor, time constraints and compliance issues, managed all activities of the ground-up construction of a 300,000 square foot manufacturing facility. Led cross-cultural team of contractors, engineers, technologist and laborers to complete project 60 days ahead of schedule and 15% under budget.

- Designed and installed the plant's production and operating systems, and assembled a highly qualified leadership team of manufacturing executives from the US, Europe and Asia. Directed a group of 8 first-line reports in the development of HR policy and procedure. Hired and trained over 5,000 employees and introduced class 10 clean rooms.

- During the first 12 months of operation, received numerous awards for meeting extremely challenging deadlines and revenue goals. Won the "Eye of the Tiger" award from the Asian Business Advisory Counsel (ABAC) for the most innovative solutions to increase growth in one year.

PRESENTATIONS

Kennedy School Of Business – Harvard University,
"US Multinational Companies in Asia"

East Asian Executive Leadership Conference – Harvard University
and Nanyang Technology University – Singapore
"Supply Chain Management Concepts"

Pepperdine University and University Of Paris
International Management Series for Graduate Students

BOARD OF DIRECTORS

Republic Of Singapore National Productivity Board
Singapore Technical Training Committee
Singapore Data Storage Institute

EDUCATION

Hawkeye Institute Of Technology; Denver, CO
Associates of Applied Science – Electrical Engineering, 1987

DeVry Institute of Technology; Chicago, IL
Associates of Applied Science – Industrial Engineering, 1982

DONALD B. BAUMER

1-28-3 Toyosatonomori
Tsukuba, Ibaraki ken, 300.268
Phone/Fax: 0.298.471.555
E-mail: dbbm@donbaumer.prserv.net

SENIOR MARKETING & BUSINESS DEVELOPMENT EXECUTIVE
EXPERT IN INTERNATIONAL EXPANSION

**Strategic & Tactical Marketing & Sales / Competitive Market Intelligence / B2B Marketing
New Territory Development & Penetration / New Product Launch & Positioning / Foreign Nationals Leadership**

Results-oriented, confident and creative spearheading successful marketing and business development programs in the global arena. Combines expertise in strategic alliances, organizational leadership, engineering and project management. Consistent success in identifying opportunities for product launch, market penetration and accelerated growth. Practical knowledge and understanding of Asian/Japanese management techniques, culture and business trends. Excellent skills in team building, quality performance and productivity improvement.

PROFESSIONAL EXPERIENCE:

Independent Consultant, 2000 – Present
HSLD LTD, INC., Tokyo Japan

Created HSLD LTD to serve the Automotive and IT industries, and broaden Asian business development and program management expertise.

Clients / Activities
- *B2B Automotive aftermarket exchange – Helped to formulate business plan and Japan market entry strategy.*
- *Automotive component research Japanese market – On behalf of world's leading automotive forecast group, collected market data regarding interiors market in Japan.*
- *Automotive Forecasting – Consulted world's leading automotive forecast group concerning Japan market entry.*
- *M&A strategy Asia Pacific – Consulted with major player in automotive closure systems for strategic partnership plan.*

Director of Engineering and Sales, 1995 – 2000
MAGNA INTERNATIONAL, INC., Troy, MI, Tokyo Japan

Joined Magna International specifically to expand the Atoma Hardware & Door Systems division's Japanese customer business. The goal was to ensure all programs ran smoothly while meeting the needs of the customer. Challenged to formulate and execute sales strategies in the identification of key products. Utilized effective problem-solving skills to create solutions and work through tenuous situations.

Accomplishments
- *Grew Japanese customer base, increasing sales from $3M to $50M in five years, thus establishing a substantial Magna presence in Japan.*
- *Directed the set-up of a new Japanese office and an information systems program to a more profitable location. This move saved time, decreased costs and increased productivity.*
- *Organized and executed the Toyota Global Technical Show in Toyota, Japan and Ann Arbor, MI. – 1999 & 1996*
- *Coordinated the Tokyo Motor Show exhibit in Tokyo, Japan. – 1999 & 1997*
- *Sales Awards: 2000 – Best Sales Negotiation; 1997 – Best Team Effort; 1996 – Best Sales Presentation*
- *Program Management – Nissan TK decklid, GMT355 SAP & Endgate, Cluster*

New Business Development Manager, 1987 – 1995
ZEXEL USA, Farmington Hills, MI & Tokyo, Japan

While holding the dual roles of New Business Development Manager and Account Manager, consistently successful in identifying and capitalizing upon market opportunities to drive revenue growth, expand market penetration and win dominant market share. Demonstrated outstanding presentation, negotiation and closing skills.

Accomplishments
♦ *Secured a $32M annual account to install air conditioning units on all new Saturns.*
♦ *Procured a $13M price increase on Satum account compressors through successful negotiation.*
♦ *First American to be transferred to the corporate headquarters in Tokyo, Japan, becoming the cultural liaison between Japanese and American manufacturing facilities.*
♦ *Managed the successful launch of the Subaru account resulting in them obtaining POE air conditioning from Zexel.*
♦ *Secured, managed and serviced the General Motors GEO Storm POE air conditioning business.*
♦ *Worked on the original Navigation systems team.*

Sales Engineer, 1984 – 1987
AKR ROBOTICS, Livonia, MI

Coordinated project management and engineering for large-scale robotic paint systems – projects at major automotive and aerospace manufacturing plants in the US and Canada. Oversaw purchasing, operations, inventory systems, service, sales and installation.

Accomplishments
♦ *Established North American operations for this French multinational corporation.*
♦ *Secured and managed the program of a $2M Hyundai automated paint shop project.*
♦ *Organized profitable service/maintenance programs for key accounts.*

Owner, 1982 – 1983
SHAPE BUILDER ENTERPRISES. Farmington Hills, MI

Starting with a business concept and a personal commitment to success, launched Shape Builder Enterprises in 1982 to meet an identified market need of customized home and institutional exercise equipment. After consulting with clients, manufactured the equipment to meet specific customer needs. Attained $200K in gross sales for the year.

EDUCATION

Business Management, **Northwood University**, Midland, MI, expected graduation 2002
Industrial Engineering, **Lawrence Technological University**, Southfield, MI

ORGANIZATIONS

Kaisha Society, Tokyo, Japan – a professional Networking organization
American – Japan Society, Tokyo, Japan – enhances relations between the US & Japan
Canadian Chamber of Commerce – Board of Governors – Japan
JMEC- Executive Committee

LANGUAGE SKILLS

Japanese: Speak, read and write – Katakana & Hiragana   Japanese Government level 4 certified 1993
French: Speak – Survival level

KEVIN J. C. TAYLOR
newmediaxyz@globalxyz.com

West Shengli Road
Shaoxing, Zhejiang, P.R. China

Business 00 86 575 515
Mobile 1 971 675 3912

INTERNATIONAL PUBLISHING EXECUTIVE
Mergers & Acquisitions · Joint Ventures & Strategic Partnering · IPOs
E·Business · E·Publishing · Website Development

Ground zero strategist highly successful pioneering innovative new product lines, implementing emerging technologies and negotiating international partnerships in a large brick and mortar environment. Championed early electronic publishing initiatives with leading US publishers, and spearheaded one of the first multimedia channel programs in a print media environment. Negotiated strategic partnerships with cable television companies, telecommunications providers and newly emerging online marketing portals.

Highly Accomplished International Conference Speaker
US • Europe • Asia
MBA Degree – Columbia University

PROFESSIONAL EXPERIENCE

InternationalGuide.com (IGcom); New York, & Hong Kong   **2000 – Present**

A well-funded clicks and mortar company valued at $75 million, with 350 employees, 150 international sales reps, and 5 offices in China and New York. Negotiated joint venture start-up between Publishers, Inc. and China's only fully integrated telecommunications company. Built an Internet-based operating company in three countries, which successfully withstood the most intensive due diligence by its publicly traded investors. Negotiated a $33 million investment partnership with Infospace and the leading Hong Kong telecom.

**Currently IGcom offers the first tri-lingual online yellow pages catering
to the Chinese and Chinese/American business community.**

CHIEF EXECUTIVE OFFICER

- ❑ Established the North American subsidiary based in New York to capture the manufacturing and export business of American and Chinese American companies seeking to expand into China. Launched the Global Trade Directory and Wireless Directory Services as the second and third major product line, delivering an additional $2.5 million revenue within 6 months.

- ❑ Through 5 executive level reports, provided the strategic leadership for the print publishing operation in Shenzhen; the IT organization in Beijing; and the Internet professional services group in the US and China. Established global pricing, defined contact-to-contract relationship strategies, and designed compensation and incentives programs for the 150-member international sales organization.

**Strategies achieved a 1000% growth in monthly page views,
increased database by 1 million businesses, and improved top-line sales 250+%.**

Publishers, Inc.; Purchase, NY   1990 – 2000

Integral member of the executive leadership team to successfully separate PublishersUSA, Inc. from its parent Dun and Bradstreet, and establish Publishers, Inc. as an independent public company. With 2000 employees, $1+ billion annual sales revenue, 500,000 business customers, 370 directories to over 40 million homes and businesses in the US, Publishers, Inc. is the premier yellow pages sales agent and publisher for the nation's largest telecommunications companies.

SENIOR VICE PRESIDENT STRATEGIC MARKETING & BUSINESS DEVELOPMENT (1995-2000)

- ❑ Created the vision and strategy for the modern yellow pages directory business in South China. Negotiated complex transaction with the Chinese Ministry of Telecommunications and established the yellow pages/Internet joint venture noted in the above position.

- ❑ Led a team of senior-level executives through the intricacies of business licensing in China, including establishing HR policy and building international government relationships. Successful start-up and growth of InternationalGuide.com led to the promotion to CEO of the newly formed joint venture and relocation to China.

VICE PRESIDENT, PRODUCT MANAGEMENT (1990-1995)

- ❑ Pioneered the development of the multimedia product line including cable television, tele-communications services, audiotex, and Internet yellow pages. Grew the cable TV advertising business into the company's premier growth product, increasing operating income 52%.

- ❑ Built a multi-market business alliance with AOL and Switchboard.com which generated $5 million within 8 months. Cable and Internet sales accelerated to $14.2 million over 12 months and to $35 million by the end of the second year.

EARLY CAREER HIGHLIGHTS

Worldwide Media; NY, NY (1985-1990)
Director New Publications Division, Travel Agent Magazine
Associate Publisher, Unique Homes Magazine
Managed a national telemarketing sales force and launched 9 new travel directories
realizing combined revenues of $21 million. Returned a declining
publication to profitability yielding $6 million annual revenue.

Ziff-Davis Publishing; New York, NY
Director Business Development (1980-1985)
Spearheaded the creation and expansion of the print and electronic
publication business initiatives.

EDUCATION

Columbia University; New York, NY
Master of Business Administration – International Business, 1990
Bachelor of Science – Business Administration, 1980

United States Address:
4150 Harris Boulevard
San Luis Obispo, California 93401
U.S.A.
805.971.6119 tel

SAMUEL L. JOSEPH

China Address:
Zhong Hui Gardens Bldg. 20, Apt. 9
Lane 22, Wu Xing Road
Beijing, 500621 China
2186.2426.2801 tel/fax

josepsl@worldwide.com ▪ josephsl@online.bj.cn

REAL ESTATE DEVELOPMENT EXECUTIVE – FAR EASTERN MARKETS

PROFILE

Senior Executive with 20 years' International Business experience, predominately in Greater China; strong educational background and significant success in large, international development management. MIM credentials with advanced management education from Harvard University. *Expertise includes:*

- Asian Business Environment/Culture
- International Negotiation
- Organizational Design
- Multiple Department Management
- Leadership & Team Building
- Establishing Strategic Vision & Market Position
- Joint Venture Partnerships
- International Marketing
- Profit Optimization
- Managing Large Multi-Use Developments
- Mandarin Chinese

PROFESSIONAL EXPERIENCE

Senior Consultant for Property Development   1998 to Present
GREATER HSINCHU CORPORATION – TAIPEI, TAIWAN
(Entity made up of Taiwan's 12 largest companies developing world's largest Build, Operate and Transfer (BOT) rail project - $49 billion USD.)

Lead team in feasibility study for 10 station developments totaling 29 million square foot floor area. Includes providing development direction in creating Master Plan for entire 358 hectare area and extensive Taiwan Real Estate market research.

Deputy General Manager/Director of Marketing   1994 to 1998
SEASIDE LIMITED – BEIJING, CHINA (1988 to 1998)
(25-year partnership of The Pradami Companies (Chicago), The International Group (New York), Tajima Incorporated (Osaka) and Asia-World Development (Hong Kong) responsible for financing, design, construction, management of Beijing Centre. Foreign joint venture partner with Beijing Exhibition Center, a bureau level organization directly subordinate to municipal government.)

> BEIJING CENTRE PROJECT – A $205 million USD multi-use real estate joint venture project between Seaside Limited and Beijing Centre. Three million square foot building includes 515-room Ritz-Carlton Hotel, 575 apartments, 310,000 square foot commercial office space, 70,000 square foot retail space, 2,000-seat theater and underground parking facilities. Opened in 1989, remains one of the largest and most successful foreign investments in Beijing.

Directed staff (640 Chinese nationals and 25 expatriates of various nationalities), managed and coordinated all building operation departments including Property Management, Engineering, etc. Responsible for profit and loss and customer relations; negotiated major issues with municipal and district authorities and joint venture partner.

Led marketing effort to lease office, commercial (retail) and residential space. Included creating financial strategy to maximize return, contracting with real estate agencies for new rentals, expansions and renewals, and formulation of advertising and public relations strategies to heighten market awareness.

Key achievements:

- Established brand name and image for Beijing Centre – universally known as "Pradami" – synonymous with quality and prestige.
- Increased annual revenue from $30 million USD loss in first year to exceeding $92 million USD in five years (for which I was directly responsible).

PROFESSIONAL EXPERIENCE

Deputy General Manager/Director of Marketing
SEASIDE LIMITED – BEIJING, CHINA

Key achievements: (continued)
- Instrumental in eliminating $175 million USD debt in seven years. Beijing Centre is one of the very few developments to pay off debt.
- Successfully negotiated 10-year joint venture extension with Chinese partner; approved by Chinese government, all agencies and bureaus.

Senior Marketing Manager   1988 to 1994

Created and implemented annual marketing plans, defined marketing strategy and set $50 million USD budget goals; Managed all leasing activities including office, commercial and residential, and directed staff of seven as well as all departments associated with marketing. Included preparing semi-monthly marketing reports, presenting quarterly financial status reports, and negotiating leases and management contracts; constructing and analyzing financial models of retail outlets determining viability, and working with design departments facilitating tenant renovation.

Key achievements:
- Attained 100% occupancy within three years; world-class clientele, weak market.
- Maintained Beijing's highest occupancy and rate; most successful development.

Chief Development Manager   1985 to 1988
PRADAMI OVERSEAS – CHICAGO, ILLINOIS
(International Development and Management Company; part of the Pradami Group of companies.)

Based in Beijing, China, served as liaison and negotiator with joint venture partner and Chinese authorities, developed marketing strategy and operations of Beijing Centre during and after construction. Included meeting and negotiating with government agencies regarding tax issues, loan guarantee, foreign exchange, importation and customs, building and code requirements, personnel and legal requirements. Performed company registration for subcontractors and management companies.

Sinologist & Travel Consultant   1980 to 1985
BAI TRAVEL, INCORPORATED – STANFORD, CALIFORNIA/HONG KONG, CHINA

Led teams of foreign experts/travelers through China, Southeast Asia and Sub-continent.

ACADEMIC CREDENTIALS

HARVARD UNIVERSITY – CAMBRIDGE, MASSACHUSETTS
Advanced Management Program   1999

AMERICAN SCHOOL OF INTERNATIONAL MANAGEMENT – GLENDALE, ARIZONA
Master of International Management (MIM)   1994
Concentrations: Marketing, Management, International Finance and Trade.

STANFORD UNIVERSITY – STANFORD, CALIFORNIA
Graduate studies in computer studies and Chinese language   1983

NEW YORK UNIVERSITY – NEW YORK CITY, NEW YORK
Bachelor of Arts (BA)   1980
Double major: History and Philosophy

THE CHINESE UNIVERSITY OF HONG KONG – HONG KONG, CHINA
Exchange student   1980
Concentrations: Chinese Modern History, Philosophy and Economics

FJ JEN CATHOLIC UNIVERSITY – TAIPEI, TAIWAN
Accelerated courses in Chinese language   1979

United States Address: SAMUEL L. JOSEPH   *China Address:*
4150 Harris Boulevard   Zhong Hui Gardens Bldg. 6, Apt. 701
San Luis Obispo, California 93401 U.S.A.   Lane 22, Wu Xing Road, Beijing, 500621 China
805.971.6119 tel   josepsl@worldwide.com ▪ josephsl@online.bj.cn   2186.2426.2801 tel/fax

BARRY A. WAHL

FB 25-11
Singapore, PS DIE 05330-770

Home: 212 44 12 383-1133   *E-mail:* DieSingapore@aol.com

SECURITY PROFESSIONAL

More than 20 years' experience in drug enforcement administration with a consistently outstanding performance. Strong narcotics investigative skills with excellent qualifications in strategic planning/ coordination of investigative operations, resource allocation, information gathering and reporting. Excellent briefing and presentation skills. Extensive experience in the U.S. and abroad (Indonesia, Brunei, Singapore, Pakistan, Saudi Arabia, United Arab Emirates). Conversant in Bahasa Indonesian language.

- Developing Liaison Contacts & Sources
- Electronic Surveillance
- Interviews & Investigations
- Knowledge of Asian Laws & Culture
- Leadership & Team Building Skills

- Tactical Field Operations
- Technical Advice & Expert Testimony
- Training Seminar Presentations
- International Drug Designation Negotiations
- Clandestine Laboratory Certified

PROFESSIONAL EXPERIENCE:

DRUG INVESTIGATION & ENFORCEMENT (DIE) — Washington, D.C.   1980-2001

Assistant Country Attaché — Singapore (10/97-10/01)

Assigned to Singapore DIE Country Office and challenged to direct investigative operations throughout Singapore, Indonesia and Brunei. Tracked suspected ships and containers transiting Singapore. Conducted large-scale investigations targeting high-profile drug traffickers involving heroin, methamphetamine, marijuana, cocaine and ecstasy (MDMA). Conducted investigations on precursor and essential chemicals for the manufacturing of designated drugs. Presented professional training seminars on various security and drug-related issues. Instructed mail service employees (e.g., Federal Express, DHL, UPS, TNT) on mail and parcel drug interdiction.

Established liaison contacts with primary Singapore Country Office (SICO) affiliates, the Central Narcotics Bureau (CNB), Singapore's Commercial Affairs Department (CAD), the Indonesian National Police Narkoba Directorate (INP/Narkoba), and the Bruneian Narcotics Control Bureau in developing strategies to disrupt and immobilize drug trafficking.

Served as case agent or co-case agent in *numerous major* drug investigations.

- Spearheaded the *first*-ever joint DIE and INP/Narkoba precursor chemical investigation. Resulted in seizure of 4,400 kilograms of acetic anhydride, precursor used in heroin production.

- Conducted joint investigation with the INP/Narkoba, DIE New York and DIE Kuala Lumpur C.O., resulting in the seizure of heroin and the arrest of a Jakarta-based source of supply.

- Managed (co-case agent) joint DIE Singapore and Singapore CNB investigation leading to the arrest of 3 Pakistani nationals and the largest seizure of heroin in Singapore (destined for New York City) in more than 2 years.

  - Case represented the *first* time DIE agents testified in a Singaporean court.

- Commended in joint letters of appreciation from Malaysian and DIE host officials (Director, Narcotics Department, Royal Malaysia Police (RMP) in Bukit Aman, Kuala Lumpur and DIE Country Attaché, U.S. Embassy in Kuala Lumpur) for expertise in a joint operation between the 2 agencies, which resulted in an undercover delivery of heroin and the arrest of 1 suspect.

  - Operation marked the *first* joint accomplishment with the RMP in several years.

103

· Participated in negotiation of the *first* drug designation agreement allowing exchange of financial data on drug-money laundering suspects, reciprocal honoring of asset forfeiture requests, and the sharing of assets between the Government of Singapore and U.S. Department of Justice.

· Established, developed and maintained dynamic, ongoing relationships with key INP officials throughout Indonesia, ranging from brigadier general to sergeant major, to expand DIE's network. As a result:

- Arrested and deported 8 suspects, high-level drug traffickers, with outstanding DIE/U.S. Federal arrest warrants.

- Arrested 32 foreign national drug dealers responsible for distribution of heroin, ecstasy, marijuana, hashish and cocaine. Worked directly with the Naval Criminal Investigative Service (NCIS) Far East Field Office and the INP in this *first* joint NCIS-DIE-INP narcotics suppression operation based in Bali. Operation was recognized by Vice Admiral Natter, USN, Commander, 7th Fleet in a "personal for" message.

- Orchestrated the *first* clandestine methamphetamine/ecstasy laboratory seizure in Jakarta, representing sufficient finished product to produce 2.4 million tablets.

- Led investigation netting the *largest* seizure of methamphetamine in Jakarta.

- Conducted surveillance and provided technical expertise for joint DIE/INP operation, resulting in the *largest* seizure of hashish in Indonesia.

· Developed and instructed numerous training conferences to increase knowledge of drug surveillance, mail and drug parcel interdiction, international controlled drug deliveries, undercover techniques, informant management, drug equipment/clandestine laboratory, drug trafficking trends and other related topics.

· Recognized with "International Award of Honor" in 1998 for outstanding performance in a major heroin investigation by the International Narcotic Enforcement Officers Association at the 40th Annual International Drug Conference.

· Won a U.S. DIE "Exceptional Performance" award (1999) for the aggressive, successful investigation, arrest and prosecution of a drug trafficker.

Senior Special Agent — Sierra Vista, Ariz. (6/90-10/97)

Challenged to establish a DIE post of duty in Sierra Vista, one of the primary smuggling corridors between Mexico and the U.S. Established DIE presence in southeast Arizona and 2 customs ports (Douglas and Naco). Supervised new agents and served as back-up supervisor for 7 agents. Developed working relationships with major law enforcement agencies, organizing and directing a joint provisional task force to combat illegal drug activities along the U.S. and Mexican border.

· Spearheaded the initial detection of an underground tunnel between the U.S. and Mexico, designed by a Mexican drug cartel, to smuggle large quantities of cocaine.

· Acknowledged with 1987 "Exceptional Performance" and "Special Achievement" awards.

· Achieved the highest conviction rate among 8 agents in Southwestern region.

Special Agent — Karachi, Pakistan (3/85-6/90)

Worked on international heroin cases originating from Pakistan, Iran and Afghanistan. Traveled worldwide, often serving as an undercover agent.

Special Agent — Atlanta, Ga. (3/81-3/85)

Handled corruption cases involving the security of drug smuggling loads entering Henry County, Georgia through high-level local law enforcement officials.

· As an undercover agent, participated in the investigation, arrest and prosecution of the Henry County Sheriff, Chief of Police, County Judge and County Commissioner, all of whom received sentences ranging from 30-35 years. Testified as the DIE cases' main witness.

DIE Special Agent Trainee — Washington, D.C. (12/80-3/81)

Appointed Trainee, December 1980. Graduated #1 in class.

BOSTON POLICE DEPARTMENT — Boston, Mass.   1971-1980

Police Detective — DIE Task Force (1978-1980)
Police Detective — Narcotics Squad (1974-1978)
Patrol Officer (1971-1974)

MILITARY: U.S. Marine Corps   1967-1970
- Vietnam Veteran, 9/68-10/69
  - Assigned to 15th Counterintelligence Team, 3rd Marine Division, Dong Ha, Vietnam.
  - Awarded Individual Commendation Medal.

EDUCATION: B.S., Criminal Justice, University of Virginia, Charlottesville, Va., 1977

PERSONAL: Runner enthusiast; scuba diver (Advanced Certificate and Underwater Cavern Certification); avid camper and hiker.

Resumes for Latin America

LINDA A. BONITO
Licensed Architect

1227 Oak Avenue
Lantern, Texas 77391

telephone: 331-271-9952
facsimile: 331-271-9953

ARCHITECT / PROJECT MANAGER with experience in the planning, design, and construction of diverse project renovations (major and minor) and architecture projects such as institutional, recreational, and health care facilities. Extensive background in **urbanism** and all infrastructure directing all project phases, from design through completion of construction, coordinating the efforts of contractors, architectural, engineering and landscaping consultants, and government agencies. Excellent technical qualifications complement an **innate sense of creativity** in the design of aesthetically attractive, architecturally strong, and utilitarian space. Highly organized and proficient in AutoCAD. Meticulous, detail-oriented, perfectionist; work well under pressure.

AREAS OF PROFICIENCY

Experienced in all phases of design from program definition through working drawing; expertise in
- construction estimating, cost analysis, feasibility studies, and project budgeting
- negotiation and contract administration
- inspection and supervision of construction

< Solid design and construction experience in commercial projects including landscaping, office buildings, schools, churches, hotels, and restaurants.

< Established a **regional reputation** for excellence and developed a loyal following. Highly successful financial results in project profitability and investor ROI.

< Strong **management skills**, including personnel and project scheduling, employee and subcontractor supervision, budgeting and finance, problem solving, client relations, and quality control.

< Seasoned **sales and marketing skills**. Demonstrated ability to gain trust and confidence of prospects. Personable and highly ethical.

< Proven **communications ability** that is straightforward, honest, articulate, yet tactful and diplomatic. Sincere sensitivity to unique needs and aspirations of all segments of a community. Active listening and consultation skills with talent for respecting and responding to divergent opinions and interests. Strength in blending idealism with political reality, and devising new methods to improve procedural and system efficiency.

< Computer literate: Microsoft PowerPoint, Aldus PageMaker, CorelDraw, Harvard Graphics.

< Fully bilingual: Spanish and English.

CAREER HIGHLIGHTS

ARCHITECT
Planin Consultores, S.A., Caracas, Venezuela

1999   Designed, drafted, and supervised the building project for the new emergency area for Adults and Pediatrics at the Hospital Clinico de Caracas.

1997   Remodeled living quarters on the second floor of the Caracas Hospital (4 models).

1996   Designed individual family units for private owner.
Participated in all project phases from initial client contact and presentation through conceptual design, production of contract documents, interface with engineers and outside planning consultants, and development of interiors, finishes, and specifications.

ARCHITECT
G.P. Arquitectura, S.A., Valencia, Venezuela

1998   Assigned as architect in charge for the Main Control Room project at the Energia
                Eléctrica (Electrical Energy) of Venezuela (ENELVEN / CAUJARITO).

1996   Designed and drafted the remodeling of the main offices at the Investment Bank of
                Welles Orvitz. Served as Director of Field Operations. Reviewed project specifications,
                researched previous designs, and prepared designs for customer presentation and
                approval. Maintained in-house library of design materials and references.

ARCHITECT
Faculty of Architecture, University of Apure, Cabimas, Venezuela

1992 – 1995   Supervising Architect on several relocation projects among which were the communities
                of *El Hornito* (252 acres, $300 million budget, 325 houses from 7 different models, a
                church, elementary school, community center, clinic, and fishing processor center).

                Reviewed development proposals for adherence to county zoning and other ordinances,
                and aesthetically-based design guidelines. Dealt with:
                - zoning administration   - community development
                - site plan review and approval   - stormwater drainage
                - subdivision regulation   - surface hydrology
                - wastewater distribution   - parking lot design
                - design ordinance administration   - environmental impact
                - economic development   - public relations
                - historic preservation   - urban redevelopment
                - environmental impact and planning   - administrative management
                - policy analysis

                Directed and facilitated the design and construction of new development projects and
                improvements to transportation facilities, streets, sidewalks, and utility systems.
                Coordinated/supervised an interdisciplinary team of professional consultants and
                construction inspectors to meet individual project time and cost objectives.

                Prepared graphic files for inspection and critical path schedules; analyzed construction
                schedules from contractors. Monitored project construction daily and represented the
                interests of client at progress meetings. Prepared design revisions when required by
                unknown field conditions.

LANDSCAPE ARCHITECT
Faculty of Architecture / Agronomy, University of Apure, Cabimas, Venezuela

1993   Collaborated with horticulturist Carmen Avila (partner in El Guacamayo Company) on the
                design and development of the exterior landscaping at *La Cabana Hotel* (Aruba, Antilles).

PATENTS AND PUBLICATIONS

- Authored and published *Informe Final*, Relocation Project of the community of *El Hornito*. Presented
  material in Barcelona, Spain (1996).
- Authored, designed, and published *Memoria Descriptiva*, Relocation Project of the community of *El
  Hornito,* which became permanent reference in the library at the Faculty of Architecture.

EDUCATION

Diploma, **Architect**, University of Apure, Cabimas, Venezuela.

EDUARDO CADENAS

Phone: (919) 620-2886
Cell: (919) 545-9632

Email: cadenas414@aol.com

121 Johnson Mill Road, Apt. 11
Durham, North Carolina 27712

CHIEF FINANCIAL OFFICER – INTERNATIONAL MARKETS
Start-up, High-Growth & Multinational Corporations

Corporate Finance Executive with over 15 years' experience leading the financial, treasury, general accounting, and human resource management of world-class multinational corporations. Diverse financial experience across advanced technology and telecom industries. Multilingual, with expertise in the Central and Latin American markets. Consistently delivered strong and sustainable financial gains in highly competitive business markets worldwide through expertise in:

- Strategic Financial & Business Planning
- Financial Modeling
- Corporate Banking & Lending
- International Banking Relations
- Risk & Investment Management

- Transaction Structuring & Negotiations
- Merger & Acquisition Review
- Corporate Treasury Management
- Debt Restructuring & Reduction
- Financial Reviews, IPO & SEC Reporting

PROFESSIONAL EXPERIENCE

COMMUNICATIONS.COM   January 2000 to Present

A 2½-year-old, $5 million capital-infused Internet company specializing in a full range of Latin American e-commerce business solutions for small- and medium-sized businesses in Latin America. Communications.com develops, markets, licenses, and supports a suite of high performance software products allowing customers to deploy Internet-based business applications facilitating B2C and B2B e-commerce.

Chief Financial Officer

Corporate CFO leading the development of all financial, treasury and accounting models plus S-1 IPO filing documentation. Assumed responsibility for human resources and led development of HR infrastructure, benefit programs and payroll functions. Developed nine-person management team overseeing a staff of 40 professionals.

- Established appropriate procedures to comply with SEC regulations, including implementation of corporate policies and procedures for quarterly reviews and annual audits.
- Created all aspects of corporate financial reporting systems, cash management systems, and corporate treasury functions.
- Aggressively facilitated completion of a 2½ year audit being conducted by a Big Five accounting firm within two months to meet scheduled IPO launch date.
- Assisted senior executives in negotiation and completion of agreements with strategic partners and international banks throughout the US and Latin America.
- Assisted in negotiating multinational on-line credit card transaction contracts with VISA's international and local networks.

CASTILLA USA PUBLISHING COMPANY, INC.   1998 to 1999

A $300 million, privately-held multinational publishing company based in Spain with a portfolio of 20 entities in 15 countries throughout North and South America (2000 employees) generating in excess of $150 million annual revenues.

Chief Financial Officer

Corporate Financial Executive recruited to lead formation and financial management of a Miami-based holding company overseeing all 20 of the Americas entities. Coordinated corporate treasury functions, capital budgets, cash management systems, debt restructuring, and financing. Oversaw 15 Directors of Finance. Consolidated and executed all financial reporting functions to Spain's holding company.

- Established standardized financial models, reporting systems, and budgeting processes for all 20 entities, including implementation of a Microsoft SQL-based data warehouse with online analytical tool capabilities.
- Developed and managed critical relationships with international banking institutions to fund Americas operations.
- Led aggressive restructuring, consolidation, and renegotiation of all existing corporate indebtedness and slashed the number of lending institutions from 45 to 5, yielding a $1.2 million interest savings.
- Conducted merger and acquisition feasibility reviews, advised executive management teams, and led financial integration/consolidation.

PROFESSIONAL EXPERIENCE (Continued)

WORLDWIDE HOLDINGS, INC. (WHI)   1994 to 1998

A $500 million holding company with a portfolio of premier video, audio, data, and programming service entities throughout 20 countries worldwide.

Vice President / Chief Financial Officer – CCN Communications (1997 to 1998)

Executive member of a four-person management team selected to lead start-up of a Latin American cable television network.

- Established entire corporate infrastructure including finance, treasury, accounting, operations, human resources, and administration, as well as programming acquisitions.
- Directed financial planning functions and presented final results to Board of Directors and investors.
- Structured transactions and contracts and managed negotiations with operational facility, production company, talent, and artists.

Chief Financial Officer-Latin America – WHI (1995 to 1997)

CFO overseeing all financial, accounting, and audit functions for Latin American investments in excess of $250 million throughout five countries. Reported directly to President of Latin America.

- Coordinated financial reporting functions for WHI properties in Mexico, Venezuela, Brazil, Peru, and Chile in accordance with GAAP and International Accounting Standards.
- Conducted due diligence processes and made final recommendations regarding acquisitions or investments prior to presentation to Board.
- Instrumental in assisting WHI properties in obtaining local financing for operational management and expansion.
- Negotiated with international banks to consolidate debt funding worldwide.

MADRID TELECOM CORPORATION   1990 to 1994

An $8 billion industry-leading manufacturer of telecom equipment and wireless products.

Manager, Finance – Latin America (1993 to 1994)
Director of Finance – Madrid Subsidiary (1993)
Manager of Offshore Accounting (1990 to 1993)

Managed financial operations throughout Latin America and provided support to Vice President of Sales in Central America, Venezuela, Peru, and Argentina.

- Designed a collection system with local banks as part of a joint venture with a major company in Colombia.
- Designed and implemented local accounting functions for Colombia, Venezuela, Brazil, and Argentina offices.
- Designed and implemented an entire billing and collections system supporting annual revenues of $36 million for a telephone company with over 250,000 lines.
- Assisted in the execution of expatriate program including housing, legal and tax matters.
- Set up an Oracle accounts payable/receivable system and slashed receivables 85% within 10 months.

DELOITTE & TOUCHE   1985 to 1990

Senior Accountant-Audit Division

Five years' experience with an industry-leading consulting firm. Participated in audits of international banks, financial institutions, non-profit organizations, captive leasing companies, local government, and public companies.

EDUCATION

BS, Finance and Marketing, Rockhurst College, Kansas City, Missouri, 1984
CPA, North Carolina and Missouri

COMPUTER SKILLS

ProSystem Accounting, Oracle, Platinum, QuickBooks, Microsoft Excel, Lotus, Access, MAS 90, Peachtree

EDUARDO RENDON

3617 Pinnacle Road
San Diego, California 95174

(415) 672-6792
edrendon@aol.com

SENIOR HUMAN RESOURCES & ORGANIZATIONAL EFFECTIVENESS EXECUTIVE
US & International Organizations ... High-Growth, Turnaround & Fortune 500

Business Partner to senior operating and leadership executives to guide the development of performance-driven, customer-driven, market-driven organizations. Recognized for innovative leadership and counsel in transitioning under-performing organizations into top producers and guiding other organizations through accelerated growth and global market expansion. Decisive, energetic and focused. Talented team leader, team player and project manager. Fluent in Spanish, German and English.

Strategic HR Leader with expert qualifications in all generalist HR affairs. Particular success in:

▪ Performance Management Systems	▪ Quality Improvement Processes	▪ Change Management
▪ Process Redesign & Reengineering	▪ 306-Degree Feedback Systems	▪ Job Process Design
▪ Employee Satisfaction & Retention	▪ Rewards & Incentive Programs	▪ Self-Directed Teams
▪ Training, Coaching & Team Building	▪ Organizational Assessments	▪ Cycle Time Reductions
▪ Leadership/Competency Development	▪ Business & People Strategies	▪ Large Scale Change

---

ACCOMPLISHMENT HIGHLIGHTS

☑ **International Experience**: Extensive management and consulting experience with companies operating in Central America and U.S. In-depth understanding of regional labor codes. Managed HR programs for expatriates.

☑ **Organizational Development (OD) Initiatives**: Led many large-scale change programs involving change management, organizational redesign, corporate restructuring and productivity, performance and efficiency improvement. Delivered multi-million dollar cost savings.

☑ **Human Resource Programs**: Instituted 306-degree feedback processes. Designed new HR strategies including new employee orientation programs, rewards and recognition systems, and flextime schedules. Coached corporate executives through leadership and change management initiatives.

☑ **Training & Development**: Trained all levels of staff including executives in one-on-one, small and large group settings. Expertise in adult learning principles, instructional design, program organization and experimental learning methods such as low-rope courses and survival experiences.

☑ **Management/HR Instruction**: Taught courses in change management, team building, coaching, self-directed teams, experimental learning activities, customer service, facilitator skills, train the trainer, leadership development and new business development.

☑ **Executive, Management & Leadership Development**: Designed and implemented Leadership Executive Development Program with Wharton School of Business for business leaders in El Salvador. Currently leading supervisory/management development program for middle managers, incorporating action learning processes.

☑ **Team Building**: Instituted Team Base Programs for numerous organizations implementing large-scale change or single-department initiatives. Marketed brand-name product, TEAMS, in Central America that increased employee satisfaction levels and delivered gains in quality improvement and cost savings for other companies.

☑ **Benefits & Compensation Plans**: Redesigned compensation systems using variable pay system. Restructured salary scales based on competency models creating career ladder for technical employees. Implemented innovative performance-based reward systems minimizing costs of turnover, workers' compensation and low attendance.

111

PROFESSIONAL EXPERIENCE

Best Services International, San Diego, CA   2000-Present
$7 billion corporation with 12 million customers in more than 40 countries. Named #1 most admired outsourcing company in the world by Fortune Magazine.

ORGANIZATIONAL EFFECTIVENESS DIRECTOR

Recruited to lead large-scale change initiative in Best Service's Hospitality Service Management Division. Contracted to SoCal Healthcare System to manage non-clinical services for 2 major hospitals in San Diego. Implement strategy design, process improvement, human resources systems redesign, coaching, teambuilding and leadership development.

Operate under matrix organization reporting to VP of Integrated Support Services, Regional Organizational Effectiveness Director for the West Region and the Advisory Board including hospital COO, VP of Human Resources and VP of Operations for Best Services.

- Restructured 7 non-clinical service departments into single integrated department, requiring staff downsizing and implementation of new systems and processes. Sustained same service quality levels through transition.

- Instituted integrated service model and organizational effectiveness tools: key focus indicators (balance score card), performance management model, Ready for Healthcare (employee orientation system), We S.E.R.V.E. (customer service program), Feeding the Roots (leadership development), Service Center (call center), continuous value improvement program and service partner selection process.

- Revamped hiring selection process for hospital's Support Service Department including behavioral-based tools for hiring/developing employees, standardization of hiring selection tools and team base interviews that include employees. Retrained hiring managers. Reduced selection process cycle time from 4 weeks to 1 week.

- Ensured 5-year cost savings projected at $2.5 million. Improved employee satisfaction levels by 20%.

Escuela Superior de Economia y Negocios, El Salvador, C.A.   1995-2000
Prestigious, non-profit economic development organization offering organizational development consulting services for private and government sector, executive training programs and economic research studies through Economic and Business University in Latin America.

ORGANIZATIONAL DEVELOPMENT CONSULTANT

Program manager for undergraduate business and organizational development extension program at University. Professor of Management, New Business Development and Leadership/Teambuilding programs.

Consulted with corporate clients on organizational development initiatives to drive gains in productivity, quality, cost control and employee satisfaction such as process improvement, operational effectiveness, human resources strategies, reengineering, downsizing and self-directed teams. Clients included Xerox, Pizza Hut, Convergence Communications, Cablevisa, Intercontinental Hotel, La Constancia and others.

- **Convergence Communications, Inc.:** Spearheaded new HR initiatives designed to boost OE competency, employee satisfaction, quality and service. Redesigned compensation and performance/evaluation systems. Led company restructure and downsizing. Reduced overhead expenses by 15% and improved productivity from 73% to 85%. Trained employees to integrate new products and service requirements with no loss of productivity and sustained high levels of service and quality.

- **La Constancia, S.A.:** Guided Central America's largest brewery through "Whole System Change Process" that increased productivity, increased employee satisfaction and reduced costs over $1 million.

- **Viper, S.A:** Led strategic planning effort to streamline key operations, reduce cycle times and improve productivity. Repositioned company as leader in pager service.

- **Xerox:** Instituted work groups for technical service department that increased employee satisfaction levels from 73% to 94% in one year.

- **Pizza Hut**: Supported launch of HR strategy to increase quality, productivity and employee satisfaction. Trained 100+ managers and employees in change management, team building and coaching. Positioned company as #1 in fast food industry in local market.
- **Cablevisa**: Reorganized largest cable network in El Salvador, facilitating reengineering project to reduce cycle times, increase customer satisfaction, eliminate bottlenecks and reduce overhead costs.
- **Additional assignments** included work with Intercontinental Hotel, Banco Capital, Toyota and others.

Duramas, El Salvador, C.A.   1993-1995
Largest shoe manufacturer and retailer in Central America, producing top brands including Bally, Sebago and Hush Puppies.

ORGANIZATIONAL DEVELOPMENT MANAGER

Spearheaded process reengineering initiative. Facilitated, coordinated and motivated workforce to form self-directed work teams and implement change initiatives that reduced cycle times and improved productivity.

- Reduced shoe manufacturing costs from $22 to $19.

General Electric, Moorestown, NJ & Louisville, KY   1991-1993

MASTER IN MANUFACTURING PROGRAM MEMBER

Completed 500+ hours of graduate coursework and 4 manufacturing work assignments in high-volume manufacturing of consumer products and low-volume manufacturing for government contracts. Focused on quality, information systems, industrial engineering, production and supervision. Assignments included:

- **Quality Leader, GE Aerospace.** Managed 1st and 2nd shift quality team (70 employees) inspecting 5 major components. Motivated workforce to meet business plan goals. Fostered communication between functional groups. Addressed customer concerns with proactive, corrective action. Improved process yields by 15%.
- **Industrial Engineer, GE Aerospace.** Led process measurement initiative by GE-IUE union to reduce cycle time and established type-2 engineering rates for work center. Supported Characteristic Verification Process (CVP), a quality improvement effort, during pilot runs in 2 work centers. Reduced cycle time by 10%.
- **Production Engineer, GE Appliances.** Supported production design in shop operations, initiating changes through idea generation and feasibility/evaluation testing. Managed quality improvement projects, enhanced product production, and reduced service call rates and material cost take-outs. Helped to implement self-directed work teams by leading steering committee to develop team guidelines. Oversaw process improvement project to reduce cracked liners. Captured total cost savings of $200,000+.
- **Systems Support Engineer, GE Appliances.** Key implementation team member for Material Scheduling & Quick Response Information System that included billing, inventory control, material flow control, parts scheduling and engineering. Facilitated work-out sessions and trained staff on repair parts scheduling system.

EDUCATION

M.A., Organizational Design & Effectiveness, UCLA, 2000
Executive Certificate Program in Business Administration, University of Barcelona, Spain, 1995
Master in Manufacturing Management, GE Leadership Executive Development, 1993
B.S., Mechanical Engineering, Marquette University, 1991

AFFILIATIONS

Organizational Development Network ▪ Society for Human Resource Management
Competitiveness Network for El Salvador ▪ Founding member of ROTARY International of Ciudad Merliott

Juan Gonzalez

54389 Berlin Avenue • Berlin • Germany
Tel/Fax: +49 55 4 32 53 66 • E-mail: jgonz@email.com

Personal Information:

Born: Quito, Ecuador • 15 March 1958
Marital Status: Married, wife is German; one child
Work Status: Authorized to work in Germany

IT PROJECT LEADER / BUSINESS DEVELOPMENT
Delivering critical team leadership in the design, development, implementation & communication of IT deliverables.

Twenty years IT experience within the European and Brazilian Financial/Banking arena with strong technical and business knowledge of the Card and Transaction Processing Industry:
Acquiring and Issuing • Online Authorization Systems • Security and Key Management
Cardholder and Merchant Systems • Clearing and Settlement Processing

---

Key Strengths:

- Creative, innovative and holistic project leader committed to the delivery of quality and excellence to clients and management. Natural talent and ability to connect, organize, motivate, and inspire team members of diverse nationalities to achieve business objectives within budget and in a timely manner.

- A strong communicator who blends people, business, and technical skills to bring focus and vision to projects, is able to secure commitments and obtain desired results, and knows when to negotiate compromise in order to move projects forward. Strong knowledge of all components of project and software development lifecycles.

- Talent for analyzing problems, developing and simplifying procedures, finding innovative solutions, and integrating projects into the total business solution. Innate curiosity and drive to learn. Committed to professional development.

- International experience in Brazil, Germany, UK, France and Canada. Strong knowledge of South American culture and business practices. Extensive international travel with a strong global network of IT associates. Speaks Portuguese, Spanish, English, and German. Available for global assignments in South America and Europe.

Employment History:

1989-Present   INTERNATIONAL PROCESSING SERVICES, London, UK
                        Formerly belonged to Bank of America, Banco de Santander, Ricos and Beta Group.
                        A global company providing customized card processing and merchant processing services including all system developments and technical support related to such services.

                        Project Manager, Team Leader, Telecom Senior Programmer, Programmer Analyst-IT-Transaction Processing, Cardholder Application, Telecom., & Merchant Development
                        Remained with company through several international mergers and management restructuring.

1987-1988   BANKER'S TRUST, Frankfurt, GERMANY
                        Programmer Analyst / Quality Assurance Department

1986   CANADIAN UNIVERSITY, Halifax, CANADA
                        Programmer Analyst / Administrative Computing Services

1981-1986   BANCO CREDIBANCO, Rio de Janeiro, BRAZIL
                        One of the top 5 private banks in Brazil.
                        Senior Programmer / Application Development

1976-1981   BANCO SUDAMERIS, São Paulo, BRAZIL
                        Brazil's largest private bank.
                        Programmer / Data Processing Department

Career Highlights:

International Project Management

- Worked on international 3-year project with IPS in France to link one of France's largest banks with partner banks outside France to the VISA Net. Developed a complete solution, "The International Interchange Routing", that included Online Authorization (BASE I) interface to VISA via our VISA Access Points (VAPs), and Clearing and Settlement (BASE II) Processing and Routing. This international project involved both the EU and CEMEA regions with 4 different organizations in Germany, France, and the UK. Built and led cross-functional team.
- VISA Bi-Yearly Business Enhancements - BASE I & BASE II.
- Y2K Pre-Certification and Certification Testing for VISA and Europay/MasterCard.
- Contributed to several projects for VISA International including Euro, EMV, CVV Enhancement, VISAPhone, Plus Card, Electron Card, ATM TIER II, Edit Package Upgrades, VAP Upgrades.
- Participated in the development, testing, and implementation of the JCB Project.

Communications and Business Development

- Recognized for developing and maintaining strong worldwide networks and communication with co-workers, contractors, in-house users, software houses, and organizations such as VISA International and Europay International.
- Strong business and technical knowledge of all aspects of software development with the ability to communicate, motivate, and negotiate with applications developers, clients, and senior management to successfully resolve problems and keep projects moving forward.
- Attend vendor meetings in the Card Industry through Europay International and VISA International, as well as international IT fairs and forums such as CeBIT, Cartes, Card Forum, and European Banking Technology.
- Regular contributor to the IPS corporate journal *"IPS INSIDE."*
- Keep senior management team updated on current projects and critical issues with weekly reports.
- Promote corporate activities by founding the "IPS Sports Team." Organized, trained, and motivated group of 60 runners to participate in the "Chase Corporate Challenge" for past three years. Assembled team of 6 runners for the 2000 Frankfurt Marathon.

Applications Development & Change Management – Germany, Canada, Brazil

- Managed the 24/7 On-Line Authorization System (UM20) running on Stratus fault tolerant machine. Directed staff of 4 team members in performing programming, design, development, installation, and testing. Served as liaison with several departments and groups including Authorization, Fraud, Merchant Development, Cardholder Application, Telecommunication and Customer Business Solution, as well as external software houses, ATM Network providers, and financial institutions such as VISA International, Europay/MasterCard, and JCB.
- Worked with cardholder management system (HOGAN), primarily the Transaction Editing Routing System (TERS) and the Clearing & Settlement interfaces to Visa & Europay/Mastercard.
- Configured and maintained the VISA BASE II Edit Package System for all CIBs/BINs.
- Programming experience on the STRATUS fault tolerant machine and IBM Mainframe Host including analysis, testing, implementation, trouble-shooting, and support of applications written in COBOL and EASYTRIEVE. Experienced with Unit Testing, System Testing, Stress Testing, System Integration, QA Acceptance Testing, Implementation, and System Review.
- Improved error-free rate of applications. Analyzed and prioritized requests for service from end-users. Worked with software houses to resolve problems quickly and with quality outputs/results.
- Trained end-users, support staff, and development staff on use of new applications.
- Developed, implemented, and maintained COBOL programs in batch and on-line environment for the following banking applications systems: Leasing, Insurance, Stock Control, Saving and Checking Accounts. Served as interface between applications development team and DBA group and computer centre. Participated in overall system testing and prepared systems documentation. Provided end-user support and training and resolved user requests and problems. Served as mentor to new programmers.

Technical Experience:

Environments:	IBM OS/390, STRATUS/VOS, RS/6000, IBM 3090, MVS/XA JES2 IMS DB/DC, CICS, TSO/ISPF, CONTROL-D Report, CONTROL-M Job Scheduling
Languages:	COBOL, EASYTRIEVE, JCL
Software:	MS Word, MS Excel, MS Project, MS PowerPoint, MS Outlook Express, MS Visio, Lotus Notes, ABC Flow Chart
Protocols:	SNA, TCP/IP, X.25, ISDN
Message Format:	ISO8583, GICC, KAAI, MAKATEL, ACS
Test Tools:	VISA Test System (VTS) 2000, Europay ECCF Simulator

Education:

1979-1983 **Bachelor in Economics**
Universidade Estacio de Sa, Rio de Janeiro, BRAZIL

1975-1977 **Technician in System Programming (Fortran, Assembler & COBOL)**
Escola de Tecnicia (Technical High School), Rio de Janeiro, BRAZIL

Languages:
Fluent: Portuguese (native tongue), Spanish, English and German
Basic: French and Italian

Recent Professional Development:

- **Certificate in Bank Card Management**, 12-month self-directed class; expected completion April 2001 October 2000 Intake, VISA International & The Chartered Institute of Bankers, London (www.visacertificate.co.uk/cibcm.htm)
- **Leadership and Communication Management Development Course**
Krauthammer International, Germany; an intensive 6-month course (www.krauthammer.de/)
- Project Management: Instruments of Project Planning and Realisation, Frankfurt, Germany
- Time Management, Personal Development and Self Management, Frankfurt, Germany
- ECCF Workshop, Europay Academy, Lisbon, Portugal
- Clearing & Settlement Services for Members, Europay Academy, Lisbon, Portugal
- Using Base II & VSS More Effectively, VISA International, Frankfurt, Germany
- MS Excel 97 & MS Word 97, MS Project 4.0, Frankfurt, Germany
- HOGAN Cardholder Management System, Lisbon, Portugal
- MVS and JCL Advanced Course, Frankfurt, Germany
- CA-EASYTRIEVE Plus, Frankfurt, Germany
- Security through Europay Security Module & Key Management, Rome, Italy
- Introduction to Europay International Processing, Frankfurt, Germany
- Risk Management Consolidated PIN Security Standard Training & Awareness, London, UK
- Payment Service 2000: POS94 German Member Technical Workshop, London, UK
- Systematic Software Testing: Methodology, Techniques & Tools, Munich, Germany
- Procedures for Maintenance of Software Development Projects, Frankfurt, Germany
- Online Authorization System (UM20), Advanced Course, London, UK
- STRATUS Application Analysis and System Administrator, Maarsen, Holland

Memberships and Affiliations:

- **Project Management Institute (PMI)**, Newtown Square, PA, USA (www.pmi.org)
- **Ganthead IT Project Manager Community**, Fairfax, VA, USA (www.ganthead.com)
- **Innovation Network**, Denver, CO, USA (www.thinksmart.com/home.html)
- **International Association of Students in Economic and Management (AIESEC)**
Served on the Public Relations and several local committees in Brazil and Canada. Attended events and seminars organized by AIESEC in Brazil, Canada, Germany and France. (www.aiesec.org/alumni/)

HENRY SIGNOROTTI

222 Brant Drive, Burlington, Ontario, L5N 7V2, Canada
905.824.4498

International Trade

North America ↔ South America
English • Spanish • Portuguese
GATT and Andean Trade Agreements

Dynamic business professional with an outstanding background in business development, cross-border trade and marketing. Network of contacts, companies and senior executives, specifically in Ecuador. Acutely aware of differences in culture with particular attention to South America; thrives on a challenge in a fast-paced environment, works diligently and directly to accomplish goals and objectives. Effective, tactful and diplomatic communicator in three languages; patiently builds profitable rapport and strategic partnerships with clients, staff, supervisors and peers. Entrepreneur, strong business acumen and thorough knowledge of all facets of company operations. Exercises leadership and vision, and creates a workplace that supports quality work and products.

PROFESSIONAL EXPERIENCE

Tia Susuna Banana Farms, Ecuador   1995 - 2001
PRINCIPAL/OWNER
Accomplishments:
- Purchased under-performing 30-hectare banana farm in 1995; conducted operational and fiscal evaluation resulting in purchase of a further 90 hectares at $15,000 U.S. per hectare.
- Selected by Dole Inc. to join the prestigious "Elite Group" of 40 farms (out of a total of 400) in Ecuador to provide bananas for their global clients.
- Given the much-revered "High Quality/High Production Award" for bananas, only the third time this award has been given in 25 years. Achieved 98.1% quality per box.
- Chosen for the "Second Best Quality" Award in the 1998 harvest.
- Honored with the "Highest Production per Hectare" Award in Ecuador.

Responsibilities:
- Recruited and managed 150 farms and 10 administration employees; oversaw all human resource issues.
- Positioned the banana plantation to deliver strong and sustainable financial results through prudent but aggressive farming.
- Spearheaded the continual logistics involved in banana processing in a time-sensitive environment ensuring consistent supply.

Rico Riasa S.A., Ecuador
GENERAL MANAGER
Successful company importing pipeline equipment to refinery installations within Ecuador. Prior to selling partnership in early 2001, Riasa's gross revenue grew to $3 million U.S. per annum.
- Met with senior Ecuadorian Government officials and President of Petro Ecuador to commence a profitable business relationship.
- Liaised between U.S. pipeline equipment manufacturer and government officials to obtain a $6 million U.S. contract for fluid measurement equipment.
- Prospected new business, set and maintained high sales goals.
- Recruited, trained and led a dedicated operational staff of 8 persons.
- Maximized sales and gross revenue by negotiating and signing agency and importing contracts with several U.S.-based companies.

Escudos, Ecuador   1993 - 1997
GENERAL MANAGER
Built and directed a successful importing company solely supplying the second-largest household electronic retailer in Ecuador, Mave Orichin.

- Orchestrated the agency negotiations and exporting agreements with leading international manufacturing companies (Sony, Aiwa, Panasonic, Goldstar) through the Panama Duty Free Zone. Complex negotiations involved extensive research into export/import regulations.
- Achieved positive cash flow every year, and carried no debt.
- Negotiated a favorable shipping contract with transportation companies for 4-5 containers per week with a 22% cost reduction over previous rates.
- Worked in partnership to comply with Customs to allow uninterrupted delivery of products.
- Constantly monitored JIT process to ensure adequate supply in position across Ecuador.
- Held full strategic planning, financial, operating, marketing and administrative leadership during a time of growth with revenues increasing from $450,000 U.S. to $3 million per annum in 4 years.

Reaventas S.A., Ecuador   1990 - 1993
IMPORT MANAGER
Imported household and electronic items from the U.S. for the T.V. Shopping Network of Ecuador on a JIT basis. No inventory or sales required, permitting low importation and transportation cost and lowering the FOB significantly.

- Guided all facets of business operations: finance, import/export, operations, transportation contracts, supplier sourcing and purchasing negotiations.

B. Robno Jewelers, Rio De Janeiro, Brazil   1983 - 1987
INTERNATIONAL PUBLIC RELATIONS EXECUTIVE
Fourth largest jeweler in the world with agents and stores located across the globe.

- Acted as the company agent on board cruise ships advising prospective clients on their jewelry purchases prior to their Rio De Janeiro disembarkation.

EDUCATION

Centennial College & Forum to International Trading (F.I.T.T.), Toronto, Ontario   Enrolled
International Trader Certificate
Modules include:

- International Marketing
- International Trade Finance
- Legal Aspects of International Trade
- International Trade Management

- International Trade Logistics
- International Market Entry & Distribution
- International Trade Research
- Global Entrepreneurship

University of Babahoya, Ecuador   1997
BUSINESS ADMINISTRATION DEGREE
Major: Commerce – Management

Getuho Vargas Foundation, Rio De Janeiro, Brazil
Applied Mathematics Certificate   1985
Foreign Trade/Import – Export Certificate   1983

Tulane University, New Orleans, Louisiana   1985
Investment & Security Analysis Certificate

SANDRA L. NUÑEZ

79 Henry Avenue   215-459-7168
Philadelphia, PA 19144   267-251-0446
slnunez@hotmail.com

PROFILE

Effective and competent legal professional offering significant experience in collections, settlement negotiations, and contract, employment/labor and real estate law. Background includes appearances before courts and government bodies. Relevant skills: case management, attorney supervision, negotiation, legal document preparation, and contract writing and review. Fluent in English and Spanish. Authorized to work in the U.S.

EDUCATION

PHILADELPHIA UNIVERSITY   **Philadelphia, PA**
  L.L.M., International Law Emphasis   **1998**
  Minor, French; Certificate, ESL

COLEGIO BOGOTA   **Bogota, Colombia**
  J.D.   **1994**
  Ranked 5th in a class of 150.
  Represented the college at an intellectual property conference in Venezuela.

LEGAL RESEARCH

Examined criminal and civil procedure pertaining to indigenous law. Presented findings to the Interior Department for use in multi-level governmental meetings. (1992 to 1993)

EXPERIENCE

FINANCIERA GENERAL   **Bogota, Colombia**
Assistant to the General Secretary   **1993 to 1995**

- Initiated legal proceedings to collect on delinquent loans or leases. Utilized legal property seizures to recover the highest annual amount; recording an index of 10% late payments, compared to the average of 30%.

- Provided representation before courts and governmental entities such as the Superintendent of the Financial Agency and the Superintendent of the Societies Corporation, both of which reviewed compliance with lending, investment, collection and other financial laws.

- Participated on a conciliation panel that initiated a successful class action lawsuit against Vehicle International Co. over "lemon" automobiles; negotiated a settlement in which the company paid customers' outstanding loans and leases.

INTERNATIONAL LABORATORIES, LTD.   **Bogota, Colombia**
Legal Advisor   **1992 to 1993**

- Reviewed labor contracts to ensure compliance regarding wages, year-end bonuses, hirings and terminations. Completed contract revisions and updates.

URBANIZACION BAVARIA   **Bogota, Colombia**
Legal Assistant   **1990 to 1991**

- Produced commercial and residential real estate and property titles. Examined blueprints for conformance to legal titles. Filed documentation before government agencies.

Carlos Juan Santiago

USA
56 Second Ave.. Suite No. 3324, Tampa, FL 12345
Fax 555-555-5555

carlos.santiago@peras.com

Brazil
Amalfa #355 Los Condes, Rio De Janeiro
Phone (H) 55-2-222-2222 • Phone (B) 55-2-555-5555
Fax (B) 55-2-111-1111 • Cell 55-2-0-000-0000

International Marketing Professional

Fortune 100 strategic business / marketing specialist and expert on Latin American markets. Currently Marketing Director for Procter and Gamble, Brazil, managing the full market-cycle from concept, to development, to market.

Respected as a dynamic business builder, hands-on leader, and creative solutions provider, delivering impressive bottom-line impact. Thrive under the challenge of planning and managing demanding assignments. Energized by the development of entrepreneurial marketing strategies that generate maximum results.

Use systematic, bottom-line approach to development — engage in cross-departmental research and author future-forward marketing plans to determine products' viability. Have produced a continuous stream of profitable marketing initiatives, cost-reducing measures, and innovative solutions.

Entirely fluent in English and native Spanish. Broad background in international cross-cultural relationship building. Working and living experience in the United States and Latin America. Accustomed to the rigors of frequent business travel.

Areas of Expertise

- Strategic marketing
- Global market study / research
- Product / market identification
- Business plan creation
- Short- and long-term forecasting

- Long-term market analysis
- Competitive and value analysis
- Profitability, EVA, ROI analysis
- Multimillion-dollar budgets
- On-time and on-budget projects

- Project management
- Solutions sales / marketing
- Cross-function teaming
- Marketing materials design
- Boardroom presentations

Recent Marketing Milestones

Led outstanding results in P&G's beauty care business in Brazil, behind excellent performance in hair care, increasing Pantene's volume +54% and sales +64%. (2000)

Revitalized feminine care category in Brazil with volume and sales of the Always brand up by +16% and +18% respectively over previous year. (1999-2000)

Managed several new category launches for Latin American subsidiaries, creating new market segments for Secret cream antiperspirant, Pringles potato chips, and Pampers baby wipes. (1999-2000)

Restored profitability of P&G's Latin American personal cleansing business, delivering above target results, improving profits by +56% over previous year, and creating first-ever profits for a P&G Latin American sub-region. (1999)

Recommended a trade program in Venezuela to improve the diapers and hair care businesses in the Drugstore channel. With an annual sales potential of $5 million, initiative became a P&G top priority. (1999)

Led P&G's sales improvement in diapers in Venezuela, lifting unit price by +15% over previous year. (1998)

Turned around P&G's Venezuelan bleach business. Elevated sales by 85% and reversed negative profit margins, achieving 10% margin by June 1997, versus -16% margin in last six months of 1996. (1997)

Increased P&G's diaper volume 28% above previous year to $4.3 million, with profit improvements of 100%, and cost savings of $1.7 million by recommending an expansion of an optimized diaper product. (1995)

Representative Marketing Initiatives

Revitalized subsidiaries' second largest business.

Category had experienced a two-year downward trend, losing 30% in past 18 months.

Proposed plan to increase sales by 60% in three years. Championed plan through P&G channels and pushed local team hard to quickly relaunch one of the product lines.

Plan's key elements included relaunch of top-performing product line using better technology and new advertising... introduction of new product presentations, adding 3% to 7% incremental business... revising pricing strategy... leadership of the sales platform recovery behind two major price increases in 12 months... a progressive plan to increase unit level sales by +25% from its base... implementation of a business plan to recover wholesaler / distributor business (25% of category volume)... relaunch of the basic performing brand behind better technology and re-establishment of marketing support.

- **Bottom-line**
  Top performing line grew 16%... total category trend was stabilized, declining only 4% in the last 12 months vs. 15% decrease in previous two years... pricing leads were followed by category competitors.

Improved results of strong, yet stalled, category.

Category was not growing past its 50% share.

In response, implemented holistic marketing program with strong media support to all product lines... proposed pricing above what was needed to recover inflation and devaluation... implemented a promotional program to surpass competition and significantly grow business out of the basement of a 35% share key category channel... managed a product line relaunch using better technology and a new advertising campaign.

- **Bottom-line**
  Recorded record-high profits... improved unit price by 15%... increased market share by two points over previous year.

121

Established focused regional direction of major global brand's Latin American expansion plans.

Needed to reverse effect of company's haphazard white spaces investment in several Latin American countries that did not have proper business-building fundamentals or adequate investment support.

Designed a Mexican regional learning market to measure the effect of a high-investment model and the plans to develop a new product form that could be reapplied in the Latin American rollout. Used strategic thinking, initiative, and follow-through to

develop marketing plan elements (including concept qualifications that received excellent scores)... to work with geographically scattered teams... to produce consistent communications... to execute entire project with excellence and within time frame.

- **Bottom-line**
  Mexican learning market is in line with objectives and results will be reapplied to Latin American expansion plans.

Increased profitability of one of the largest Latin American beauty care categories.

Category was suffering from poor cost structure.

Recommended and championed simplification and standardization measures to cut costs. Teamed with engineers and R&D to transfer all production to one Latin American manufacturing site... standardized all brand presentations in all Latin American countries... streamlined regional product line menus, reducing presentations by 33%... standardized brand names across all countries, requiring a name change in one of the major brands.

- **Bottom-line**
  Initiatives improved profits by +56% over the previous year and created first-ever profits in one of the Latin American sub-regions.

Career Development

PROCTER & GAMBLE	**1989 TO PRESENT**
Marketing Director, Brazil 1999 to present	**Marketing Manager, Liquid Detergents, Venezuela** 1996 to 1997
Marketing Director, Venezuela 1998 to 1999	**Brand Manager, Pampers** 1993 to 1996
Marketing Manager, Beauty Care, Latin America 1997 to 1998	**Assistant Brand Manager, Hair Care and Pampers** 1989 to 1993

P&G manufactures, sells, and distributes mass consumer goods, marketing 300 brands. P&G has 136 employees in Brazil, and operates in 140 locations around the world.

As Marketing Director, Brazil
Manage Paper (Diapers, Wipes and Feminine Care), Beauty Care (Hair Care and Deodorants/ Antiperspirants) and Food (Snacks) categories, with $120 million in sales and a $14 million marketing budget.

Charged with organizational restructuring following "Organization 2005" principles. Coordinated efforts with General Manager, four Brand Managers, and one Administrative Assistant reporting directly, and with eight indirect reports at supervisory level.

As Marketing Director, Venezuela
Directed Pampers (Diapers and Feminine Care) and Food categories with $105 million in sales and a $10 million marketing budget.

As Marketing Manager, Beauty Care, Latin America
Managed Personal Cleansing, Deodorants/Antiperspirants, and Hair Care lines with $70 million in annual Beauty Care categories sales in Latin America, working directly with each country's local line management.

As Marketing Manager, Liquid Detergents, Venezuela
Directed Bleach, Household Cleaners, Fabric Softeners, and Dishwashing categories, with $25 million in annual sales and a $15 million marketing budget.

As Brand Manager, Pampers
Reported to Marketing Director, Paper, Venezuela. Managed sales of $55 million.

As Assistant Brand Manager, Hair Care and Pampers
Coordinated day-to-day business management, budget proposals, and control. Developed and implemented plans at trade and consumer level.

L'OREAL OVERSEAS CORPORATION, NEW YORK, NY　　　　　　**1987 TO 1989**
Human Resources Supervisor – Caracas, Venezuela

Maintained payroll control, benefits, enrollment and terminations, and training with the Human Resources Director. Supervised day-to-day activities of one Administrative Assistant.

Education / Professional Development

MBA , Marketing, 1990	**BS in Business Administration, 1986**
Universidad de Columbia, Caracas, Venezuela	Cornell University, Ithaca NY, U.S.A.

Have participated in over eleven years of extensive marketing training within Procter and Gamble.

Cecilia M. Diaz

55 Magnolia Lane, Oakland, NJ 07436
(201) 405-5555 Home ▪ (201) 203-6789 Mobile ▪ cmdiaz@worldnet.net

Objective: Public Relations / Promotions in an international organization
focusing on business in Central and South America

CAREER PROFILE

☑ Native Chilean with PR experience in the medical, education, and non-profit industries.
☑ Poised professional with marketing, promotions, and project management experience.
☑ Strong presentation and communication skills; languages – Spanish, Portuguese, Italian, French.
☑ Windows 98, Microsoft Office 2000, Word, PowerPoint, Excel, and the Internet.

PROFESSIONAL SKILLS

Public Relations & Promotions

▪ Promote managed care products and services to prospective clients in a four-county territory within central and northern New Jersey, producing a strong and sustainable market lead.
  Result: HMO membership has grown 70% within the last year to over 170,000 members.

▪ Created and launched innovative marketing strategies in targeted Spanish-speaking territory to respond to Medicaid market changes.
  Result: Received award for overachieving market quota.

▪ Participated in task force that successfully recruited medical providers in assigned territories.

Communications

▪ Conduct bi-lingual group sales presentations to physicians, HMO members, community-based organizations, schools, and small businesses to promote healthcare products and services.
  Result: Diversified and increased revenue stream through ever-increasing HMO memberships.

▪ Design, write, and produce promotional materials and communications for sales presentations.

▪ Deliver 9 workshops/month to HMO members on service access and other identified needs.

Project Management

▪ Partnered with Latinas Unidas and the Hispanic Affairs and Resource Center of Somerset County to develop and deliver monthly member resource and educational workshops.

▪ Created a volunteer program to provide telemarketing training to member Medicaid recipients.
  Result: Volunteers hired full-time for telemarketing sales due to their success rate in cold calls.

▪ Designed and compiled a database of community groups to facilitate community outreach.

EMPLOYMENT HISTORY

1997 – present **Community Relations Specialist / Managed Care Consultant**
          Allied Health Care Plan of New Jersey, Summit, NJ
1991 – 1997 **Adjunct Professor / Counselor**, Instituto Superior Santiago, Chile
1988 – 1994 **Child Psychology Counselor**, Regional Education Council of Chile

EDUCATION

MS, Educational Psychology, Del Rio University, Santiago, Chile
Professional Development Courses: Consultative Sales Training, Territory Management,
Professional Presentation Skills, and Event Planning (company-sponsored)

COMMUNITY AFFILIATIONS

Board Member, Hispanic Affairs & Resource Center, Somerset County
Advisory Committee Member, Literacy for America, Summit and Chatham, NJ

Resumes for the Middle East

FAREED AHMED

1550 Old Connecticut Turnpike
Framingham, MA 09254
U.S.A.

Residence: 781.528.3309
Mobile: 781.223.4765
ahmed21@zzzz.com

ELECTRICAL ENGINEER
Technical Sales • Instrumentation Engineering • Design Consulting

Eleven years of international engineering experience, with particular emphasis on the nuclear power, petrochemical and saline water industries. Landed multi-million dollar contracts as a member of a sales engineering team. Acted as key communications link between technical and non-technical personnel. Fluent in English and Arabic.

EDUCATION

BACHELOR OF SCIENCE IN ELECTRICAL ENGINEERING (1990)
Boston University, Boston, MA

Continuing Professional Education and Certification
- Fundamentals of Mechanical and Pneumatic Instrumentation — Acton Industries
- Control Maintenance and Engineering — Gillette Corporation
- Certified Vibration Analyst — Hopkinton Engineering Associates, Inc.

PROFESSIONAL EXPERIENCE

Walsh & Anderson Engineering Corporation, Electrical Division, Boston, MA
INSTRUMENTATION ENGINEER (1999-Present)

Developed and revised instrumentation and control diagrams for testing and calibrating electrical and mechanical equipment. Prepared scoping documents for system turnover packages. Interfaced with vendors to complete field reports and identify testing processes.

- Contributed to the preparation of a nuclear plant system turnover.
- Reviewed and approved drawings according to NRC (Nuclear Regulatory Commission) and IEEE (Institute of Electronics and Electrical Engineers) standards.

SAN Corporation, Dammam, Saudi Arabia
Sales & marketing / distribution company for process instrumentation and control valves.
TECHNICAL SALES ENGINEER (1994-1999)

Performed needs assessment. Designed and implemented technical solutions. Prepared specifications for control valve calculations.

- Key contributor to the team effort that won a $2.5 million contract to supply electronics and instrumentation to the Saline Water Commission Project.
- Provided technical design and implementation support to multi-million dollar alarm system safety projects for gas-fired power plants.
- Provided consulting expertise to 43 international companies.

Al Khobar Consulting Engineers, Al-Khobar, Saudi Arabia
CLASS IV INSTRUMENT ENGINEER (1990-1994)

Developed and revised instrumentation and installation detail drawings for hydrogen sulfide monitors at a nuclear power plant. Reviewed and approved piping and instrumentation drawings during site visits. Performed field inspection during design and construction phases.

- Designed explosion proof equipment for use in power plants.
- Redesigned suppliers' equipment to meet specifications, improving efficiency.

Seeking to Relocate Internationally

Harold J. Standard

147 Woodchuck Court • Walson, WA 98666 USA

(300) 355-7777   email: hjs@slowmail.com

Nuclear Medicine Technologist

EMPHASIS

- Nuclear Cardiology
- Nuclear Oncology
- Radiation Safety
- Radionucleid Treatment for Thyroid Disease, Prostate Seeds Implantation, and Brachy Therapy
- Radio Pharmaceutical Lab Management
- Quality Assurance and Control in Nuclear Medicine

EDUCATION

Nuclear Medicine Technology Degree, 1981
> St. Joseph's School of Nuclear Medicine Technology, Plantation, New Jersey, USA
> Recognized top student in graduating class.

Master of Science Degree, Chemistry, 1967
> University of Peshawar, Peshawar, Pakistan
> First-Class in graduating class.

Bachelor of Science Degree, Chemistry, Botany, and Zoology, 1964
> University of Panjab, Lahore, Pakistan

PROFESSIONAL BACKGROUND

Hospital Appointments

1988–present	**Nuclear Medicine Technologist / Assistant Radiation Safety Officer** St. Vincent Hospital, Langham, Washington, USA
1981–1988	**Supervisor, Nuclear Medicine,** Winne Hospital, Winne, New Jersey, USA

Teaching Appointments

1983–1985	**Instructor in Nuclear Medicine Technology** St. Joseph's Hospital and Medical Center, Plantation, New Jersey, USA
1975–1979	**Education Officer / Head of Chemistry Department,** Bauchi State of Nigeria, West Africa
1971–1975	**Head of Chemistry Department,** Aga Khan Mzizima Secondary School Dar-ES-Salaam, Tanzania, East Africa
1968–1971	**Lecturer in Chemistry,** Forman Christian College, Lahore, Pakistan
1967–1968	**Lecturer in Chemistry,** Edwards College, Peshawar, Pakistan
1964–1965	**Demonstrator in Chemistry,** Forman Christian College, Lahore, Pakistan

MEMBERSHIPS / ACCREDITATION

The Society of Nuclear Medicine
Technologist Section of Society of Nuclear Medicine
American Society of Clinical Pathologists
The American Registry of Radiologic Technologists
The Nuclear Medicine Technologist Certification Board
Licensed State of Washington Nuclear Medicine Technologist

PERSONAL   Date of Birth: January 8, 1940; Married; two children; Christian by faith; US Citizen

REFERENCES   Will be supplied upon request.

Theopolis Rajman

US address 222-30 210 Street, Bayside, NY 11360   ■   718-555-5555   ■   fax 718-000-0000 ■ ThoR@All.com

International Sales and Marketing Executive

Action-driven multilingual senior area manager with over fifteen years of experience in the on-site opening and management of profitable multimillion dollar sales territories and distributorships in the Middle East, the Mediterranean Basin, Europe, and the Indian Subcontinent. Territories generate $8.5 million in annual sales.

Produce double-digit growth and profit margins through the development of high-level contacts, competitive niche markets, culture-specific marketing materials, and innovative sales techniques. Open closed markets using patience, contact network, sophisticated investigative techniques, and street-by-street local market research.

Fluent in written and spoken English, French, and Arabic, with working knowledge of Italian and Spanish. Educated at Purdue University. Have lived and worked in the United States, Europe, and the Middle East, with current residences in both the United States and in the Middle East. Work "on the road," on three continents, over 250 days a year.

Key Areas of Expertise

- Multimillion-dollar sales generation
- Profit / loss responsibility
- Sales / business plan development
- Business-to-business selling
- Competitive business capturing
- Marketing materials / sales tools
- Sales training / sales promotions
- High-level presentations
- Distributor / factory interface

- New global market development
- Executive-level contact development
- Strategic partner identification / evaluation
- International negotiations
- Contract evaluation
- Distributor recruitment / management
- Local market and consumer research
- Cross-cultural business practices
- Trade show exhibit creation

Career Development

The HomeStyle Company, New York, NY, USA	1983 to Present
Senior Area Manager, Middle East	1988 to Present
Sales Area Manager, Middle East and Europe	1986 to 1988
Sales Area Manager, Middle East	1982 to 1986

Currently direct strategic planning, sales / marketing, and training operations across all product lines and business units on three continents. Markets include the Middle East, the Mediterranean Basin, and the Indian Subcontinent.

Produce an annual volume of $8.5 million, with a net (after expense profit) of over $2 million. Have personally grown business consistently by 20% a year for over ten years.

Create wholesale and retail sales and distribution channels for HomeStyle products including basic and luxury plumbing products, furniture, generators, and engines.

Executive Performance Highlights

■ **Developed virgin territories that now represent over $8.5 million in annual sales. Grew Saudi market twelve-fold and created distribution networks in Saudi Arabia, Kuwait, Qatar, Bahrain, Oman, United Arab Emirates, Israel, Lebanon, Jordan, and India.**

Established and managed a low-overhead, "one-man-show," client-accessible Middle East sales office. Created immediate growth by intense re-training of a small group of existing distributors. Fostered long-term growth by adding distribution, reaching out directly to non-represented clients, identifying potential clients, and providing exceptional customer service from order, to installation, and beyond.

■ **Developed and implemented culture-specific marketing materials and sales strategies that produced consistent double-digit growth and changed project-based vs. retail-based sales from 95% project / 5% retail to a more profitable 70% project / 30% retail.**

Produced an exclusive Middle Eastern end-user product catalog designed to simplify choices and increase add-on sales in a product-saturated market. Developed an eight-magazine ad campaign focusing on end-user decision-makers, contractors, architects, and consultants. Produced informative product video tapes that allowed "home-shopping" for Middle Eastern women and luxury consumers who are often reluctant to enter showrooms.

■ **In three years, grew European start-up business in Belgium, Netherlands and the United Kingdom into a $1 million operation with annual gross margins averaging 40%.**

Determined that niche marketing was the key to this market as most Europeans are quite proprietary about using European products. Did catalog and shop-to-shop field research to discover small gaps in product selection that HomeStyle could fill. Networked with architects and builders to identify consumers that wanted American products for large 20- to 50-bathroom residences.

■ **Built $1.5 million-plus business by identifying, building and opening previously closed markets in Egypt, Turkey, and Pakistan.**

Developed Pakistan to current $.5 million, Turkey to $.5 million, and Egypt to current $.5 million with potential to $3 million. Worked for three to five years to take these "import-banned" markets from conception to fruition. Used street-research techniques, determined market viability, and established contacts. Went in early and built organization, showroom, and staff to have workable structure in place to do immediate business when import bans were lifted and market duty / customs rates dropped to create favorable sales climate.

■ **Identified and developed strong regional distributor networks and multimillion-dollar opportunities in existing and virgin territories.**

Discovered an Israeli manufacturer who had the wrong product but the right financials, contacts, and organization. His HomeStyle products are now 90% market share of the Israeli cast-iron kitchen sink business. In Saudi Arabia, approached the largest contractor in the region and persuaded him to open an exclusive HomeStyle trading division. Business grew from start-up to $4 million in an eight-year period. In India, where no distribution network has yet been established, work with major Indian hotels to produce $.5 million in sales.

Key Customers and Contacts

Established excellent working relationships with all key construction companies, architectural firms, industry consultants, building material wholesalers, various government agencies, and private luxury clients. Representative contacts include:

Construction / Architectural Firms:
Bechtel, USA; Saudi Oger, Saudi Arabia; J&P, Cyprus; Philip Halsman, Germany

Hotels
Marriot, Sheraton, Four Seasons, Hyatt, Intercontinental, Holiday Inn

Building Materials Distributors
Mesma, Cyprus; Paul Weil, Lebanon; Alnajran, Saudi Arabia; King, Egypt; Van Marcke Belgium; Hadayat, Pakistan

Consultants / Agencies / Private Contacts
Royal Family of Saudi Arabia; Ministry of Public Works, Jordan; Aramco, Saudi Arabia; Dyar Consulting, Saudi Arabia

Professional Activities and Honors

Received The HomeStyle *Salesman of the Year* Award.

Profiled in the HomeStyle company magazine over a dozen times.

Lead HomeStyle bi-annual regional distributors' meeting.

Lecture on international trade issues and Middle Eastern / European business practices to academic and business groups:

- Purdue University
- Lakeland College
- US/Arab Management Association
- Rotary and International Lions Clubs

Education and Development

Columbia University; New York, NY USA
MBA in International Business, 1982

Queens College; Flushing, NY USA
Bachelor of Science in Electrical Engineering, 1978

HomeStyle Sales and Management Training Programs
Professional Sales Management, Effective Negotiations, Effective Presentations, Conflict Management, Project Management

Resumes for Western Europe

Highlights

Drafter / Designer

Design / build
Commercial interior design
Residential & commercial
design

Academic Credentials

BA Honours Interior and
Spatial Design

Design Skills

Schematics
Contract drawings
Materials & standards
research
Specifications
Freehand drawing
Presentation boards and
models

Executive Capabilities

Project management
Sales & marketing
Price negotiation
Organizational ability
Delivering projects on time
under budget

Interpersonal Skills

Architect & contractor
interface
Customer service

PROFESSIONAL EXPERIENCE

Linda Sorenson Designs, London, England, UK
INDEPENDENT DESIGN CONSULTANT   1999 - Present

Projects included law offices, dental offices and residences.

- Co-designed a 3,000 square foot restoration of a 1650 residence.
- Designed complete furnishings for an 11-room home.

Gained a reputation for sensitive restoration of period properties.

London Building Interiors, London, England, UK
DESIGN COORDINATOR / HEAD DESIGNER   1995 - 1999

- Designed a model office showcasing the company's products and services.
- Established a library of design resources and materials, successfully attracting a customer base of sales and design professionals.
- Recruited, selected and trained design personnel.
- Coordinated and evaluated work plans and supervised projects on-site.

Exceeded sales goals and landed repeat business.

Architectural Concepts, Inc., London, England, UK
SENIOR DESIGNER   1992 - 1995

Rapid promotion to Senior Designer in an architectural office. Designed and managed million-dollar bank projects. Worked on design / build projects, floor plans and ATMs.

- *Marketing:* Performed needs assessments, designed work flow systems, prepared and presented schematics, and made formal presentations. Prepared bid packages to be sent out to contractors and sub-contractors. Handled price negotiations.
- *Visual Presentations:* Produced design boards showing detailed millwork and special finishes. Created full-color sketches in perspective of interior and exterior site plans.
- *Technical:* Specified interior finishing, furnishings and exterior materials. Drafted specifications and full working drawings.

Brought projects in on time, under budget, every time.
Personally assured quality of workmanship through on-site supervision.
Designed a stage set for the "Bank of the Future," Bristol, England, UK.

Graves & Thompson, London, England, UK
DESIGN CONSULTANT   1992

- Completed floor plans for a 160-unit condominium project.
- Produced drawings for framing, electrical and HVAC.

Contributed to bringing the project in under cost projections by designing meticulous plans.

Central Episcopal Hospital, Herefordshire, England, UK
ARCHITECTURAL DRAFTER   1991

- Collaborated with the designer in collecting data and drafting plans.
- Ensured existing drawings conformed with engineering, construction and repair plans.

Facilitated timely completion of projects and minimal disruption to residents by providing accurate design materials and precise instructions to contractors.

Hampstead Road ▪ London, SW3 6LS UK ▪ 011+44-20-7815 6977 ▪ l@sorenson.cc.uk

Interpersonal Skills

Team player
Public relations
Tact and diplomacy

Computer Skills

AutoCad 13/14, 3-D
DataCad
Lotus Notes
MS Word
PowerPoint
Excel

EDUCATION

South Bank University, London, SE1 0AA England, UK
Masters Program in Interior Architecture   2000 - Present
Coursework to date: Algebraic Structures I & II; Theory/Forum; CAD 2-D;
Design Studio A1/A2; DataCad II/3D Modeling; Design Studio B; Values; Perspective
Drawing; AutoCad 3-D.

Hereford College of Art and Design, Hereford, England, UK
BA Honours Interior and Spatial Design   1991

Architectural Association School of Architecture, London, England, UK
Coursework: Architectural Design, AutoCad   1996

AFFILIATIONS

Member, Association of Architects and Designers   2000 - Present
Member, Institute of International Business Designers   1991 - Present

References Available Upon Request

Bernd Hieber

c/o Giraud, ch du Baguier
06650 Opio
France
Telephone from USA 0113-366-635-51898
Telephone from Europe +33-666-355-898
Email **career@abc.org**
Online résumé portfolio http://www.abc.org/career/html

E-Business Specialist / Business Development Strategist / Marketing Executive
Creating & Driving Winning E-Business Strategies for the New Economy

Dynamic planning expert offering fresh insight and a passion for innovation; proven record of contribution to high-profile, international business. Powerful strategist able to map creative budgeting, resource planning, and business development. Empower organizations with the tools, technologies, and strategies to bridge the digital business gap.

Respected leader, able to build team cohesion and inspire individuals to strive toward ever-higher levels of achievement. Exceptional relationship and management skills; relates and interfaces easily at the top executive levels. Keen, in-depth understanding of Internet tools, trends, and business models. Solid background and qualifications in all core business functions – finance, marketing, sales, and operations.

AREAS OF EXPERTISE

- Budget Planning / Management
- Resource Management
- Personnel Training / Supervision
- Team / Group Leadership

- Strategic Planning
- Organizational Planning / Analysis
- Presentations / Public Speaking
- Multi-lingual; fluent in 3 languages

HIGHLIGHTS OF PROFESSIONAL ACHIEVEMENT

Inventoried existing budgetary controls, reinventing goals, strategies, and models to meet the changing demands of the new digital economy. Achieved increased competitiveness, heightened market valuation, and long-term and sustainable revenue gains.

Formatted strategies and action plans that exceeded IPO and shareholder requirements for financial planning and reporting.

Facilitated negotiations and consensus for selection / integration of numerous development plans in company budgets.

Identified opportunities to accelerate monthly financial reporting, resulting in substantial extension of management's response options.

Pioneered and promoted the award-winning Total Customer Satisfaction Project, responsible for increasing competitiveness by reducing packaging costs 8%, storage 17%, and shipping 23%. Recruited to present model during the final round of Motorola's worldwide project presentation competition in Toronto, Ontario.

Designed and built creative Internet portal for the high-growth organization abctriplets.org, credited with national awards and recognized by international health care professionals.

Noticed for developing highly complex and effective projecting tools for sales, costs, orders, and manpower planning requirements. Integrated marketing, product, and resource plans in budget models now being employed as the corporate-wide standard.

PROFESSIONAL EXPERIENCE

Aristotle Global Distribution – Sophia-Antipolis, France 1998 – Present
Senior Officer Cost Control

Senior consultant managing long-term plan, budget, forecast, and analysis for manpower, travel, training, recruitment, and running cost in an increasingly competitive global marketplace. Provide reporting support for mergers, joint ventures, and partnership agreements. Coordinate and consolidate all company functions including 17 divisions, 62 departments, 158 cost centers, and 185 projects. Lead, motivate, train, and coach teams comprised of talented cost control officers, producing standard and ad-hoc analysis reporting as input for crucial, top management decisions.

Motorola Multiservice Networks – Crawley, United Kingdom and Darmstadt, Germany 1994 – 1998
International Financial Assistant

International financial specialist with collaborative responsibility for the re-organization, centralization, and re-location of administration, manufacturing, and customer support for Europe, Middle East, and Africa Markets (EMEA). Played a key role in the implementation of new tools and management systems in finance and operations. Creative participant in innovation of centralized stock and shipment management.

EDUCATION AND SPECIAL TRAINING

M.B.A., Business and Marketing
University of Paderborn, Germany
Degree awarded 1995

Business and Marketing Studies	**Business and Marketing Studies**
St. Olaf College, Minnesota, USA	University of Paderborn, Germany
1990 – 1991	Degree awarded 1990

Effective Presentation Training – Motorola University
Working As A Team / Six Sigma – Motorola University
Working Smarter – Leadership Development, Ltd.
Six Steps to Best Quality – Motorola University
Trans-Cultural Competence – Motorola University

PROFESSIONAL AFFILIATIONS

Member, International Sales and Marketing Executives
Member, Internet Marketing Association
St. Olaf Career Advising Network

PUBLICATIONS

Standards, Certification, and Accreditation in the European Union, 1994, VDE Verlag, Berlin, Germany

Author / Co-Author of 7 scientific and non-scientific articles. Complete list of titles can be found at:
www.abc.org/certifications.html

Supporting documentation, additional information, and references available on request
View complete online résumé portfolio at http://www.abc.org/career/english

WILLIAM RASAUCK

Current Address
The Fairmont Hamilton Princess
P.O. Box HM 664
Hamilton HM CX Bermuda
(W) 541 675 7658 • (H) 665 675 8768
(E) rasauck@hotmail.com

Permanent Address
Wiesbachhornstr. 67
80825 Munich, Germany
(H) 089 6520872
(F) 089 6580876
(E) rasauck@hatmail.com

PROFILE

Experienced in **Food and Beverage Management** for exclusive hotels around the world. Possesses an aggressive management style and creative talent for *making things happen*. Demonstrated expertise in planning, quality management, operations development, budgeting, cost control, negotiations, procurement, staffing, training, and marketing. Achieved turnaround success of declining F&B departments and non-producing outlets that contributed to significant profits, revenue gains, and expense reductions. Advanced skills in relationship building, team development, and staff motivation.

Pre-opening and multinational experience with worldwide travel throughout the U.S., Bermuda, South America, Germany, Portugal, England, and Switzerland. Fluent in English and German; business proficiency in French, Spanish, and Portuguese. PC skilled.

PROFESSIONAL EXPERIENCE

FOOD & BEVERAGE DIRECTOR
The Princess Hotels (six outlets, 413 rooms and member of *The Leading Hotels of the World*)
Hamilton, Bermuda 04/1999 to Present

Recruited to guide transition efforts of the F&B department of this Bermudan property. Challenged to create a grand strategy for F&B, restructure and streamline current processes to improve efficiency and reduce costs, prepare hotels for renovation, and develop a new concept for future property. Supervised a staff of 170.

CONTRIBUTIONS
➢ Streamlined departmental operating infrastructure, consolidated administrative functions, developed new budgets, slashed entertainment expenses 40%, cut food & beverage costs 3%, and reduced staffing levels from 170 to 120.
➢ Eliminated non-performing staff, hired new staff, and trained and prepared local staff for increased responsibility.
➢ Established effective union relationships.
➢ Developed new budgets.
➢ Created a new, high-impact corporate image introduced through new menus, wine lists, aggressive marketing presentations, and planned festivities.

FOOD & BEVERAGE DIRECTOR
Hotel Oro Fuuer (nine F&B outlets, 254 rooms and member of *The Leading Hotels of the World*)
Guayaquil, Ecuador 03/1997 to 02/1999

Led revenue increase and quality improvement initiatives despite culturally challenging environment. Guided F&B departmental restructuring efforts to improve service style including enhancement of kitchen facilities, menu presentation, and staff/guest interaction. Eliminated non-performing staff, hired new staff, and trained/motivated existing staff. Additionally, developed budgets, oversaw banquet sales, negotiated with vendors and suppliers, and served as entertainment director. Oversaw a total of 150 employees.

Continued...

136

FOOD & BEVERAGE DIRECTOR EXPERIENCE (CONTINUED)

CONTRIBUTIONS
- Increased revenue 10%.
- Dramatically improved quality standards and hotel reputation.
- Implemented various food and music festivals (i.e., Cuban, Italian, Argentinean, German, Smokers Nights with Aurora and Leon Jimenez, etc.)
- Created and opened a highly successful Californian–concept restaurant.

FOOD & BEVERAGE MANAGER
Sorenskii Hotel Fürstenhof (five F&B outlets, 92 rooms and member of *The Leading Hotels of the World*)
Munich, Germany 09/1995 to 03/1997

Brought in as pre-opening F&B manager of this exclusive hotel catering to high-profile individuals and Hollywood celebrities. Oversaw construction of all food and beverage areas and procurement of $1M in equipment/supplies. Streamlined hiring process to eliminate excessive paperwork and expedite qualified staff recruitment. Developed F&B budget, performed pre-opening market research/analysis to create concepts for restaurants, designed menus including print materials, installed cost control systems, oversaw installation/operation of Micros computer system, organized grand opening party, negotiated highly sought after supplier contracts, and organized sponsorships for hotel. Oversaw a total staff of 45.

CONTRIBUTIONS
- Successfully established food and beverage department, client base, and excellent reputation.
- Contributed lasting design for menu, glassware, plates, and uniforms.
- Organized wine dinners with Caroline Krug, Chateau Lynch-Bages, Roederer, etc.

ASSISTANT FOOD & BEVERAGE MANAGER / RESTAURANT MANAGER
Tudor's Hotel (seven F&B outlets, 167 rooms and member of *The Leading Hotels of the World*)
Madeira, Portugal 06/1993 to 06/1995

Promoted from Restaurant Manager overseeing an à-la-carte restaurant with 80 inside seats and 50 terrace seats to Assistant Food and Beverage Manager of seven F&B outlets.

CONTRIBUTIONS
- Achieved turnaround profitability and tripled revenues.
- Developed incentive programs to drive continuous performance and efficiency improvements.
- Converted Portuguese restaurant into an Italian concept in five months.
- Successfully restructured F&B department, performed quality control, budgeted, planned/organized special events, developed menus, created monthly reports, and directed activities of 120 employees.

PRIOR EXPERIENCE

TRAINEE IN THE CONFERENCE AND BANQUETING DEPARTMENT
The Hyon (a member of *The Leading Hotels of the World*)
Broadway, England 03/1992 to 07/1992

FOOD AND BEVERAGE ASSISTANT
Hotel Babulsr (a member of *The Leading Hotels of the World)*
Basle, Switzerland 02/1991 to 07/1991

Continued...

FOOD AND BEVERAGE CONTROLLER
Hotel Sofriier (a member of *The Leading Hotels of the World*)
Munich, Germany 02/1990 to 07/1990

APPRENTICE CHEF
Hotel Thayerishcher Hof (a member of *The Leading Hotels of the World*)
Munich, Germany 05/1998 to 01/1990

EDUCATIONAL ACHIEVEMENTS

- **Swiss Hotel Management Diploma**
  Hotel Institute Montreux
  Montreux, Switzerland

- **Hospitality Management Diploma**

- **American Hotel and Motel Association Diploma**

- Studied marketing and sales, financial accounting, convention services, supervision, F&B management, front office and housekeeping procedures. — Hotel Institute Montreux

CONTINUING PROFESSIONAL EDUCATION

Completed extensive continuing professional education throughout career. Course highlights include:

- Leadership 2000, Hamilton Bermuda 1999/2000
- Vision 2000 for Food and Beverage Administration, Toronto, Canada 1999
- Sales Seminar, Guayaquil, Ecuador 1998
- International Convention for Conference and Catering, Baltimore, USA 1997
- Extensive Wine Seminars with Drug Champagne, Chateau Lynch Bages, etc., Leipzig, Germany 1995/96
- Middle Management Seminars in HR, Marketing and F&B, Madeira, Portugal 1994
- Entrepreneurial Management, Madeira, Portugal

MILITARY

Lance Corporal of the German Armed Forces, Honorably Discharged, 1984

EXCELLENT REFERENCES AVAILABLE

Thomas Skovsö-Hansen

Freiherr-V-Steinstr 4
63950 Gollhiem, Germany
Residence 011-49-6351-756325
tskhansen@xzy.com

GOLF DIRECTOR / CLUB MANAGER / TEACHING PROFESSIONAL / CONSULTANT

Private Clubs, Group & Individual Instruction Since 1973

- Professional Club Fitter
- Tournament Playing Professional
- Sales & Marketing Management
- Membership & Guest Services
- Pro Shop Management
- Competition Management
- Budget Administration
- Property Development
- VIP Relations

Consistently successful in increasing revenues, member service / satisfaction and profitability.

HIGHLIGHTS OF QUALIFICATIONS

Entrepreneurial golf professional with full PGA status and more than 20 years of experience in pro shop management, custom club design and repair, instruction, tournament organization and supervision, and direction of all aspects of successful course maintenance and operations. Personally trained by John Jacobs and by Denis Pugh of the David Leadbetter Golf Academy. Bi-lingual; fluent in German and English. Willing to travel and relocate.

Golf Instruction
- Provide on-site computer digital swing analyses using Interactive Frontier's V1 equipment to teach golf swing methods from beginners through top professional standard.
- Increased private instruction by 37% to 140 half-hour sessions per week generating over $65K USD.
- Experience teaching top national players and professionals, including two PGA winners.
- Designed academy practice facilities from the ground up, now supporting membership of over 700.
- Regularly called upon to conduct summer junior camps, weekend clinics, group, and individual instruction.

Operations Management
- Recruited to superintend new construction from grow-in through start-up of 18-hole golf club in Rehburg-Loccum, Germany. Course opened on time, signing 150 members within three months.
- Lengthened hours of operation for young club in Rehburg-Loccum, resulting in a 92% increase in membership and 20% gain in pro shop revenue.
- Delivered a 35% increase in driving range revenue, 100,000 DM in club sales, and 250,000 DM in golf school fees to secure a top-50 rank in 2001 for the Donnersberg Golf Club for the second consecutive year.
- Selected to design and oversee course and driving range upgrades including new bunkers, facilities, and advanced security systems. Project was completed on time and within budget.
- Drove revenues to record highs by introducing quality services and amenities for a new club in Munstor, Germany. Increased membership 85% to capture position as one of top two clubs in the area.
- Experience producing and presenting highly effective multi-media promotions, aggressively marketing facilities and events to secure sponsorship for a Professional Tournament in 2001.

Playing Career

Earned player position in PGA Tour events in the Midlands Region
Placed 2nd and 3rd in fields of 100 at Surrey Assistants Tournaments
1st place finish at British Car Auctions' Pro-Am Tournament
Qualified through Regional Rounds for the British Open
Qualified for playing position at the Scandinavian Open
Finished 1st in the Surrey PGA Golf Championship
Placed 2nd in the Surrey Professional Golfers Association Championship

RECENT PROFESSIONAL POSITIONS

2000 – Present	**Head Professional**, Skovsö-Hansen Golf Academy – Donnersberg Golf Club - *Roderhof, Germany*
1996 – 1999	**Head Professional**, Skovsö-Hansen Golf Academy – Golf Park Münster-Tinnen - *Munster, Germany*
1993 – 1996	**Head Professional**, Golf Club Rehburg Loccum - *Rehburg Loccum, Germany*
1990 - 1993	**Co-Sponsor with Ian Woosnan**, Maruman UK, Ltd. Golf School - *London, England*
1986 – 1992	**Head Teaching Professional**, Silvermere Golf Club – South East Academy of Golf - *Surrey, England*
1985 – 1986	**Teaching Professional**, Tilgate Forest Golf Club - *Crawley, Sussex*

Hildi Johanes   Global ICT Consultant

W. van Templantsoen 55, Loudekerk aan den Bijn 1122 VK, The Netherlands • E-mail: hildijohanes@all.com
Tel: +31 55 555-5555 • Fax: +31 00 000-0000 • US Tel: 201-555-5555 • US Fax: 201-000-0000

Knowledge Management • Systems Integration • Project Management

- Globally experienced multilingual information technology professional with a comprehensive background in development and oversight of leading-edge technologies for the support of international businesses. Expertise includes experience with world-class banks and financial institutions, global manufacturers and distributors, telecom groups, call centers, and government agencies.

- Effectively communicate technological concepts, finding the simplicity in complex business structures and integrating end user needs into system requirements. Improve systems and solve problems through a solid foundation of personal initiative, persistence, and dedicated customer support. Meet the challenges presented by a rapidly changing global economy.

- Fluent in spoken and written English, German, and native Dutch, with a working knowledge of French. Adept at relationship building and the understanding of countries' characteristic business cultures. Have worked in the United States (30 extended assignments within six years), England, and nearly every European country. United States "green card" application process close to completion. Married to a United States citizen.

Areas of Ability

- Project Planning / Management
- Multi-Project Development
- Applications Design / Development
- Systems Implementation
- Global Operations

- Knowledge Management
- Computer Telephony Integration
- Global Transport / Logistics
- Branch Automation
- Data Communication

- Global Information Exchange
- Global Systems Standardization
- EDI Message Standards
- Call Center Management
- Intranet Development

Summary of Technology Expertise

Masters in Business Administration, Information Systems, 1996 ● Bachelor of Science, Computer Science, 1991 Princeton University, Princeton, NJ, USA

Operating Systems – Windows 95 / 98 / NT/ XP, UNIX, (AT&T, Berkley & SCO), Message Handling Servers (IATA Protocol)

Web Technology – IIS, VBScript, HTML, ASP, DHTML, CCS, JavaScript, ActiveX Development, ISAPI, PWS, FrontPage, Image Composer, and Liquid Motion

Programming Languages – COBOL, UNIX sh/ksh, SQL, C/C++, Visual Basic 3.0/4.0/5.0/6.0, PowerBuilder, GUI (Graphical User Interface), HTML, Uniface, Microsoft Application Programming Interfaces (MAPI, API, TAPI & SDK), DAO, RDS, ADO, ODBC (Open Database Connectivity)

Database Environments – Sybase, Oracle, Microsoft SQL Server, Microsoft Access JET

Design Methods and Techniques – SDW, ISAC, IDEF, SDM, DSA, OO (Object Orientation), Erwin, Blues, RAD (Rapid Application Development), Client/Server Technology, Distributed Object Technology (OLE/DLL/DCOM)

Data and Telecommunications – Bridges/Routers, TCP/IP (Telnet/ftp), UUCP, ISDN, ACDs, Computer Telephony Integration, Data Switches, Voice Processing

Hardware – Apple Macintosh, PC's (i286/i386/i486/Pentium), NCR 4000/5000/9000/10000 (ITX), NCR 3000/3400/3600 (UNIX), HP 9000 (UNIX)

Applications – Microsoft Excel, Word, PowerPoint, Office, FrontPage, Outlook, Access; Internet Explorer; Microsoft Exchange and Outlook Forms; CorelDraw; and Visio

Recent Project Highlights

Knowledge Management

- Developed projects for *ExteBank's 64-branch, main system Global IT department* consisting of main aspects such as project management, tracking of internal costs, time registration, and order invoice / HR administration.

- Currently using project documentation and repository tools, such as SourceSafe, to *set up standards and guidelines for the integration and use of Microsoft Exchange Mail Services in a multi-developer environment, and Public Folder Structure with Intranet Services* to stimulate global communication between ExteBank's large internal research groups.

- Researched tools and languages, and *developed standards and guidelines for the design and implementation of a company-wide Intranet* to provide ExteBank with a new way to bring globally gathered information directly to the research departments. Set up a suite of frameworks to jumpstart the development and implementation of departmental sub-Intranets.

- *Implemented document management systems using Exchange Client Server Technology* for several ExteBank global research groups. This system is now used on a global scale throughout the bank.

Management Information Systems

- *Reengineered Global IT time registration and project management systems* using the e-mail client as a communication layer, allowing end users and team leaders anywhere on the ExteBank's Global Network to fill in and verify time sheets according to a complex project / task structure. Information is downloaded to a database using Crystal Reports as a tool to disseminate project information in various formats.

- *Developed new tracking methods for extensive Global IT department travel costs* that resulted in large-dollar reductions through procurement of airline and hotel chain discounts that became available as a result of concrete information on travel costs / volumes. In addition, all travel costs are now allocated to the proper projects.

- *Redesigned the order / invoice and human resource administration for the Global IT Management Information Department* using Rapid Application Development and Object-Oriented design methodology. Designed and built class libraries and several OLE servers to give fast, flexible, and accurate insight into global financial status and resource availability.

Computer Telephony Integration

- *Implemented a Call Center Solutions scripting tool for the Dutch Governmental Tax Service.* Developed this customized product as an emergency, interim solution to answer questions regarding a new road tax law involving six million drivers.

- *Provided expertise on Object-Oriented Design Methodology* to Dente, a Dutch telecom supplier. Team leader for *Call Center Management Information System projects* to supply tools for call statistics and real-time queries. Evaluated various companies for their ability to provide large-scale billing services for calling card applications.

International Transport and Logistics

- *Saved S. Schwedrdel, the world's largest fresh flower distributor, over $200,000 annually* through the elimination of brokers formerly necessary for the production of import / export documents. Designed and implemented an efficient import / export invoicing and order system that determines order status and weight of every box of flowers on over 100 trucks leaving daily, signals when truck is processed, produces all necessary perishable goods export documentation, and automatically stores information for Customs and the Central Bureau of Statistics.

- *Designed inventory-based "local-standards" order entry / invoicing systems* for several European and U.S. branches of   S. Schwedrdel. Selected hardware, operating system, and developing language. Negotiated contracts with vendors, handled implementation and continuity. Conducted extensive end user and system administrator training.

- *Saved Schwedrdel at least $100,000 per year on personnel, and third-party shipping and handling costs* by the development of several ground-breaking IT projects involving electronic information transfer (EDI). Partnered with the Dutch government for increased flexibility in the import of perishable goods from non-European markets. System is still being used as a reference for other Dutch companies.

Career Development

Trans-Euro Consultants, Loudekerk, The Netherlands   1996 to present
Owner and Principal Consultant to these representative clients and industries:

ExteBank International — a triple A status global bank currently expanding into investment banking with total assets of over $10.5 billion; 3,500 employees; and 90 branches in over 30 countries.

- Streamlined global communications and improved information sharing using all available information technologies.
- Currently designing and developing project management information software and procedures for ExteBank Global IT.

LOD Finance — a large international ICT consulting firm serving clients such as ExteBank International. LOD is listed in the London and Amsterdam stock exchanges, had a 1998 turnover of $600 million, and operates in the United Kingdom, Germany, Belgium, France, and The Netherlands.

- Work with Global IT, Global Service Management, Human Resources, and Global Research departments.
- Provide direction on technical, functional, and organizational issues for Management Support, Project Management, Global Product and Service standardization, and Global ITIL implementations. Handle new project acquisition.
- Consulting Project Manager and onsite supervisor of five programmers and three database administrators.

Dente International — a solutions provider for the telecommunications industry and call center market. Dente was established in 1988 as part of the Regent Group.

- Served as Senior Systems Analyst for various client projects.
- Implemented scripting in the Dutch Governmental Tax Service.

JKJ Telecom — an international telecommunications corporation (formerly known as RSS Telecom) with revenues of $1.7 billion. Currently ranked eighth in the European telecommunications sector and listed on the New York and Amsterdam stock exchanges.

- Acted as Senior Systems Analyst / Developer.
- Designed and developed pricing and configuration tools for the Dutch RSS Telecom.

S. Schwedrdel and Company, The Netherlands   1986 to 1989
Senior Systems Analyst / In-House Development

World's largest flower exporter, with 15 worldwide branches, $259 million turnover, and 600+ employees.

- Directed day-to-day operations of information systems for worldwide branches.
- Managed company-wide information exchange using telex, fax, e-mail, and EDI.
- Automated the invoice, transport documentation, and export documentation departments.
- Handled several groundbreaking EDI projects in conjunction with the Dutch government.
- Established four satellite branches in Spain and the US.

Education

Princeton University, Princeton, NJ, US

- Masters in Business Information Systems, 1995
- Bachelors in Computer Science, 1993

Institute of Computer Science, The Netherlands

- Computer Science Degree, 1989

JACQUES PHILIPPE

500 Maple Avenue, Lincoln, Nebraska 68508

Residence: 402-555-1212   JPhilippe3@email.com   Fax: 402-555-2121

SENIOR LEVEL MANAGEMENT / INTERNATIONAL BUSINESS DEVELOPMENT

Global Sales & Marketing · Turnaround Leadership · P & L Accountability

Results-oriented **Multinational Business Executive** driving innovation by creating and implementing unique market entry strategies. Expert international sales and marketing skills achieving consistent records of aggressive growth in industries with slow buying cycles. Ability to access top officers of targeted companies, recruit in-country sales professionals, create top-performing sales support offices, and establish prominent local brands. Officer/shareholder of travel company and advertising agency. Multilingual in French, English, and German. French citizen with work permits in 15 countries.

PROFESSIONAL EXPERIENCE

FANFARE, INC., Omaha, Nebraska   1996 to Present

Privately owned US-based manufacturer of cleaning maintenance products with operations in US and Europe, staffing 650 employees and reporting $50 million annual sales with 15% in exports.

DIRECTOR, INTERNATIONAL SALES

Manage high-growth international sales and marketing operations with full P&L responsibility for newly built European manufacturing plant. Administer annual $550 thousand international division operating budget. Establish and meet international sales goals exceeding $5 million per year for parent company and international subsidiary. Supervise European sales office, organizing and leading marketing activities related to global markets. Appointed United Kingdom subsidiary Officer, collaborating with subsidiary Managing Director on issues of personnel, administration, production planning, inventory requirements, and manufacturing process improvements. Redesigned company image from that of pure manufacturing group to a leading-edge company offering business solution systems and specialized expertise.

- Installed transfer-pricing policies between parent company and United Kingdom subsidiary. Result: Reduced import duties 18% and overall corporate tax liability $75 thousand in 2000.

- Assisted in reversing negative performance of international subsidiary within 12 months, contributing to record profits in 1998. Result: Exceeded 8% of sales after tax in 1999.

- Grew sales 75% from 1997 to 1999 by restructuring territories to strengthen European distribution including the initiation of direct sales in major European markets. Result: Steep margin increases.

- Triggered 90% increase in sales in 1996 by securing 2 new accounts with exclusive 5-year contracts valued at $1 million per annum. Result: Stimulated subsidiary turnaround profitability.

- Recommended $300 thousand new production equipment investment to boost expansion with new products in new markets. Result: 65% of equipment capacity sold within 6 months with ROI on track to be under 24 months.

- Established, staffed, and supervised European sales office, successfully hiring outside talents with proven industry track records. Built high-performing, self-motivated, autonomous sales staff that achieved consistent under-spending despite sharp sales increase and requirement for more resources.

143

JOHNSON HYGIENE PRODUCTS, INC., Essex, United Kingdom   1989 to 1996

Wholly owned subsidiary of Garçone, a French-based company of $850 million sales per annum, employing 70 people and reporting $10 million sales in 1996 with 70% in exports.

EXPORT SALES MANAGER, 1993 to 1996
COMMERCIAL ADMINISTRATION MANAGER, 1989 to 1993

Directed export sales for leading world manufacturer of hygiene and sanitary equipment. Exceeded goals by selling to top officers of key accounts. Collaborated with marketing director to launch new products. Appointed distributors and provided ongoing support. Planned and directed international trade shows. Organized and presented technical training for customer sales representatives. Built effective management information system by introducing PC-based office software. Implemented new key accounts database system with exhaustive account details, revenue analysis, short- and medium-term product needs, plus other key elements to drive future account strategy.

- Increased value of territory from $650 thousand in 1993 to $1.7 million in 1996.
- Accelerated sales growth 27% over 3 years despite loss of 2 major accounts representing 34% of all export sales in 1996.
- Recommended $125 thousand investment to successfully adapt standard range of products to specifications for export market.
- Captured largest single distributorship in company history valued at $450 thousand per annum within 12 months of activity in Japan.
- Closed largest single stock order sale in South Africa valued at $75 thousand.
- Consistently exceeded sales goals for 3 years with 20% under-spending in departmental operating budget.

ADDITIONAL EXPERIENCE:
FOOD & BEVERAGE CONTROLLER, HOTEL INTERNATIONAL, Nice, France   1989
MARKET RESEARCH ASSISTANT, UNITED TELESALES, Paris, France   1987 to 1988

EDUCATION

BACHELOR OF SCIENCE (US equivalent)   1989
Business Administration/General Management
French Academy of Business, Paris, France

Hautes Études Commerciales (Business school preparatory course)   1986
Mierse College, Nice, France

PROFESSIONAL ACTIVITIES

Affiliations
- Textile Rental Service Association
- Textile Service Association

Presentations
- *"Joys and Challenges of International Business Careers,"* Guest Speaker International Business Immersion Week, University of Nebraska, 3/96
- *"Concept Selling – the Four-Step Sales Process,"* Guest Speaker International Cleaning Products Asia Show, Singapore, 8/98

NIGEL R. CUNNINGHAM
45 Mullin Green, Surrey CR2 9BL, U.K.
Telephone: 44 890 677 9988
E-mail: NCunningham@composerve.com

COMPETITIVE INTELLIGENCE ♦ INVESTIGATIONS ♦ LEGAL RESEARCH

PROFESSIONAL PROFILE

Accomplished investigative and law enforcement professional recognized for thoroughness in research, case management, documentation and report writing. Expertise in diverse legislative issues and industries. Equally strong skills in team leadership, staff training, negotiations and management of multiple projects concurrently. Consistently deliver project results within deadlines and on budget.

Strengths: Analytical, intuitive, tenacious, business knowledge, creative problem solver, effective communicator, adept interviewer/investigator. Proficient in various computer applications.

CAREER EXPERIENCE

BOROUGH OF CONSUMER PROTECTION, London, U.K.	1987-Present
Senior Officer – Special Investigations & Enforcement Team	1992-Present
District Officer – Special Investigations Team	1990-1992
Inspector	1987-1990

Promoted through progressively responsible positions in the detection and prevention of business fraud and unfair trading practices. Diverse scope of responsibilities includes:

Research/Investigations – Investigate alleged unfair business practices, including fair trading fraud and counterfeit products; ensure compliance with laws. Document cases and prepare comprehensive reports. Develop contacts and foster collaborative relationships with law enforcement agencies in joint prosecution efforts to achieve positive outcomes. Conduct extensive legal research. Serve as an expert witness/present cases in court. Advisor to businesses and consumers.

Management/Training – Assume managerial functions during supervisor's absence; regularly deputize for the manager and oversee junior staff members. Plan and execute departmental projects, supervise project teams and administer budget. Represent senior management at meetings and deliver presentations at local and national levels. Monitor impact of new legislation and train staff.

Quality Management/Audits – Representative on Quality Improvement Team designed to review systems, identify needs and develop continuous improvement initiatives; establish audit plans for enhancement of customer service while saving costs. Accountable for assessment, analysis, consulting, implementation and staff training on quality/process improvement.

Accomplishments

- Effectively investigated and managed a wide range of highly sensitive and complex cases. Results include successful criminal prosecution of an organized software counterfeiter with over 3,000 illegal PC and business software products seized and of a major international corporation for serious safety act offenses. Case frequently quoted by British law students.

- Contributed to a major decline in illegal business start-ups through education of property owners and effective collaboration with law enforcement officials.

- Planned and executed several comprehensive quality audits of the department's business processes/systems and assisted in highly technical audits conducted at similar internal departments.

- Recognized for contributions to the establishment and launch of customer-focused initiatives that improved quality processes.

continued...

145

BOROUGH OF CONSUMER PROTECTION *continued...*

- Conducted SWOT analysis of department and delivered recommendations to the performance review management team on service and operations improvements to address changing customer needs.

- Advanced department's use of technology and improved system effectiveness, saving department money while enhancing efficiency. Created documentation and trained staff on new technology.

- Awarded a highly competitive international scholarship to study diverse aspect of business law enforcement practices in the U.S. One of only 5 U.K. business professionals to win the coveted scholarship.

EDUCATION & TRAINING

Post Graduate Diploma in Management
University of Sussex, London, U.K., 1999

Business & Technology Education Council Certificate in Management Studies
Manchester College, Manchester, U.K., 1995

Diploma in Consumer Protection
Manchester College, Manchester, U.K., 1990
- Rigorous training program in Civil and Criminal Law, Local Government and the European Union, Metrological Control Principles, Information Technology Systems, Food and Agriculture, Quality Management and Assessment Techniques, Structure of Trade.

Quality Assurance Lead Assessor (5-day course)
Vanguard Associates, London, U.K., 1991

References available on request.

GIANCARLO M. DI MAIO

49 Spring Avenue
Elkins Park, PA 19027
(215) 551-4642

ITALIAN INSTRUCTOR & TRANSLATOR

Native Italian and longtime U.S. resident with extensive educational experience on the collegiate and professional adult levels providing language instruction from beginning to advanced levels. Additional abilities in education administration. Four-year degree.

Background includes providing translation for World Cup ice skating, as well as for legal firms and corporations. Presently authoring an Italian instruction book and companion CD. Current member, Sons of Italy, and periodically deliver lectures on Italian history, culture, and political leaders.

EMPLOYMENT

1989 to 2002   **Administrator/Instructor**   **School of Languages**   Philadelphia, PA

🕮 Provided both group and individual Italian instruction to working professionals from the beginning through the advanced stages. Employ teaching methods which focus on the mechanics of the language in order to ensure students' self-reliance in learning and using the language. Addressed administrative issues including program design, curriculum development, and design and selection of teaching materials. Directed business and financial functions.

1988   **Italian Teacher**   **Western University**   Philadelphia, PA

🕮 Conducted five-hour compulsory instruction sessions for undergraduates.

1988   **Italian Teacher**   **Italian Institute**   Philadelphia, PA

🕮 Tutored adults in beginning through advanced Italian.

EDUCATION

B.S., Education, The University of Cincinnati, Cincinnati, OH, 1987

MILITARY

Smef, Italian National Army, 1973

ATHLETICS

Regional Champion Boxer, 1972; Top Italian Traveling Soccer Athlete, 1971

Gunnar Ericsson

United States: 248.555.1048 / facsimile: 248.555.1049
Singapore: (65) 8741.1212 / business: (65) 8742.6996
E-mail: gericsson@yahaamail.com

CAREER PROFILE

International Business / Marketing Specialist

Dynamic management career spearheading successful international marketing and business development programs. Combined expertise in strategic market planning, organizational leadership, and project management with strong qualifications in product representation and brand management. Expert at identifying markets, prioritizing objectives, and representing/ promoting products and services.

Entrepreneurial-driven business professional with significant Asian/Middle East/European/Latin American expertise and contact networks. Strong ability to establish and maintain long-term relationships. Successful at building brand name recognition that leads to greater profit margins.

Expertise includes:

▪ New Market Identification & Entry	▪ Export Program Development
▪ Multicultural Team Building & Leadership	▪ Key Account Management
▪ Multinational Alliances & Contract Negotiation	▪ P&L Responsibilities
▪ International.Marketing & Business Development	▪ Sales Forecasting & Budgeting

Fluent in English, Scandinavian languages, and French. High proficiency in German. Extensive international travel; strong international culture understanding. MBA and MIM degrees.

EXPERIENCE

HABTECH CORPORATION – 1985-current

(Fortune 300 corporation and $4 billion international manufacturer of building products.)

Director, Far East Sales – Singapore Regional Headquarters, 1993-current

Member of executive team with full responsibilities for establishing presence and directing operations in the Asian market. Manage all P&L, finance, recruiting/hiring, budgeting, sales, and marketing efforts. Initiated the development and launch of the regional headquarters office in Singapore. Direct a staff of nine professionals representing multiple product lines, as company's largest international office in sales. Negotiate new product offerings.

▪ Formulate annual business plans for various divisions in addition to corporate plans, forecast overhead, plan budgets/expenses, and determine marketing goals and objectives.

▪ Develop new missions including aggressive sales and profit projections.

▪ Create programs to grow company; adjust plans to compete in competitive markets.

▪ Solicit companies for potential acquisition. Conduct market studies on product lines; analyze marketability and profitability. Identify viable channels of distribution.

Results:

▪ Fostered international brand awareness in new cultures. Led cooperative efforts that promoted understanding and encouraged international business agreements into the region.

▪ Consistently attained, and frequently doubled, division sales projections. Delivered profit margins among the best of company's divisions.

▪ Built confidence and positions with numerous divisions; conferred executive titles (VP International - [Brand]; Director of Sales - [Brand]; Export Sales Manager - [Brand]).

▪ Developed exceptional brand name positioning for product lines throughout Asia.

Associate Director, International Sales – Michigan, 1988-93

Promoted to a position of greater responsibilities including hiring and supervising a sales and administration staff. Responsible for all corporate international trade show participation.

- Strong involvement in identifying and cultivating key high-growth international markets.
- Developed and implemented marketing programs that enhanced key brands and delivered effective sales campaigns.

International Account Executive, 1985-88

- Developed lead follow-up systems for several divisions including import/export.
- Identified and commissioned more than 20 distributors in Asia, the Middle East, Central America, and South America for key brand distribution.

International Sales Manager (Division of Belcorp United), 1984-85

Directed analysis of international market potential for new products. Identified new geographical market opportunities.

- Led aggressive campaign to broaden overseas sales and market share.
- Promoted highly competent and productive distributors to the network, including eight new accounts in three months.

TOPLAND INTERNATIONAL CORPORATION (Division of Highland Global Inc.)
European Marketing Sales Manager, 1981-84

TRANSAIR NORWEGIAN AB (NAS) – **Airsteward**, 1976-80. While completing MBA degree.

NORWEGIAN AIR FORCE – **Sergeant**, 1975-76. Military obligation as Air Traffic Controller Assistant.

EDUCATION / PROFESSIONAL DEVELOPMENT

AMERICAN GRADUATE SCHOOL OF INTERNATIONAL MANAGEMENT
Master of International Management; Glendale, California, 1981
Specialization in international marketing, selling and sales management, business communication, and import/export operations.

UNIVERSITY OF AZLUND, NORWAY
Master of Business Administration, 1980 – Marketing major

Continuing education/training:

UNIVERSITY OF GRENOBLE – Certificat Pratique De Langue Francaise; France, 1979
Intensive study of French and French culture

NORTHWESTERN UNIVERSITY, Kellogg Graduate School of Management – International Marketing Strategies, 1992

THE UNIVERSITY OF MICHIGAN, School of Business Administration – Managing International Joint Ventures, 1991

PERSONAL INFORMATION

Date of Birth: October 9, 1955	*Marital Status:* Married
Dual Citizenship: United States & Norway	*Health:* Excellent
	Children: Two

BERN HERTENSTEIN, M.D.

87 Lawrence Road
Trenton, New Jersey 98000
Residence: (555) 555-5555
E-mail: bernhert@compaserv.com

PROFILE

Pharmaceutical Research & Development Management Professional with expertise in the design and management of clinical trials for OTC skin care, sunscreen and cosmetic product lines. Clinical and managerial competencies combine with thorough knowledge of dermatological and other pharmaceuticals plus bioengineering. Strengths include marketing support, product innovations, product training, relationship building and contract negotiations. Successful in cultivating relationships with opinion leaders in the field of dermatology as well as with clinical test institutes and clinical research organizations (CROs) in the U.S. and Europe, collaborating on clinical studies. Adept in international arenas and cross-cultural communications with business experience in Europe, United States and Japan. Bilingual in English and German. Computer literate.

EDUCATION & TRAINING

M.D., in Dermatology, *graduated magna cum laude*, 1979-1986
University of Hamburg, School of Medicine, Hamburg, Germany

- Thesis: "*Comparative Study of Systemic and Local Side Effects of Prednicarbate Conventional Corticosteroids with Halogen Groups*"

Internship – Internal Medicine and Anesthesiology, 1985-1986
General Hospital, Hamburg, Germany

Completed University Entrance Qualification (B.S. equivalency in U.S.), concentration in Economics
Albright Gymnasium, Hamburg, Germany

PROFESSIONAL HISTORY

PHARMADORF INC.   Trenton, New Jersey
A $150 million U.S. subsidiary of a multi-billion dollar, German-based pharmaceutical, cosmetic and OTC skin care products company with 68 subsidiaries worldwide. Pharmadorf is #1 market leader in skin care products throughout Europe.
Director, Medical and Scientific Affairs • 1999 to Present

Develop, conduct and manage an average of 20 clinical studies per month, ranging from several weeks to 3 years; supervise research staff. Assess test results and provide scientific support of claims and new indications for existing as well as new skin care product lines. Research, audit, negotiate contracts and supervise independent product test sites. Team with Marketing and Consumer Affairs Departments to provide scientific, advertising/promotion and customer relations support. Perform analyses of new technologies and potential applications for new product development initiatives. Manage $1.5 million budget for all clinical testing in the U.S.

Contributions:

- Designed and instituted procedures for conducting safety and efficacy studies on all products in the U.S. Managed clinical studies for 21 product launches since 1996.

- Sourced, conducted comprehensive audits and negotiated contracts with 10 new independent sites for product testing throughout the U.S. and Canada.

- Cultivated and maintain productive relationships with dermatology industry experts/leaders, resulting in successful product promotion in "Dermatologic Surgery, Cutis, Cosmetic Dermatology" and other publications.

Director, Medical and Scientific Affairs *continued...*

- Trained marketing and sales professionals on various product lines, expanding their product knowledge and contributing to successful marketing/sales results.

- Partnered with company's Japanese joint venture to source, develop and conduct clinical trials to meet the needs of the Japanese market.

Manager, Medical and Scientific Affairs – Munich, Germany • 1993 to 1999

Designed, conducted and directed clinical research on the safety and efficacy of company's medical skin care product line (25 different products) at European headquarters in Germany. Managed budget and staff of research professionals. Developed strategies for new and existing cosmetic and pharmaceutical skin care products, including scientific support for claims and indications. Provided scientific, medical and product development support to Marketing Department.

Contributions:

- Initiated and managed joint international research projects (new product efforts) with Clinical Research Organizations in England, Germany and the U.S.

- Conducted and led clinical studies for 6 new product launches over 3-year period.

- Introduced new technologies and applications for new OTC pharmaceutical products.

PHARMASCHEIN AG   Hamburg, Germany

A multi-million dollar global company specializing in pharmaceutical, herbal and vitamin product lines.

Manager, Medical and Scientific Affairs/Medical Marketing Advisor • 1990 to 1993

Diverse scope of management responsibilities included designing and conducting clinical studies to support new and existing product lines, overseeing regulatory affairs, serving as medical advisor and facilitating product training. Accountable for providing all scientific and medical support regarding any aspect/issue of each product.

Contributions:

- Directed clinical trials on over 28 products and fostered positive relationships with regulatory agencies.

- Collaborated with the Marketing Department in development of product brochures, ensuring scientific accuracy in product claims and indications.

- Presented product training seminars to sales teams; provided medical consultation as advisor to the Marketing Department of another company division.

SCHERSON AG   Berlin, Germany

Scientific Assistant in Experimental Dermatology • 1987-1990

Managed research project entitled, "Comparative Study of Systemic and Local Side Effects of Various Corticosteroids," published in *Yearbook of Dermatology* in 1990.

Additional Experience: Department of Clinical Chemistry, General Hospital, Hamburg, Germany (1986-1990).

PROFESSIONAL MEMBERSHIPS

Society of Investigative Dermatology
International Society for Bioengineering and the Skin

References Available on Request.

BRANDY G. DUGINS

Georg-Rieser-Str. 7
62804 Kitzingen, Germany

49-6291-7860 (h)
brandydugins@yy-onlin.dy

CAREER SUMMARY

Skilled business and office manager with extensive experience and knowledge of the following:

· Import & Export Operations	· Quality Customer Service	· International Trade
· Research (Internet)	· Public Relations	· Office Organization
· Communications	· International Regulations/Customs	· Sales & Marketing
· Account Management	· Financial Transactions	· Administration
· Economics	· Windows 2000 & NT	· Outlook
· Excel	· Adobe	· Hardware

- Strong background in the import/export business managing international regulations and assisting international clients.
- Expert knowledge of international trading practices and laws. Organize and manage office administration.
- ***Fluent in German and Spanish.***

EMPLOYMENT EXPERIENCE

Customer Service/Account Representative   1996 to Present
MEISTER GMBH & CO.KG, Germany
* Meister sells automobile accessories worldwide with an annual volume of $14M.

- Manage export sales and process orders. Travel internationally to customer locations to review purchase orders. Discuss purchases with clients and prepare required documentation including required export/international and customs records. Check credit and determine customer qualifications. Access financial records for credit checks.
- Review collections lists and compose collections/credit/reclamation letters. Investigate and resolve customer complaints. Examine pertinent data to ensure correctness of collections/money owed.
- Attend major fairs as an official company representative. Respond to questions and direct potential customers to the purchase of appropriate products.
- Work closely with customers proving superior quality customer service. Speak to customers with tact and politeness (in German, Spanish or English). Manage complaints and diffuse problems.
- Control logistical requirements and set up transportation for orders. Prepare required paperwork including customs forms for sending sample products.
- Meticulous in organizational skills. Manage myriad of administrative requirements: maintain extensive files, prepare mailings, create Excel tables, prepare statistics, and translate documents.

Commercial Executive/Hardware Sales   **1993 to 1996**
Schmidt Computers, Germany (Headquarters-Atlanta, GA)

- Sold computer hardware and managed a client load of 70 plus.
- Created and prepared exhibitions and served as an official company representative at major international exhibitions/computer fairs in Germany. Met and spoke directly with customers regarding hardware, equipment, and specific requirements.
- Assisted customers, maintained accounts, and resolved customer complaints/problems. Researched inquiries. Conducted Internet searches.
- Built computers, installed software, and instructed customers in basics of computer hardware. Operated computer equipment.

Collections Representative   **1989 to 1993**
United Parcel Service, Germany

- Controlled the collection of the drivers' packages and money. Maintained and reviewed a constant checklist. Ensured a free balance. Assigned packages for certain routes.
- Proofread and corrected all C.O.D. money. Processed manual financial transactions.
- Assisted customers in locating packages, researching lost money, resolving problems, and receiving packages. Responded to inquiries.

EDUCATION

- IKH (Recertification Training), 1995 to 1996
  Administration Development, 525 hours of class time and a six-week internship. Courses included: Memory Training · Administrative Organization · PC Windows 3.1 · Data Processing WinWord 6.0 · Excel 5.0 · Workshop in PC · Economics and German Trade Law · Business Math · Modern Office Communications · Correspondence Training · Writing Techniques · Writing on a PC Keyboard · Social Training · Work Methods · Career and Family · Interview Training · Interaction in an Interview

- Groß Außenhandel Kauffrau (Import/Export Euro-School), 1994 to 1995 (USA equivalent to a Vocational License as a Wholesale and International Trade Specialist). Courses included: International Trade · English · German · Spanish · Computer · Economics · Government · Business Math

MARIA GUARINO

De Lairessestraat 154-III   m.guarino@nlondon.net   Home: 31.22.771.2134
11225PJ Amsterdam, The Netherlands   Mobile: 31 (09).315.12506

SENIOR SALES PROFESSIONAL
Broadcast Media & Technology Industries – US & International Markets
Expertise in New Business Development & Key Account Management/Retention

Creative and confident professional with 13+ years of progressively responsible sales/business development success across highly-competitive markets. Expert in forging win-win business relationships, negotiating high-level deals, and facilitating communications among multinational players; recognized for the ability to establish trust and loyalty among intermediaries. Worldwide traveler with knowledge of cultures in countries around the globe, particularly in Europe and Asia-Pacific. Comprehension of the Dutch, Italian and French languages; dual citizenship – American/Italian.

Characterized as multi-tasked, versatile, persistent, self-motivated and results-driven. Exceptional relationship management, communication, interpersonal and cross-cultural skills combined with an entrepreneurial attitude, energy and style. Motivational team leader and mentor. Excellent reputation for highly professional ethics and integrity.

- New Business & New Market Development
- Large & Key Account Management
- Relationship & Consultative Sales
- Executive Sales Presentations & Negotiations

- Business Infrastructure & Budgeting
- Strategic Alliances & Partnerships
- Customer Relationship Management
- Marketing & Promotions

PROFESSIONAL EXPERIENCE:

Emerge Europe, Amsterdam, The Netherlands   2001 to Present
REGIONAL SALES MANAGER, NORTHERN EUROPE

Recruited to provide strategic/tactical sales leadership to accelerate the business development pipeline for this subsidiary of Emerge@home. Venture is projected to evolve into a global broadband company with content offerings via multi-platform distribution (narrowband, broadband, Interactive TV, mobile phone portals) upon completion of merger with Promo, a major European broadband Internet company.

Given full autonomy for developing business plans, structuring/negotiating complex business partnerships, prospecting new accounts, recruiting/training sales team and building the organizational infrastructure.

- Identified potential market opportunities projected to deliver 200% annual average growth. Prospected clients, assessed needs, delivered high-impact sales presentations and secured key accounts.

- Encouraged a solutions-selling and needs analysis methodology to enhance performance of sales team. Built consensus among cross-cultural teams through open communications and understanding of diverse cultural/business ideologies.

- Guided teams in the vision, strategy and appropriate action plans to generate leads and drive revenues through the sale of advertising via narrowband/broadband portals.

Essex Technology Partners, Amsterdam, The Netherlands   1999 to 2001
SENIOR BUSINESS DEVELOPMENT MANAGER

Joined this 4200-employee, $600+ million global management consulting firm specializing in e-business and e-integration solutions to effectively transition clients into the "new economy" business arena. Provided an intense focus on needs analysis, problem-solving and strategy development for Global 1000, middle-market and start-up client companies.

- Conducted market research and developed a comprehensive business plan outlining a value-propositioning strategy. Accelerated market penetration and capitalized on profitable market opportunities.

- Partnered clients with consultants and directed teams in strategic account planning. Secured client accounts in the broadcasting/publishing/entertainment industries valued at $2.8+ million in revenues.

- Emphasized a solutions-based paradigm to foster long-term client development, relationship management and retention.

- Developed new management processes that strengthened sales, productivity and customer service.

BCB Europe and CBCB Europe, Amsterdam, The Netherlands   1995 to 1998
INTERNATIONAL SALES MANAGER

High-profile sales, marketing, business development and account management position for the European affiliate of this major television network. Challenged to accelerate revenues through television advertising/sponsorships and lead the sales management cycle, from consultation through presentation, negotiations and final closing. Managed, motivated and mentored a six-person sales/marketing team based in Italy.

Partnered with international research/marketing teams in support of marketing programs, created business development initiatives, developed sales strategies and launched country-wide market entry in Italy. Concurrently, managed the Netherlands, Belgium and Luxembourg territories.

- Achieved recognition for forging, strengthening and protecting key account relationships in a volatile marketplace. Captured a 65% renewal rate.

- Led account development programs with key focus on objective setting, pre-call planning and relationship management strategies. Demonstrated outstanding sales presentation, negotiation and closing skills.

- Penetrated non-traditional advertisers and built multinational account base from the "ground floor." Increased annual billing by 500% in 18 months and delivered consistent year-over-year growth.

- Created a marketing strategy/advertising campaign for a major high-profile global account. Encompassed agency relations with advertising firm, fostering relationships with managers in several countries and providing strong attention to detail. Represented the "highest dollar" in global revenues.

- Planned and orchestrated special events and seminars. Secured guest speakers, profiled programming line-up and effectively demonstrated viability of programs.

DCV/GTV & Cartoon Network International, Hong Kong   1993 to 1995
SALES MANAGER

Challenged to facilitate the start-up of a sales/service/support organization in Asia and accelerate advertising revenues throughout the Far East. Provided strong organizational leadership and active participation in key account sales and business development.

- Managed and secured a critical account generating $2.2 million in annual revenues.

Early Career (1990 to 1993): Played a critical role in the strategic development and profitable performance of local/network affiliate stations and a major advertising agency through dramatic growth and financial success. Exceptional performance in identifying market/business opportunities and creating the programs, promotions and client relationships to outpace the competition and dominate the marketplace.

- *Account Manager* – *WWLB-FM, WWTJ-FM, WOPV-AM, WTHG-FM*, Boston, MA. Managed local, regional and national accounts. Won several awards for "top biller" status and outstanding performance.

- *Sales Assistant* – *WVVA-TV*, Boston, MA. Executive-level administrative position supporting General/National Sales managers and local sales team for Boston's leading ABC-TV affiliate network.

- *Broadcast Traffic Manager* – *Johnson, Smith & Bishop* (leading advertising agency), Boston, MA.

EDUCATION: **BS, Broadcasting & Film, 1992 – Boston University**

KATERINA HOESCHLE

18 Yellowstone Blvd., New York, NY 11375
(718) 268-5555 • khoeschl@wurldnet.net

Field Producer / Associate Producer for TV Documentaries

Creative professional with 15 years' experience as a freelance documentary field producer and published writer and editor in Germany and France. Highly effective in translating complex technical information into easily understood language. Adept interviewer with a natural talent for building rapport with subjects. Thorough researcher, who obtains the details that become the "turning point" for the story. Expertise areas in:

☑ International Business	☑ Management	☑ Engineering	☑ Financial Markets
☑ Economics	☑ Technology	☑ History	☑ Food / Consumer

PROFESSIONAL EXPERIENCE

1998 – 2001 Freelance Producer, Writer, and Editor, Frankfurt, WEST GERMANY
- Supervised technical editing and English translation for Lufthansa's in-flight video magazine.

- Wrote text and treatment, shot film and created montage for TV documentary on the history of the Volkswagen Group for Deutsche Welle. Broadcast worldwide in German, Spanish and English.

- Produced 3–5 minute films for the public broadcasting channel's economic TV program "Trends", one of which was on WorldCom affiliate MFS and their optical fiber network.

- Contributed articles regularly for VDI Nachrichten, a weekly hi-tech and engineering newspaper.

- Conducted pre-production and field production research, interviews and translations for ABC-TV documentary series "Turn of the Century" with David Frost. Obtained interview with key figure who was previously unreachable for segment on WWII potential bombing of the city of Paris.

- Researched, developed and wrote articles in English for European Sources & News (targets computer industry), and for The International Cookbook Review, published by Edouard Cointreau.

1995 – 1998   Freelance Writer and Editor, Berlin, WEST GERMANY
- Penned and edited feature articles on industry, business and management issues as an ongoing contributor for Frankfurter Allgemeine Zeitung (a business economic daily), VDI Nachrichten and Fairchild Industries Publications (translations from French into English).

- Researched and wrote treatments on economic topics for Zebra Film, a TV production company.

1986 – 1995   Freelance Writer and Correspondent, Paris, FRANCE
- Produced economic news coverage for VWD (Germany's economic news agency), VDI Nachrichten, Deutsche Welle (Radio and TV), other trade publications for the advertising, food and related industries, and stock market coverage for two large economic newspapers.

- Created magazine pieces for European Television Service (broadcast in US as European Journal); served as field producer performing research and interviews for English language service.

- Wrote general articles for magazine supplement Profitravel, articles in English for The International Herald Tribune and a press kit for the German state of Saarland, in French.

EDUCATION

College-equivalent education in Journalism in Germany
Professional Workshops: Production Management (Frank Dohmann),
Script Writing (Syd Field, Thomas Frickel), and Industrial Films (Frank Haller)

LANGUAGES: English, German, French, Russian and Italian
TRAVEL: Extensively throughout Africa, Australia, Europe and USA
COMPUTER: Windows 98, MS Office 2000 – Word, Excel, Access, MS Outlook

5

Resume Examples
By Special Populations

MOST OF THE RESUMES IN THE PREVIOUS CHAPTER WERE FROM experienced professionals, many of whom command six-figure salaries. Most have years of experience which they are able to translate into impressive statements about their skills, competencies, and accomplishments. Their resumes usually command the attention of employers and recruiters because they showcase patterns of accomplishments throughout their career history.

All of the individuals in Chapter 4 began careers when they were young and inexperienced. In many cases, their first job had a significant impact on their overall career development. In this chapter, we include examples of resumes from individuals just out of college who wish to embark on an international career. Although they have limited experience, most of them have clear goals, marketable skills, enthusiasm, and a passionate drive to land an international job. Within a few years their resumes should include a much greater depth of experience as found in the resume examples in Chapter 4.

Our final group of resumes are from Americans seeking employment opportunities abroad. Most of these individuals have international experience as well as skill sets that are desired by employers around the globe. Examining how they present their objectives, career profile, experience, accomplishments, and education can be very instructive for developing your own resume.

The language of our resumes speaks to the hiring needs of employers who seek the very best talent for enhancing the productivity of their organizations. This is the language of skills, accomplishments, and productivity, a universal resume language that continues to transcend different cultures and nationalities. It's the language you, too, should increasingly speak as you seek your international dream job.

157

Resumes for Graduating Students Seeking International Opportunities

Karen Mo Sha Lo

AUSTRALIA: 403/22 Victoria Street, Bathurst 2795 NSW Australia • +61 2 5445 6677
HONG KONG: Flat H, 3/g, Block 19, Happy Gardens, Pa Of Man, Shatin, Hong Kong • 4565 4321

FOCUS: GRADUATE OPPORTUNITIES IN:
• Banking & Finance Analyst • Business Development Analyst • PR • Marketing

New University Graduate, educated in Australia and keen to commence a career in Hong Kong. Distinctively qualified for employment opportunities requiring superior analytical, organisational and creative strengths, combined with a natural team spirit and the drive to succeed.

KEY SKILLS SUMMARY

"Hands-On" Experience in:
- Data Collection
- Critical Problem Solving
- Data Entry
- General Clerical Functions
- Confidential Records Management
- Inbound/Outbound Telephone Calls

Expertly Trained in:
- Statistical & Financial Analysis
- Business Forecasting
- New Business Development Investigations
- Product/Brand Management
- Corporate Communications/PR
- Strategic Planning

Computer literacy: MS Word, Excel, Access, PowerPoint; Minitab for Introductory Statistics, Minitab for Economic & Business Forecasting, Internet and Email.

QUALIFICATIONS & TRAINING

Bachelor of Commerce, Majors: Economics and Marketing, *Australia University,* Australia...........2001

Diploma of Market Research, *Marketing Society of Australia*..2001

Certificate in Commerce, *University of Sydney,* Australia 1997

Certificate in Computing Literacy, *University of Sydney,* Australia 1997

Certificate in Advanced EAP, *University of Bathurst,* Australia 1997

Certificate of HKCEE, *Immaculate Heart of Mary University,* Hong Kong 1996

EXPERIENCE PROFILE

Organisational Examples

- Proven track record for completing all tasks quickly and precisely; swiftly and accurately entered data into computerised systems meeting all productivity and volume objectives for international law firm in Hong Kong.

- Maintained complex filing systems to aid easy records retrieval for all staff.

- Managed hectic reception area with professionalism. Juggled the demands of a multi-line telephone system, while simultaneously greeting visitors and sourcing personal assistance.

Communication Examples

- Fluent in three languages.

- Selected for front-line reception role based on personality and capacity to communicate effectively and persuasively with people at all levels.

Leadership Examples

- Intrinsic leadership and motivational strengths have been regularly recognised by teachers and peers throughout employment and education. Appointed Prefect and Girl Scout Team Leader during secondary schooling, and assumed administrator role of the International Student Society in 1998.

159

EMPLOYMENT SUMMARY

Harry Smith Law Firm, Hong Kong..Jan 01 – Feb 01
International law firm with multiple specialisations and offices throughout Europe and Asia.
Marketing Department
Library Data Entry Clerk (Temporary)

- Entered alphanumeric data into the computerised system for the marketing department's library of marketing resources.

- Maintained accurate record files of all confidential marketing materials. Assisted staff with sourcing information and cross-referencing archived and filed data.

Core Technology Computers, Australia... Feb 00-Nov 00
Clerk (Temporary)

- Supported administrative staff by handling a range of general clerical duties. Included mail receipt, recording and distribution, telephone answering, records handling and updating, filing, and information research to aid problem-solving efforts with missing or erroneous data.

Bank of China, Hong Kong .... Dec 98
Receptionist (Temporary)

- Acquired on-the-job training in a range of clerical and front-line reception tasks. Demonstrated quick ability to learn and carry out required tasks effectively.

MEMBERSHIPS

Student Member, Marketing Society of Australia
Former Administrator, International Student Society, Sydney University (1998)
Committee Member, Hong Kong Association (Secondary school) Hong Kong (1995)

PERSONAL DATA

Hong Kong ID No: 11190908 (1)
Languages: Fluent in English, Cantonese and Mandarin.
Leisure interests include swimming, travelling, badminton and reading.

REFERENCES

Available Upon Request

Ping Lin

414 Ruby Village, UF, Gainesville, FL 32603

352.846.6806

t_lin@grove.ufl.edu

BIOINFORMATICS SCIENTIST

BIOINFORMATICS PROFILE

- Intensive experience in DNA and protein sequence analysis using GCG, BLAST, genefinder, ORFfinder, and Grail.
- Gene discovery, including protein domain identifications, EST blast, and unfinished sequence database mining.
- Proficient in structure-function relationship, both in experiments and molecular modeling based on three-dimensional structure using Sybyl and Insight II packages.
- Adept at structure-function relationship analysis (protein domain) based on primary sequences and PDB crystal structures.
- Development of applications for genomic sequencing data, including algorithms and implementation.
- Skilled at signature sequence analysis, including protein domains and protein family classification for protein and DNA sequences.
- Practiced at writing 3-tier applications development in microarray and sequence data analysis.
- Accomplished object-oriented programming language (OOPL) designer for applications development.
- Experienced in development of computer applications for genomic data analysis.
- Proficient in writing programs for microarray data analysis.
- Database design and implementation.

EDUCATION

Ph.D., *Molecular Biology and Protein Chemistry*, Pathobiology Department, University of Florida—May 2001

M.S., *Computer and Information Science*, Computer and Information Science and Engineering Department, University of Florida, Gainesville, Florida—(May 2002)

KEY SUBJECT AREAS:

- Bioinformatics
- Programming Languages
- Computation Algorithms
- Computer Architecture
- Software Testing
- Database Management
- Data Structure and Algorithms
- Neural Network (Audit)

M.S., *Entomology*, Entomology Department, Kasetsart University, Bangkok, Thailand—December 1994
B.S., *Entomology*, Entomology Department, Nanjing Agricultural University, Nanjing, China—September 1985

COMPUTER SKILLS

SYSTEMS	UNIX, Linux, Windows 95/98NT/2000, Macintosh
LANGUAGES	Basic, C++, SQL, Java, Java Servlets, JSP, Perl, OOPL
DATABASES	Oracle, Access
APPLICATIONS	SAS, Oracle Tools, MS Office

161

RELEVANT EXPERIENCE

MOLECULAR BIOLOGY

- Developed DNA library of *Anaplasma marginale*.
- Purified, hybridized, and sequenced DNA of plasmepsin genes from *P. falciparum*.

COMPUTER SCIENCE

- Designed and implemented web-based application—*MDB Interface*—based on Microarray Database Management System (MDMS), using JAVA/JSP.
- Wrote applications—*GeneConversion and TrimBase*—for Malaria Genome Tag project, using Visual Basic.
- Developed diagnoses applications based on microarray data, using artificial neural network and Matlab.
- Built program for automating collection and analysis of kinetic data, using Visual Basic.
- Composed microarray transformation algorism based on entropy, using Matlab.
- Developed application for screening of pest-resistant varieties of soybean.
- Constructed discriminate analysis for microarray data, using Visual Basic.
- Compiled CPU performance data transformation program, using Perl.
- Assembled and implemented MDMS, using Oracle.

PROTEIN SCIENCE

- Expressed, purified, and enzymatically assayed plasmepsins, a family of aspartic proteinases from malaria parasites, (plasmepsin IV from *P. falciparum*, plasmepsin from *P. vivax*, plasmepsin from *P. ovale*).
- Mutated amino acid residues in plasmepsin sequence to test functions in vitro, based on analysis of structure-function relationship.
- Made molecular models of plasmepsins using Sybly for structure-functions relationship analysis.
- Designed established protocols for protein purification/quantification.
- Created established FPLC protocols for protein purification.
- Discovered three proteinase genes of *P. falciparum*.
- Developed kinetic assay for plasmepsins.

EMPLOYMENT CHRONOLOGY

Postdoctoral Associate	University of Florida College of Medicine, Pathology,	**2001—Present**
Research Assistant	University of Florida College of Veterinary Medicine, Pathobiology, Gainesville, FL	**1995—2000**
Research Scientist	Guangxi Academy of Agricultural Sciences, Plant Protection Institute, Nanning, Guangxi, China	**1986—1994**
Research Assistant	Guangxi Academy of Agricultural Sciences, Plant Protection Institute, Nanning, Guangxi, China	**1985—1986**

HONORS and AWARDS

Presidential Recognition, University of Florida—1999

Presidential Recognition, University of Florida—1997

First Excellence Award, Beishe Commission of Sciences and Technology—1991

Third Excellence Award, Guangxi Commission of Sciences and Technology—1991

Ding-jiajun Scholarship, Agricultural Sciences Study and Research, Thailand—1991-1994

PROFESSIONAL SOCIETIES

American Association for the Advancement of Science

American Society of Tropical Medicine and Hygiene

JEAN FERARD

2464 Oakwillow Lane
Cary, North Carolina 27608
Phone: (919) 782-9923
jeanferard@mailpost.com

CAREER OBJECTIVE

A public relations, marketing or account management position with a company that values outstanding and transferable skills, proven experience and expertise. Focusing on international communication/entertainment industry marketing positions in the British West Indies or European markets.

EDUCATION

LONG OAK COLLEGE, Long Oak, SC
Bachelor of Arts in Art History, May 1998
- Year Abroad, Florence, Italy; Instituto de Lorenzo de' Medici and The Art Institute of Florence. Honors: charcoal drawing chosen and exhibited for student exposition.
- Researched, developed and built web site that is still used today to teach art history - www.arthistory.sbc.edu/artartists.html
- President and Disc Jockey, WAMV 1410 AM Sweet Briar Radio station

SUMMARY OF QUALIFICATIONS

- *Diverse responsibilities and skills include successful marketing/communications experience. Training and strong internship experience and activities; able to develop and execute event plans to build productive and positive company image.*
- *Develop and implement short- and long-range programs to promote and enhance the company's public relations efforts; initial promotional and research work obtained through magazine and television internships.*
- *Software skills: WIN 95/98; Microsoft Word; Excel; PowerPoint; extensive Internet work.*
- *Writing skills: creative writing, editing and copyediting.*
- *Able to perform in high-visibility areas, on multi-task assignments and use leadership skills to rally "the team" around business strategies and goals; develop and implement innovative solutions.*
- *Extensive travel entertainment experience includes Italy, France, Spain, Portugal, Germany, Switzerland, Poland, Czech Republic, Slovakia, England and Holland.*

PROFESSIONAL INTERNSHIP EXPERIENCE

Arts & Antiques Magazine, Paris, France
Assistant to the Photography Editor (2001 - Present)
- Ensured maximum acceptance and support of photography editor's plans for the European unit of the magazine. Assisted in choosing images, layout and photo returns. Contacted major museums, auction houses and galleries. Assisted editors in content analysis and proofreading. Supported advertising sales efforts.

CRL, New York, NY (France)
Communications Internship-European Division (1999)
- Assisted in editing, transcribing, research and development of French correspondence between public and producers. Presented ideas to New York and European producers that were produced for the CBS Evening News. Coordinated guest interviews in support of various CBS European correspondents.

Flowers by Cecelia, Jackson Peak, WY
Assistant Planner/Coordinator; Floral Designer/Landscaper (1999)
- Responsible for wedding planning and corporate parties at remote locations. Special project work included all floral designs and landscaping for selected parties.

Jackson Hole Aviation, LLC, Jackson Peak, WY
Customer Service Representative (1998 - 1999)

References Available Upon Request

JANET LAING

1234 Keen Crescent, Oakville, Ontario, L7X 1K8, Canada
Home: 905.999.1534 E mail jlaing@inure.com

Objective	A Student Chef position to gain practical knowledge in French cuisine.
Profile	• Industrious, proactive student chef with a passion for food and the culinary arts. • Exudes energy and confidence; works well with peers and supervisors and independently. • Thrives on challenge; patient and diligent; completes work efficiently. • Organized multi-tasker; efficient and methodical in food preparation/presentation. • Effective communicator, written and oral; advanced knowledge of French. • Culturally sensitive; works well under pressure in a deadline-driven environment.

Education

George Brown College, Toronto, Ontario   Graduate April 2002
CULINARY MANAGEMENT DIPLOMA

BASIC.fst Food Safety Training Certificate #938   2000

Iroquois Ridge Secondary School, Oakville, Ontario   2000
Honours OSSD (Ontario Secondary School Diploma)
Awarded: Arts Letter, 100 points over 5 years for extracurricular activities
     Academic Letter, Honours in 4 years
     Silver Key for receiving 2 letters

Professional Experience

Holiday Inn Express Toronto Airport, Mississauga, Ontario 2000 - present
BUFFET COOK
• Cook omelettes and pasta dishes to order during breakfast, brunch and dinner.
• Prepare, assemble and display food in buffet format.
• Serve and carve at the roast meat station during dinner service.
• Provide service at the short order station.
• Render support and service to the Garde Manger stations – salad/fruit, meat platter and seafood.
• Officiate at various catering functions throughout hotel: wedding, banquets and conventions.
CO-OPERATIVE EDUCATION PLACEMENT   1999 - 2000
• Undertook all the duties outlined above.

Salvation Army Camp, Jackson's Point, Ontario   Summers 1998, 1999
COOK'S ASSISTANT
• Assisted 3 cooks preparing and cooking 750 meals per day during summer camp.
DISHWASHER   Summer 1997

Membership Generations of Talent   2001

Community Involvement

Salvation Army Family and Community Services Centre, Mississauga, Ontario 1997
• Provided support and guidance to staff dealing with persons seeking financial and material help.

CHOUA VANG

1725 Butternut Road ◆ Columbus, GA 31907
(706) 555-3408 (cell) ◆ cvang@yahoo.com

PROFESSIONAL OBJECTIVE

Strong desire to make a difference for each individual by providing excellent patient care to achieve a positive outcome in oral hygiene.

SUMMARY OF QUALIFICATIONS

- Strong desire to provide quality patient care to a diverse population of people.
- Capable of providing interpretation and translation services to Southeast Asian community.
- Exceptional ability to work with colleagues in a team environment to give all patients excellent care and keep the work flow moving smoothly.
- Significant training in hands-on clinical setting, with student selected patients based on the level of oral hygiene needs.

◆ Periodontal assessment	◆ Dental sealants	◆ Patient education
◆ Polishing	◆ Radiography	◆ Scaling / root debridement
◆ Intra / extra oral exam	◆ Infection control	◆ Medical dental history
◆ Fluoride treatment	◆ Ultrasonic scaling	◆ Dental charting

EDUCATION

SOUTHEASTERN TECHNICAL COLLEGE, Columbus, GA
ASSOCIATE DEGREE IN APPLIED SCIENCE – DENTAL HYGIENE PROGRAM
Anticipated Graduation: May 2002
- Participated in clinical rotations to Columbia Clinic, King Veterans Home, and Golden Clinic providing care for all patients.

CERTIFICATIONS

- Certified in Local Anesthesia – specially trained in the administration of eleven different injections.
- CPR Certified – Health Care Provider
- Registered Dental Hygienist – State of Georgia

CAREER EXPERIENCE

RDH ON-CALL, Columbus, GA   2001 – Present
REGISTERED DENTAL HYGIENIST
- Educate public regarding preventative oral hygiene.
- Work closely with dentists and dental assistants in offices located throughout Georgia as a replacement hygienist.
- Complete dental hygiene assignments, including medical history, scaling, and probe readings.

PRUDENTIAL INSURANCE, Columbus. GA   1994 – 1999
MICROFILM PROCESSOR
- Operated image-link to microfilm claim files and process films through developer.
- Used print reader and IDW to locate and print files as needed.
- Worked collaboratively with other staff members to efficiently process files.
- Assisted in training night crew in machine operation and internal policies.

PROFESSIONAL AFFILIATIONS

- Member, American Dental Hygiene Association

Dora Swimmer

Curriculum Vitae

Department of Spanish and Portuguese
University of Washington
Seattle, WA 98195
206-543-2020

P. O. Box 1212
Langham, WA 98204
560-767-5230

EDUCATION

1985-89   **Ph.C., Romance Languages and Literature**, University of Washington.
Expected Graduation: January 2000

Dissertation: *"The Detective as Social Critic: The Spanish and Mexican Detective Novel, 1970-1995."* The detective novel in Spain and Mexico and its relationship to political and social change. Director: Dr. Antonio Girard.

1983–1984   **M.A., Spanish**, Middlebury College, Madrid, Spain

1973–1978   **B.A., Spanish and Education**, Western Washington University, Bellingham

PROFESSIONAL EXPERIENCE

1994–1999   **Lecturer**—1st, 2nd, 3rd year Spanish, Western Washington University

1991–1994   **Instructor**—1st year Honors Spanish, Whitcom Community College

1990   **Instructor**—The Detective Novel, Western Washington University

1985–1989   **Graduate Teaching Assistant**—1st and 2nd year, and Equal Opportunity Program Spanish, University of Washington

1986–1987   **Instructor**—2nd year Spanish, Distance Learning, University of Washington

1984–1985   **ESL Teacher**, Powell Language Services, Madrid, Spain

1980–1983   **Secondary School Teacher**—1st, 2nd, 3rd year Spanish, Reading—Grades 7–12, DODD Schools, Okinawa, Japan

1978–1980   **Secondary School Teacher**—Spanish, Reading, Language Arts, Social Studies, Speech—Grades 7-12, Vancouver Schools, Washington.

FELLOWSHIPS AND HONORS

National Endowment for the Humanities Grant for *Improving Foreign Language Education at Community Colleges*, at Washington, D.C., conference sponsored by NEH, March 1993–June 1994; March 8-10, 1993.

Scholarship to "Contemporary Mexico" at the Colegio de Mexico, Mexico City, June–August 1989

Partial Academic Scholarship to Middlebury College, Madrid, Spain, 1983–1984

Alumni Association Scholarship, Western Washington State College, 1976–1977

OTHER PROFESSIONAL ACTIVITIES

Academic Advisor for Summerstart Program, Western Washington University, August 1998.

Academic Advisor for Summerstart Program, Western Washington University, August 1999

Freshman Advisor, Western Washington University, September 1998–June 1999.

Freshman Advisor, Western Washington University, September 1999–present

Access Program Speaker, October 1999.

Faculty participant in informational roundtable for incoming freshman, Western Washington University, March 1998.

Coordinator of pedagogical round-table in the Department of Modern and Classical Languages, Western Washington University, January 1998–present.

Participant in "Mesa Española" to enhance students' conversational skills and expand their knowledge of Hispanic culture, January 1998–June 1998

Presenter: "Communicative Activities for Large Foreign Language Classes" at Pacific Northwest Council for Languages Conference in Eugene, Oregon, April 1997.

Member: Modern Language Association; Pacific Northwest Council for Languages.

Visiting Scholar: Programa Interdisciplinario de Estudios de al Mujer, El Colegio de Mexico, Mexico City, April–June 1989.

Co-Advisor, Foreign Language Club, Kadena High School, Okinawa, Japan, 1982–1983.

Coach, Boys' and Girls' Track and Tennis, Kadena High School, 1981–1982.

Coach, Boys' and Girl's Track and Tennis, Kadena Middle School, 1980–1981.

Advisor, Spanish Club, Columbia River High School, Vancouver, Washington, 1978–1979.

Directed group of high school students in Mexico City, Spring 1979.

LANGUAGES

English, native. Spanish, near-native. French, reading. Italian, reading.

REFERENCES

Dr. Wheeler Andrews, Department of Spanish and Portuguese, University of Washington, Langham, Washington 200-354-6720

Dr. Antonio Girard, Department of Spanish and Portuguese, University of Washington, Langham, Washington 200-354-6724

Dr. Mary Thurston, Department of Foreign Languages, Whitcom Community College, Langham, Washington 200-767-7120

JUAN MORALES

1224 Normand Road
Wetumpka, Alabama 36000

☎ 334.555.5555
moralesj@hotmail.com

WHAT I CAN OFFER **Hennessy et Co.** AS YOUR NEWEST **Financial Analyst**

❑ Solid logic backed up with critical thinking ❑ Proven skill in transforming complex data into information decision makers can use intuitively ❑ People skills—even across cultural barriers—that build enduring, productive relationships ❑ Advanced capability to manage complex, changing workloads under tight deadlines

EMPLOYMENT STATUS

❑ Able to work legally in the United States.

EDUCATION WITH EXAMPLES OF PROBLEMS SOLVED

❑ MBA (Double Major in **Finance** and **Economics**), Auburn University – Montgomery, Montgomery, Alabama   Dec 01

*One of the top eight percent to have a **GPA of 4.0**. Awarded **full scholarships** throughout my college education.*

Relevant Course Work

❑ Securities Analysis and Portfolio Management	❑ Statistical Methods and Data Analysis for Managers
❑ Financial Valuation	❑ Business Statistics
❑ International Finance	❑ Global Trade and Finance
❑ Macroeconomic Analysis	❑ Public Finance
❑ Microeconomic Analysis	❑ Personal Finance
❑ Economics of Decision Making	❑ Marketing Management
❑ Managerial Accounting	❑ Managing People

❑ BA (**International Trade**) Auburn University – Montgomery, Alabama   May 00

***Completed this four-year course in two years**—starting with limited English language skills. **GPA 4.0** always maintained, even when I carried 25 credit hours a quarter.*

Sample Problems Solved

Accepted leadership role on a team that analyzed the profitability potential of a major US bank. Did my "homework," then sought out members of the bank's management team to gather key data. Helped guide comprehensive analysis and recommendations. ***Results:*** Written and oral report received the highest grades from an industry expert.

Completed—on my own—a detailed assessment of a major bank merger's future profitability. Analyzed interlocking strengths of two international industry leaders and the effects of anti-trust regulation. Condensed voluminous data into useful information. ***Results:*** Professor approved my work without change. Awarded top grade.

Designed, built, implemented, and defended a simulated capital improvement plan for a large manufacturer. Integrated more than a dozen variables and distilled mountains of data into a concise report including sensitivity analyses. ***Results:*** My one-page executive summary singled out for praise.

COMPUTER SKILLS

❑ Proficient in Excel, Word, PowerPoint, and Internet search protocols.

RECOGNITION IN MY FIELD

❑ Outstanding Student of the Year, Department of International Studies   99 – 00

❑ Runner Up in Outstanding Liberal Arts Student of the Year (from 800 eligibles)   99 – 00

LANGUAGE SKILLS

❑ Read, write, speak, and think fluently in Spanish, English and French

❑ Able to read Portuguese and Italian

3522 Jordash Avenue #2114
Minneapolis, MN 55334 USA
(612) 522-8331
Penelope_Andahazy@cartino.com

Lived Abroad
Studied in Granada, Spain
Worked in Mexico City

PENNIE MARIA ANDAHAZY

BILINGUAL: Fluent in English and Spanish
Bright / Enthusiastic / Personable / Hard-Working / Learn Rapidly / Outstanding Communication Skills
Eager to put Spanish-speaking skills and financial experience to work in Latin America

---

Education

University of St. Benedict, St. Paul, MN USA
Bachelor of Arts Summa Cum Laude Overall GPA 3.975   May 2001
Major: Finance   Minor: Spanish
Center of Modern Languages, University of Granada, Spain   September - December 1999

Work Experience

CARTINO, INC.   Minneapolis, MN USA   May 2000 - Present
Financial Markets Group / Global Capital Markets
Latin American Financial Administrator
Settle and coordinate financial operations in Latin American markets including foreign exchange,
debt, options, deliverable and non-deliverable forward contracts, certificates of deposit, and loans.
Work with changing and negotiating confirmations.
Improved options administration, management reports, efficiency, and controls.
North American Operations
Settle mortgage-backed securities, mutual funds, equities, futures, and bond options.
Mexico Treasury Projects & Audit (April - May 2001)
Conducted audit and completed various projects for Mexico Treasury.

Latin American Operations	Mexico Treasury Projects & Operations Audit
Confirm trades in Spanish and English	Documented procedures in Spanish and English
Facilitate loans in Venezuela, Argentina, Columbia	Worked with all areas of Cartino de Mexico
Maintain relationships with counterparties	Trained with accounting and payments systems
Facilitate contract openings and guarantees	Led updating of account agreements

USA EXPRESS FINANCIAL ADVISORS Minneapolis, MN   March 2000 - May 2000
Investment Equity Support Intern
Maintained accurate market and security information for analysts and portfolio managers.

FIRST AMERICAN BANK, BLONDELL FINANCIAL CORPORATION   Detroit Lakes, MN
Personal Banker - Opened accounts and assisted in credit decisions   Summer 1998 and 1999
Receptionist - Increased communication and professionalism.   Summer 1997

Proficient Computer Skills

Microsoft Office	IRIS AS400	Query-Showcase Strategy	Citibank USD software
Swift payments (STP)	Internet trade settlements	Various clearing systems	Citibank Paylink (MXN)

Activities
- Twin Cities Professional Latino Network (TCPLN) - member & Cartino representative
- Junior Achievement Volunteer - teach children in Spanish
- Association of Financial Management member
- Aquinas Scholars Honors Program - built writing, communication, and critical thinking skills

Awards
- Scholarship Key 2000 - highest grade point average in university business department
- Dean's list every semester in attendance at St. Benedict
- Detroit Lakes Women of Today Outstanding Young Adult, 1998
- Alpha Mu Gamma, foreign language honor society

Lydia Cortez

45 Grant Avenue
Smithtown, NY 11787
1+011(631) 382-2425

Passport #: 999999M
Date of Birth: May 5th, 1979
Place of Birth: USA

Education

Bachelor of Science, Latin American Studies
Top 5% of graduating class
Stony Brook University, Stony Brook, NY, 2001

Experience

Intern, Cable Network International
Hauppauge, New York
2000-2001

- Translate contracts, official documents, and marketing materials in Spanish.
- Perform administrative support functions.

Intern, Servicios de Lenguistica Legal
Madrid, Spain
Fall 1999

- Proofread legal documents written in Spanish.
- Answered incoming calls.

Counselor, Hispanic Union Center
Brentwood, New York
Summers 1996-2001

- Served as an interpreter for Spanish-speaking clients.

Other Activities

President, Spanish Culture Club
Stony Brook University, Stony Brook, New York
2000-2001

Studied Abroad (Spain)
Council of International Student Exchange
Universidad de Los Cielos, Madrid, Spain
Fall 1999

Languages

Fluent in Spanish and Catalan
Conversational Italian

BART MESIEUX   1818 Edgewater Road, Valley Stream, NY 11385 ~ (516) 223-9744
Mesieux@aol.com

OBJECTIVE:
A domestic or international position within a progressive environment where problems and opportunities are well matched to my skills in marketing, research and analytical problem solving.

EDUCATION:
< **Master of Business Administration, International Business**, Schiller International University, Dunedin, FL, 2000, GPA 3.7
< **Bachelor of Business Administration**, Schiller International University, Dunedin, FL 1998
< **Associate of Science**, St. Petersburg Junior College, Clearwater, FL, 1997

EMPLOYMENT HISTORY:
Personally financed 100% of education through the following employment:

4/2000-6/2000   Merrill Lynch, NY, NY   **Internship Program**
☐ Assisted in the implementation of a new network and database system.
☐ Conducted research and performed technical analysis on client database.

1/98-4/98   Owens Online, Quebec, Canada   **Internship Program**
☐ Performed background investigations for this international business research firm engaged by French and Canadian insurance firms. Verified school and work data along with salary verifications.
☐ Examined credit reports for accuracy and translated from French to English for e-mailing.

1998 (Summer)   E-Trade/ CPR Gestion Privee, Marseille, France   **Agent**
☐ Traded stocks, options and futures, executed orders, provided real-time stock pricing information and processed paper work for clients and prospective clients.
☐ Developed customer satisfaction survey/brochure for Marseille clients.

1996-1999 Horse Breeding International (Family Business), Brussels, Belgium
Asst. Operations Manager
☐ Utilized analytical skills and good judgment during the breeding selection process.
☐ Evaluated racing performances and represented firm at racing events in the U.S.A.

TECHNICAL SKILLS:
☐ Platforms: Windows 98, NT
☐ Presentation: Word, PowerPoint
☐ Data Management: MS Excel, ACT

LANGUAGE SKILLS:
Fluent in French (native) and English. Limited skills in Chinese and Spanish

MILITARY:
1993-1994 French Army, Infantry Regiment   **Office Administrator**
☐ Conducted statistical research, managed logistics for ground force equipment and supervised 8 personnel.

SPECIAL ACHIEVEMENTS: Honor Student, 1995-2000, President, Investment Club (Day Trading)

ANGELINA MOGUMBI
Curriculum Vitae

7325 Adams Way
Isanti, Minnesota 55040

(763) 461-9611
mogumbi@aol.com

EDUCATION

LLM	Iowa State University, Ames, Iowa	1999
MSW	Iowa State University, Ames, Iowa	1992
LL.B./JD	University of California, Berkeley, California	1990
BBA	University of California, Berkeley, California Major in Management	1983
Doctoral Candidate	University of Dublin, Dublin, Ireland	In progress

LICENSURE AND CERTIFICATION

Master of Social Work, Addiction Counselor National Board of Addiction Examiners, Isanti, Minnesota	2000
Certified Criminal Justice Specialist National Board of Addiction Examiners, Isanti, Minnesota	2000
Licensed Professional Counselor Board of Health, Isanti, Minnesota	1999

TEACHING APPOINTMENTS

Minnesota Children and Family Services Agency (CFSA), Isanti, Minnesota   1997-Present
Training Specialist
Train staff in family and child welfare practice. Develop curriculum in relevant areas in field.

Minnesota State University School of Social Work, Minneapolis, Minnesota   1995-1997
Assistant Professor/Instructor
Collaborated with Minneapolis School System to bring drug awareness program to primary schools. Partnered with MSU and community organizations to develop and manage homeless coalition program to reduce effects of substance abuse in Minneapolis.
Subjects Taught:
- Social Welfare Policy
- Human Behavior
- Social Work Practice
- Social Work and the Law

Isanti Community College, Isanti, Minnesota   1994-Present
Instructor
Subject Taught:
- Business Law

Minnesota, Training Resource Associates, Isanti, Minnesota   1994-Present
Instructor
Subjects Taught:
- Human Behavior
- Ethics for Substance Abuse Counselors

(Continued on Page 2)

TEACHING APPOINTMENTS (Continued)

University of Minnesota, Minneapolis, Minnesota   1994-Present
Instructor
Subjects Taught:
- Ethics for Professionals
- Business Law
- Professional Development
- Constitutional Law

PROFESSIONAL EXPERIENCE

Minnesota Children and Family Services Agency (CFSA), Isanti, Minnesota   1997-Present
Substance Abuse Specialist
Formulate substance abuse resources for CFSA. Originate pilot projects for women and children.

City of Isanti Human Resources Administration, Isanti, Minnesota   1986-1995
Social Work Supervisor/Social Worker Staff Analyst/Fair Hearing Officer
Initiated substance abuse treatment and prevention program for birth parents. Provided individual, group, and family therapy in field. Created and enlisted community substance abuse services providers in city.

HONORS AND AWARDS

Four-year Academic Scholarship for Undergraduate Study	1999
Social Work Award, AFL-CIO Local 563, Isanti, Minnesota	1992

PRESENTATIONS

Child Welfare System and the Impact of Substance Abuse Ahmed Rasheesh Foundation, Isanti, Minnesota	1996
United Nations and the Convention of the Rights of the Child California State University, Berkeley, California	1991

COMMITTEES AND COMMUNITY INVOLVEMENT

Member	Drug Court Development Committee, Isanti, Minnesota	2001-Present
Trainer	Train Superior Court Judges on substance abuse issues and community resources	2001-Present
Board Member	Fighting Back Initiative, *Substance Abuse Program* Roberts Wood Johnson Foundation	1999-Present
Member	Serve on review panel to draft drug status report, Drug Strategies, Inc.	1999-Present
Trainer	Foster Parents and Drug-Exposed Infants	1999-Present

AFFILIATIONS

Member	The Association of Legal Writing Specialists	1999-Present
Member	Association of Trial Lawyers of America	1998-Present

Amanda Lee Harris

9437 East St. Louis Avenue, Cheney, IL 61166
(262) 775-0023—day/evening
United States Citizen

OBJECTIVE
Internship at Bread for the World

EDUCATION
Daystar University, Nairobi, Kenya—anticipated completion of Theology credits, Aug 2001–Jan 2002
B.A., Theology, Seattle Pacific University, 3307 - 3rd Avenue West, Seattle, WA, anticipated Dec 2001

Academic Honors
Saddle University Dean's List, every quarter; GPA 3.91
Whitcom Community College Running Start Program—earned 68 credits toward degree
while attending high school, January 1998 – June 1999

WORK EXPERIENCE

Sales Associate/Card Department Manager,   12/96–6/99 and 6/01–8/01
FAITH CHRISTIAN STORES, 3560 Monroe Street, Merriweather, WA 98880
Supervisor: James Hansom—(300) 677-7777
Worked 15-30 hours per week at $6.40/hr while attending high school, 12/96–6/99; and 40 hours per week at $8/hr, 6/01–8/01

••Drew upon knowledge of entire store inventory, including Bibles, books, music, and home-schooling materials, to provide quality customer service. Successfully managed entire card department. Trained successor.

Barista, TAYLOR'S COFFEE, 228 North Quincy, Saddle, Washington 98888   2/01–6/01
Supervisor: Gleason Lyme—(200) 288-2222
Worked 20 hours per week @ $8/hr. while attending school.

••Provided customer service, waited tables, and prepared specialty coffee drinks. Studied history of coffee. Performed cashiering and closing duties.

Food Service / Cashier, NOEY'S BAGLES, 135 Quincy, Saddle, WA 98888   9-00–1/01
Supervisor: Daisy Knorr—(200) 288-6566
Worked 20 hours per week @ $8.25/hr. while attending school.

••Provided cashiering, coordinated food service, and performed back-room food preparation.

Student Academic Counselor Assistant,   9/99–6/00
SADDLE UNIVERSITY, 333 East Avenue, Saddle, WA 98888
Supervisor: Jason Anson—(200) 288-2000
Worked 10 hours per week @ $8/hr while attending University full time.

••Worked independently and as member of counselor team. Processed student files; prepared for student interviews; assembled preview packets, transcript evaluations, graduation applications, academic petitions, and other academic materials. Performed data entry. Assisted in organization of community college classes. **Created catalog of transferable classes for use by other counselors.** Provided general support to five counselors. Set and consistently met priorities and deadlines.

Sales Associate, NORTHPARK UNIVERSITY BOOKSTORE   summer 6/00–9/00
CARING CHRISTIAN BOOKSTORE, 200 West Fargo, Cheery, Illinois 60000
Supervisor: Brandon Mason—(700) 878-3767

••Provided personalized customer service by maintaining knowledge of textbook requirements for classes, as well as miscellaneous inventory.

OTHER QUALIFICATIONS
Conversant in French   Accomplished Pianist
Raised in Congo, Africa; traveled extensively within Africa, Middle East, and Europe. Volunteer Experience
Teacher Assistant—Study Group Team Leader
Worship Team Music/Drama—Youth Group Leadership—Youth Pastor's Search Committee

Resumes for Americans Seeking Opportunities Abroad

NANCY D. MORROW

165 Duke Street, Alexandria, VA 22315, (703) 371-7158, ndmorrow@mtn.com

---

SENIOR ADMINISTRATIVE PROFESSIONAL

Administrative Assistant with substantial international business experience, which includes working with top-level federal and public sector executives, political appointees, foreign ministers, and ambassadors. Skilled at working with diverse individuals and overcoming language and procedural barriers to train foreign staff members. Adept at facilitating operational efficiency, meeting coordination, and cross-organizational communication in high-profile, fast-paced environments. Familiar with various foreign cultures and customs; lived in Germany and Brazil and worked with various foreign representatives.

PROFESSIONAL EXPERIENCE

THE GLOBAL BANK, Washington, DC   1987 to 2001
Senior Program Management Assistant, Romanian Federation
(Selected from 45 applicants to assist in establishing this new executive-level, policy-making office.)

Worked in the Office of the Executive Director providing administrative support, scheduling meetings, planning conferences, arranging travel, and serving as timekeeper. Assisted in planning various conferences and meetings for Romanian representatives traveling to the United States for project negotiations.

Key Achievements:
- Acclimated nine Romanian staff members to American business operations and procedures and provided guidance in drafting correspondence using appropriate language.
- Managed all office documentation and maintained an extensive library of reference resources related to various Romanian lending projects and Global Bank policies.
- Participated in coordinating two international annual meetings, which included ensuring accommodations for up to 50 participants, obtaining conference space, and preparing briefing books.

U.S. DEPARTMENT OF PUBLIC CURRENCY, Washington, DC   1972 to 1987
(Promoted through increasingly responsible positions, throughout 15-year career, in various top-level offices including International Affairs and the Offices of the Secretary, Deputy Secretary, and Under Secretary.)

Executive Assistant, Office of International Affairs (1985 to 1987)

Provided comprehensive administrative and programmatic support to top-level, political appointees. Coordinated assignments among a staff of 260 people, ensuring that correspondence was routed correctly and received clearance in a timely manner. Scheduled various meetings and arranged extensive overseas travel arrangements for Department officials.

Key Achievements:
- Served on Secretary Callahan's transition team to oversee various administrative tasks, which included arranging interviews with the Secretary for political applicants.
- Prepared the Assistant Secretary's daily briefing books and gathered materials for Congressional Subcommittee Hearings, the Economics Council, and the U.S. Trade Liaison.

Secretary/Assistant, Offices of the Secretary, Deputy Secretary, and Under Secretary (1977 to 1985)
Secretary to Financial Attaches, Mexico City, Mexico; Hamburg, Germany (1972 to 1977)

COMPUTER SKILLS MS Word, Lotus Notes, Excel, Time/Attendance and Travel Software

LANGUAGES   Fluent in *German;* moderate fluency in *Latvian, Portuguese, Spanish, Russian.*

EDUCATION   **General Studies** (75 semester hours), Iowa University, Iowa City, IO
                                Executive Secretary Certificate, Iowa Business College, Des Moines, IO

177

115 Bay Bridge Drive

Residence Telephone: (732) 905-3991

Brick, New Jersey 08724

email: jonlyons@hume.com

BUSINESS DEVELOPMENT / MARKETING AND SALES MANAGEMENT
Asia, Europe, Middle East and United States

Solid executive career leading start-up and fast-track growth of high-technology companies. Expert in business development, product positioning and market expansion with strong operating, financial and HR skills. Forges cooperative working relationships; identifies and formulates strategic, revenue-generating partnerships. Proven "intrapreneur" with a track record in championing new organizational initiatives and employing "out-of-the-box" thinking.

CAREER HISTORY

CYLINK CORPORATION, Santa Clara, CA (2/96-Present)

Director of Business Development, 7/99 to Present

Full strategic and tactical responsibility for creating and leading a worldwide business development team in the sale of high-technology products, including security software, stand-alone WAN / LAN appliances, modules and components. Accountable for planning and orchestrating aggressive market and business development initiatives throughout emerging global markets for this $400 million corporation. Captured vertical industries such as telecommunications (network equipment manufacturers and carriers), health care (payers and providers) and wireless (e-merchants and solution providers). Performed financial evaluation of business development opportunities, including NPV and IRR calculations. Conceived and developed new product distribution channels that increased market penetration.

> Accomplishments:

* Evaluated competitive activity, competitive products, emerging technologies and new markets to determine the corporation's global market position. Performed financial evaluation of business-development opportunities, including NPV and IRR calculations.

* Recruited business development team members, built / led a global sales organization, and spearheaded business development initiatives and marketing strategies that spanned four continents. Trained new sales recruits in international liaison, marketing and business development skills.

* Negotiated an annual $4 million technology license contract with L3 Communications.

* Performed due diligence and negotiated an OEM contract with DICA Technologies for the sale of an ISDN product into the Japanese market. Drove $3.5 million in annual sales revenues.

* Negotiated and signed a global purchasing agreement with AT&T Solutions, resulting in $6 million in annual sales revenues.

* Established multi-channel distribution networks to expand in health care markets.

* Negotiated strategic alliances and signed multiple co-marketing agreements, including the establishment of partnerships with SYMANTEC and IBM/Tivoli.

* Developed Marconi Communications and ADTRAN as a re-seller channel for VPN products; estimated annual revenue of $6.5M.
* Developed business partnership with Nokia to provide wireless security technology.

Global Account Manager, 2/96-7/99

* Drove international sales revenues, launched new business development initiatives and profitably directed account development programs throughout emerging markets worldwide, including such accounts as Citigroup, AT&T Solutions, MBNA, Chase, Bankers Trust, Credit Suisse / First Boston and Fidelity Investments.
* Increased sales revenues by 200% over two-year period.

CINCINNATI ELECTRONICS CORPORATION, Mason, OH (1/95-2/96)

Regional Sales Manager, Eastern United States

Responsible for regional profit and loss, distribution network management, and the coordination of marketing and sales activities within a territory extending from the Caribbean to eastern Canada. Boosted both market penetration and company brand recognition. Increased sales by more than 90%. Revamped regional coverage to maximize productivity and enhance efficiency of the distribution network. Tracked sales and analyzed trends and market conditions to develop annual forecasts. Generated market analysis reports. Developed and implemented application-specific seminars and presentations for value-added resellers. Interfaced with advertising and public relations agencies to maximize marketing efforts.

HUGHES AIRCRAFT CORPORATION (FLIR Systems Inc.) Carlsbad, CA (12/89-11/94)

District Sales Manager, Northeast Territory

Managed and coordinated infrared imaging system sales to Fortune 500 companies throughout New Jersey and extending to eastern Canada. Cultivated this territory by developing and implementing comprehensive marketing strategies. Increased sales by 74% within a five-year period. Hired and trained independent factory representatives to exceed targeted sales quotas. Tailored an incentive program to optimize productivity.

AGEMA INFRARED SYSTEMS, Secaucus, NJ (9/87-12/89)

Sales/Service Representative

Introduced thermal imaging systems to the medical marketplace. Performed market research prior to product introduction.

EDUCATION

RUTGERS UNIVERSITY, Newark, NJ

* **Executive MBA, Finance Concentration**
* **Bachelor of Science Degree, Marketing**

ALEXANDER RENALDO

1234 Fifth Avenue
Tampa, Florida 33609
(813) 555-1212
E-mail: alexrenaldo@reallyhotmail.com

CAREER PROFILE

OUTSTANDING BILINGUAL CALL CENTER PROFESSIONAL with 5+ years of progressively responsible experience with an International Fortune 100 credit card and financial services industry world leader. Achieved numerous awards and performance-based bonuses due to exceptional sales, customer service, communication, interpersonal and self-management skills driven by a passion to succeed. Accomplished producer with solid computer and time management skills who consistently exceeds all business development goals, customer service performance and quality indicators.

PROFESSIONAL OBJECTIVE

Seeking to drive organizational growth and/or profitability by utilizing my proven leadership, management and training skills where exceptional achievement, production and teamwork are valued.

PROFESSIONAL EXPERIENCE

CREDIT CARD SERVICES, Tampa, Florida
Leadership Development Associate (2000 To Present)
Customer Relations Representative (1996 To 2000)

❖ Thoroughly learned the credit card and financial services industry, the extensive operational policies and procedures, proprietary company computer software and successful selling techniques.

❖ Achieved quota after one month of starting at Credit Card Services, and went on to consistently break records for exceeding sales goals.

❖ Enthusiastically provide excellent customer service by answering inbound calls from culturally-diverse cardholders from across the country regarding the company's products.

❖ Thoroughly research and solve cardholder problems by quickly navigating complex and extensive proprietary software.

❖ Demonstrate superior assessment, crisis intervention, interpersonal and conflict-management skills with angry or upset callers to smoothly de-escalate the situation and resolve their concerns satisfactorily.

❖ Quickly update accounts as needed in a timely manner and courteously handle inbound calls regarding direct mailings.

❖ Consistently exceed expectations for "quality, productivity, value creation, ownership of job performance, embracing change, responding to coaching, revenue generation and customer satisfaction" as rated in monthly performance reviews.

❖ Earned several Recognition Awards over the years for "teamwork, professionalism, positive attitude, flexibility, communication/feedback, initiative, excellence and ownership."

❖ Presented with an award for "Outstanding Performance and Commitment to Customer Service" for January to June, 2001.

Promoted to **Leadership Development Associate** in December, 2000, which involved: taking an active role in motivating teammates to achieve team goals and aspire to exceed department goals; to participate in the development of an action plan to help the team achieve the goals set for the team; to collaborate with peers and set goals for the team; to learn new aspects of the business and develop a clearer understanding of how individual performance contributes to Credit Card Services' success; to learn additional proprietary software; to identify business trends and to develop business action plans and forecasting.

THE UNIVERSITY OF BOLOGNIA, Bolognia, Italy
Instructor (1995 To 1996)
❖ Taught two Latin American studies classes weekly to twenty native Italian students for sixteen months as part of the educational experience with South Florida University.

❖ Learned Latin American curriculum in Italian and translated it into English for students.

❖ Addressed current Latin American events to stimulate practical application of the course material.

❖ Conducted research and assisted the Professor with grading and student achievement evaluations.

❖ Consistently rated "Excellent" by students.

BUDGET RENT-A-CAR, Ybor City, Florida
Manager, Truck Division (1993 To 1995)
❖ Worked for this nationwide transportation rental agency full-time while attending college full-time.

INTERNATIONAL TRAVEL, SOUTH AMERICA (1991 to 1993)
❖ Worked at odd jobs in the farming, industrial and manufacturing fields while travelling throughout South America.

❖ Worked in Rio De Janeiro, Brazil; Santiago, Chile; Cali, Columbia; and Guayaqui, Ecuador. Learned invaluable information about cultural differences, business practices, social, political and religious views of each city/country.

ROLLING HILLS RESORT, Ybor City, Florida
Server (1989 To 1991)
❖ Worked for this world-famous resort for athletes as a server full-time while attending college full-time.

McDONALD'S, Tampa, Florida
Cook/Cashier (1987 To 1989)
❖ Began working full-time with this successful international Fortune 100 restaurant at the age of seventeen while attending high school/college full-time.

EDUCATION

B.A., INTERNATIONAL RELATIONS, SOUTH FLORIDA UNIVERSITY, Ybor City, Florida (1989-1996)
❖ Minored in Latin American Studies.
❖ Lived abroad in Italy from 1995 to 1996 and studied Italian language.
❖ Taught classes to Italian students for the sixteen months spent overseas.
❖ Paid for 100% of education by working full-time while attending school full-time.

A.A., GENERAL STUDIES, HILLSBOROUGH COMMUNITY COLLEGE, Tampa, Florida (1990)
❖ Paid for 100% of education by working full-time while attending school full-time.

COMPUTER SKILLS

Windows 95, 98 & 2000   Internet Research   Proprietary Financial Services Software

ACTIVITIES / AWARDS / MEMBERSHIPS

Earned CCS "Tampa's Outstanding Performers" Award for outstanding performance/customer service (2001)
Community Service Award, CCS, Volunteer, "Unidos Por Venezuela," relief effort to help flood victims (2000)
Fellowship Recipient for Education (1989)
Golden Key Honor Society Member (1995)
Triathlon Competitor, Tampa, Florida (1990 To Present)

SAMANTHA L. BROWN

330 Park Avenue, #1212
New York, New York 10022

212-555-1212
heremail@home.net

SENIOR-LEVEL CONSULTANT - MANAGER
INTERNATIONAL BUSINESS DEVELOPMENT

PROFILE & QUALIFICATIONS

Senior Manager with unique experience in high-level strategy development and hands-on organizational leadership for domestic and multinational businesses. Proficient in conducting, interpreting and applying the results of critical analyses in support of finance, sales and marketing, and corporate development. Successful in driving revenues, competitive market positioning, profits and value. Fluent in Spanish, Italian, French and German. MBA Degree.

Strategic Planning & Tactical Action	**Business & Operations Management**
New Business Development & Strategic Marketing	**Global Business Development**
Market Research & Competitive Intelligence	**Marketing & Distribution Network Design**
Executive Liaison & Decision Support	**Alliance & Partnership Development**

PROFESSIONAL EXPERIENCE

PRESIDENT/CEO   1998 to Present
Intrabrand, Limited, Delaware, USA and Budapest, Hungary

Author and successful executor of the business plan for a management consulting firm specializing in international market entry, strategic partnering, investor relations and overseas operations on behalf of US-based technology and finance enterprises. Hold full P&L accountability for all aspects of operations, including new business development, proposal and scope of work development, contract negotiation and administration, client liaison affairs and every element of the consulting engagement (project planning, team building and leadership, strategic partnering, competitive analysis, business intelligence, marketing strategy, sales modeling, logistics, corporate governance). Key clients, projects and results:

International Market Expansion:

HavitTech   Performed country-specific competitive market and business feasibility studies for a major player in technology-driven business continuity services (e.g., website construction, networking, IT finance, IT assessment, IT asset management).

East Digital   Led a series of business intelligence strategies in Russia and former Eastern Bloc countries as part of a global market expansion for this industry leader in the manufacture of computer hard drives.

Strategic Marketing & New Business Development:

Leeon, Ltd.   Created and launched a cross-marketing program initiated in Madrid. Partnered with Spain's Country Manager in executing high-impact marketing campaigns to combat strong competitive pressure from IBM and Microsoft. Built a pipeline of business among key players (e.g., PPG, KMPG, PriceWaterhouse Coopers) representing 150% increase in annual revenue.

East Digital   Contributed to building and strengthening strategic alliances with business and sales partners in Russia and former Eastern Bloc countries. Implemented a series of country- and region-specific business intelligence plans to optimize sales for the Hardware and Computer Storage Media Division of East Digital. Served as direct point of contact to the European investment community.

Business & Operational Start-Up:

East Digital   Managed the start-up of East Digital's offshore corporation in Eastern Europe. Benchmarked product portfolio, sales model and supply chain structure against other international corporations.

Agrisel   Managed the start-up of 12 offshore sales offices and manufacturing facilities for this multi-billion dollar enterprise involved in biotechnology R&D and product development.

PROFESSIONAL EXPERIENCE – Continued

MANAGER – NEW BUSINESS RELATIONSHIPS   1995 to 1998
Julio Marcus, Inc., New York, New York

Led high-impact business development, sales, marketing and relationship building activities for this rapid-growth commodities trading firm. Identified potential customers, led presentations, evaluated investment needs, and executed initiatives and activities designed to support sales and marketing campaigns.

- Targeted and secured 15 new accounts within 45 days of hire. Delivered $7.4 million in immediate new business and unlimited opportunity for sustainable revenue.
- Conceived and executed strategies targeting relationships with international banks. Established market as a significant business channel.

PORTFOLIO MANAGER   1993 to 1995
Benson & Sons, New York, New York

Managed a $20 million asset portfolio on behalf of domestic and international clients. Handled high-value transactions including equity, debt, commodity and currency investment accounts, and served as Cash Manager for corporate, non-profit and institutional clients. Tracked market trends, analyzed financial research and leveraged the firm's top-notch research/analyst resources to make high-level investment decisions.

- Grew the discretionary asset base from $0 to $20 million through a series of aggressive business development and relationship building activities.
- Acquired and maintained a strong base of knowledge in international equities, corporate cash management and private placement transactions.

MANAGER – BUSINESS BANKING   1989 to 1993
Equibank, New York, New York

Built and managed relationships with 650+ high-net-worth private clients representing $500+ million in assets under management. Managed investment portfolios through a combination of commodity, currency and international trade transactions. Established high-level relationships with the World Trade Centers Association (WTCA) and 60+ commodity brokers.

- Ranked #1 in opening new corporate retail accounts, particularly in the international shipping and transportation industry (e.g., Blue Moon Lines, Somtex, The Port Authority of New York and New Jersey).
- Consistently successful in meeting and exceeding objectives for new business development and sales.

EDUCATION

MBA – Concentration in International Marketing, 1991
BLOOMSBURG STATE UNIVERSITY, Bloomsburg, Pennsylvania

B.S., Political Theory - Concentration in International Business Development, 1989
UNIVERSITY OF VERMONT, Burlington, Vermont

JOHN CHASE BENTLEY III

9 Willow Trail
Scarsdale, New York 10583
719-972-2840

EXECUTIVE PROFILE

- Accomplished **executive** with **senior management talent** in providing leadership on a **global** basis to multiple companies simultaneously.

- Successfully served in key leadership roles, directing **turnaround** of company's performance which ultimately led to its immensely profitable sale.

- Proven ability to manage and position **international** companies for **peak profits** as Chairman of the Board, President and CEO of a holding company and its subsidiary entities.

- Highly effective **builder and developer** of international organizations with broad expertise in formulating **strategic management** programs with strong financial and marketing emphasis to generate superior results. In short, a **catalyst for change**.

- Extraordinary ability to align corporate resources with financial parameters to **maximize desired performance and results**.

- Outstanding leadership ability in **recruiting and training** well-educated, knowledgeable professionals for present and future leadership responsibilities. Skilled in **evaluating talent** and **implementing changes** to enhance overall performance.

- **Valued** colleague, **respected** for development of **creative** solutions to achieve results in organizations requiring leadership and direction.

- **J.D. and M.B.A.** Degrees with advanced professional development credentials from Harvard and MIT.

EXPERIENCE

...A Sophisticated Strategic Management and Financial Ability
with a Proven Strategic Marketing Capability...

UNUM GROUP, London, England   **1998 - Present**

UNUM is a worldwide leader in financial, investment and insurance services with international operations and over 28,000 employees.

- **President/CEO**, VLADAR/UNUM North America (formerly Andrus Financial), New York, New York, 2001 - Present
- **President/CEO**, Andrus Financial Corporation, London, England, 1998 - 2001
- **Chairman of the Board**, Iliamer Securities, Boston, Massachusetts, 1999 - Present
- **Chairman of the Board**, Listrx Bankam Trust, Tokyo, Japan, 1999 – Present
- **Board of Directors**, LEXar Companies, Inc., London, England, 1998 - Present

Recruited by UNUM Group to develop from existing resources a performance-oriented financial services and investment management company, Andrus Financial.

Key Results:
- Developed a strategic plan outlining mission, goals and objectives.
- Realigned staff with colleagues more attuned to new corporate philosophy.
- Executed plan to maximize financial objectives; restructured investment portfolios to achieve higher performance.
- Exceeded benchmark by at least two percentage points per year.
- Generated $3.7 billion in new sales in first year of operation.
- Built an internal team which had the capability of assuming additional responsibilities throughout the entire corporation.

Managed and directed long-range execution of strategic plan.

Key Results:
- Established total rate of return as the new investment objective; realigned assets to achieve performance objectives.
- Eliminated non-liquid securities to align assets with new portfolio objectives.
- Led efforts which resulted in a highly liquid portfolio, higher overall credit quality, a more precise asset liability match and favorable acceptance by regulatory authorities.
- Initiated common stock portfolio to generate long- and short-term capital gains.

Profitably sold Andrus Financial in 2001 to German-based VLADAR Corporation.

Key Results:
- Sold Andrus Financial for 3.4 times book value with debt assumed by VLADAR.
- Liquidated real estate holdings to reduce risk, enhance liquidity of portfolios and realize capital gains.
- Named President/CEO of VLADAR/UNUM North America in January 2001.

JUSTAL COMPANIES, INC., San Francisco, California　　　　**1984 - 1998**

Justal Companies, Inc. is a holding company publicly traded on the New York Stock Exchange, with operations in financial services, insurance and real estate.　Justal Financial Services, Inc. managed the assets of the holding company, Justal Companies, Inc.
- **Chairman, President and CEO**, Justal Financial Services, Inc., 1995 - 1998
- **Board of Directors**, Justal Companies, Inc. 1990 - 1998
- **Chairman of the Board**, Profit Investments, 1990 - 1998

Key Results:

- Rebuilt company to provide enhanced opportunity for the distribution of registered products.
- Developed five-year strategic plan to significantly grow sales and registered dealers.
- Formulated a broader product base, restructured commission schedule and developed an active solicitation program of registered dealers on an international basis.
- Expanded technology capabilities to better support existing sales volume and future growth.
- Developed a compensation program to pay proportionately higher commissions than industry averages and in addition, paid commissions more quickly, becoming a key competitive advantage in solicitation of additional registered dealers.
- Grew sales force from 150 registered dealers to nearly 2,750 from 1993 – 1998.
- Grew sales from approximately $40 million to approximately $1 billion, 1993 – 1998.

SECURITIES INSURANCE GROUP, Dallas, Texas　　　　**1980 - 1984**

Senior Vice President/Chief Investment Officer
- One of three senior managers who set policy and direction for eight business divisions.
- Developed a strategic planning process to enhance the growth path.
- Restructured and modernized investment portfolios to maximize performance.
- Realigned and added new staff to execute investment management strategy.

INSURED RETIREMENT SYSTEMS, Alexandria, Virginia　　　　**1972 – 1980**

Director of Investment Research/Assistant Investment Officer
- One of five key investment officers who set overall investment policy.
- Built the investment management unit from ground floor to 32 member research team.
- Maximized the investment returns of a $3.9 billion equity portfolio.
- Developed and executed common stock portfolio strategy.

EDUCATION

J.D.　　　University of Virginia, Charlottesville, Virginia, 1980

M.B.A.　　University of Michigan – Ann Arbor, Michigan, 1972

B.S.　　　The University of Iowa, Iowa City, Iowa, 1970
　　　　　　 Economics, Sociology, and Political Science

PROFESSIONAL DEVELOPMENT

- Management Information Systems – Professional Development for 21st Century Executive Leaders, Massachusetts Institute of Technology, Cambridge, Massachusetts, 2000

- Advanced Executive Leadership Program – Graduate School of Management, Harvard University, Cambridge, Massachusetts, 1995

- International Trust School – Chicago, Illinois, 1993

- National Chief Investment Officers Leadership Series – San Diego, California, 1988

PROFESSIONAL AND COMMUNITY ACTIVITIES

- Board of Directors, Newman Stores of New York

- Investment Committee, Opera of London Foundation

- Board of Trustees, The Boston Foundation for International Relations

- Investment Committee, Briarwood Homes for Children

- Financial Advisory Council, University of Virginia

- Board of Trustees, Saint Michael's School of Vermont

- Guest Lecturer, University of Michigan – Ann Arbor

- The University of Iowa Alumni Foundation

MARTIN C. THOMPSON

ul. Marszalkowska 1554/155 ▪ 00-001 Warsaw, Poland
+48 999 00 000 ▪ mcthompson999@hetmail.com

FINANCIAL & INVESTMENT MANAGEMENT EXECUTIVE

Mastery in financing and driving/managing growth of companies into international emerging markets

AREAS OF EXPERTISE

Deliver dynamic, captivating presentations/speeches to venture capitalists, securities analysts and professionals

- Venture Capital Start-Ups / Acquisitions
- Global Business Financing / Development
- Strategic Planning / Organization Development
- Persuasive Communications / Negotiations
- Client / Team Relationship Management
- Management Information Systems (MIS)

- Financial, Investment, & Risk Management
- Infrastructure Formulation / Implementation
- Critical Thinking / Problem Resolution
- Sales / Growth / Market Share Acceleration
- Cultural / Socioeconomic Diversity
- Team Development / Empowerment

PROFESSIONAL EXPERIENCE

INTERNATIONAL INVESTMENTS, INC. – Warsaw, Poland / Miami, Florida (1996–Present)

(Exclusive licensee of Office Supply, Inc. in Central and Eastern Europe, operating 20 Office Supply superstores in Poland and Hungary with recent expansion into the Czech Republic)

Senior Vice President, Finance and Administration
Treasurer and Chief Financial Officer / Member, Board of Directors

Teamed with four-member American executive team and assumed challenge of financing growth and pioneering expansion of leading office supply retailer into emerging international markets. Created infrastructure to support growth and recruited/developed management teams in Poland and Hungary; faced enormous cross-cultural and socioeconomic difficulties. Manage all financial, accounting, legal, MIS, human resources and insurance functions.

Selected Projects / Achievements

- **Raised $40+ million** of debt/equity to finance growth, expansion and acquisitions. **Created infrastructure** sufficient to permit growth from one store ($5 million revenues) to 20 stores ($100+ revenues) in four years. Early entry and expansion **captured brand recognition and launched barriers against new market entrants.** Simultaneous development of store/delivery businesses created cost efficiencies and competitive advantage.

- Financed, negotiated and closed cross-border acquisition of the company's main competitor in Poland, which **boosted market share 30%, accelerated unit rollout program by a year (saving $600,000** in pre-opening costs) and **increased leverage with vendors, achieving 3% additional gross margin** and **15 additional days payable.**

- **Transformed insolvent Hungarian office products retailer** by recruiting/developing executive staff and leading them in start-up operations. **Piloted to profitability** and **integration as Company's Hungarian subsidiary.** Currently negotiating another acquisition to initiate similar start-up operations in Czech Republic.

- **Formulated/implemented complete GAAP-based reporting system** to provide monthly financial statements (by country, unit and department – in USD and consistent format) to investors; supplemented with analyses of sales, gross margins, operating expenses and corporate overhead. **Created special information package** for Board of Directors; distributed prior to meetings to increase their effectiveness.

- **Spearheaded the establishment of one of the first stock option plans by an American company** in Central/Eastern Europe. Offer of company stock options to 50+ Polish and Hungarian managers **reduced turnover in this key group to less than 5%.**

- **Successfully developed high-performance management teams** dedicated to common goals of company; achieved through astute staff recruitment/training, patient mentorship and motivational strategies.

PEACE CORPS OF THE UNITED STATES OF AMERICA – Washington, D.C. (1994–1995)

Small Business Development Volunteer / Advisor, Office of International Programs

Developed curricula for and taught undergraduates/post-graduates at private post-secondary business school (Zachodniopomorska Szkola Businessu [ZSB]) in Szczecin, Poland. Acquired funding through grants and implemented initiatives to stabilize/transform/modernize this newly established institution. Trained corporate managers and served as resource for other public and private entities.

Selected Projects / Achievements

- **Acquired $315,000 funding** through TEMPUS (European Union program supporting higher education) to fund two **Joint European Projects** entitled *"Development of a New Curriculum in Banking and Finance at the ZSB"* and *"Development of a New Curriculum in Insurance at the ZSB."* **Designed/authored both programs** and directed school's project partners from England, Belgium, The Netherlands and Germany in curriculum development, teacher retraining and classroom instruction. **Enabled MBA accreditation.**

- **Created/wrote Complementary Measures Grant Project** entitled *"Cooperation Toward the Development of Strategic Business Planning Skills in, and a Strategic Business Plan for, the ZSB."* **Obtained $85,000 in funding** from TEMPUS. Directed all strategic business plan writing and coordinated provision of business planning skills workshops presented by project partners from Belgium, Germany and The Netherlands.

- **Co-administered Managerial Training Program** funded by PHARE and Government of Flanders. Belgian academics and professionals presented 400 seminar hours to ZSB's Post-Graduate Studies Program attendees.

- **Initiated contacts with Sheridan College** (Ontario, Canada) and **organized initial meeting**, which led to signed agreement between schools and trade development visits among Polish and Canadian business people.

- **Authored/presented numerous comprehensive seminars/workshops**, covering topics as: *"Basic Financial Management"* (presented to accounting/finance staffs of 12 companies from the Krakow region); *"How to Succeed in Obtaining Credit"* (presented to 30 corporate managers enrolled in ZSB's Post-Graduate Studies Program); *"Employer Recruiting and Student Placement"* and *"The Changing Labor Market"* (presented to corporate managers and government officials from the Czestochowa region); and *"Investment Funds"* (presented to management of Fabryka Mechanizmow Samochodowych POLMO – designed to strengthen this automobile parts manufacturer's privatization efforts).

- **Lectured** on *"Basic Economics and the U.S. Economy"* at American Studies Center in Warsaw University.

- **Researched/authored** *"A Report on the Status of Former Military Sites in Poland"* for EU-funded DECODE (Diversification and Economic Conversion of Defense Enterprises) Program. Report **facilitated EBRD funding** for **environmental remediation** at former Soviet airbase in Szczecin region.

THE FINANCIAL EXPERTS GROUP, INC. – Chicago, Illinois (1988–1993)

(Prestigious, privately held merchant bank specializing in providing advisory services to corporations investing equity in tax-oriented equipment/facility leveraged leases and project finance transactions, as well as investing its own capital in operating companies)

Treasury Manager (1990–1993)

- **Devised/presented various asset-based financing proposals** to diverse lenders/investors in effort to secure financing for investment activity. Created packages of collateral which enabled the **successful closing of $40 million of debt**, resulting in **doubling the size of company's investment portfolio** within three years and **expanding it into the merchant banking business.**

- **Designed/created extensive, detailed database** to include company's entire financial asset portfolio, which consisted of approximately 100 investments with **estimated future cash flows exceeding $1 billion.**

- Examined client's $2 billion portfolio consisting of 160 troubled debt/equity investments and **devised strategic divestment plan** whereby performing assets worth $300 million were sold to institutions.

THE FINANCIAL EXPERTS GROUP, INC. (Continued)

Accounting Manager (1988–1989)

Directed staff of three engaged in performing all accounting and administrative functions. Prepared/generated monthly and annual financial statements, NASD reports for registered broker-dealer subsidiary and debt compliance reports for lenders. Administered risk management program and 401(k) and profit sharing plans.

- **Conceptualized, installed and implemented new accounting system**, which provided for creation of customized financial statements and special management reports required to support the financing of company's investment program and to analyze and manage the business. **Facilitated transition from advisor to full-service merchant bank.**

- **Introduced "self-direction" element to company's 401(k) and profit-sharing plans, establishing powerful tool** to aid in company's effort to attract and retain top industry talent.

WORLDWIDE CONSULTING COMPANY – Chicago, Illinois (1983–1987)

Senior Consultant, Special Services Division (1987)

- Engaged to analyze, determine and prepare damage estimate of fraud in case brought by client against one of its executives and create methodology that would be easily understandable by attorneys and judge during court proceedings. Integrated data stipulated by both sides and statistical assumptions. **Developed PC-based model** calculating damages of **$2.4 million with 95% probability**. Resulted in **significant out-of-court settlement** acceptable to client.

- Collaborated with and directed client personnel in **establishing cost accounting system** that complied with Federal Acquisition Regulations. Ultimately allowed participation and success in bid to provide long-distance telephone service and equipment to most federal government agencies.

Senior Auditor, Utilities and Telecommunications Division (1983–1986)

Supervised daily activity of financial audits, including financial statement preparation and development of recommendations for internal control improvement. Reviewed assumptions and methodologies used in financial forecasts submitted in support of testimony in public utility rate proceedings.

- **Met challenge of leading staff of 15 in auditing $250 million in federal funding** received by Chicago Board of Education (CBE); funds serviced needs of nearly 500,000 students in 500+ locations. Applied comprehensive knowledge of federal laws/requirements authorizing use of funds. **Discovered widespread mismanagement and noncompliance. Formulated and defended extensive management letter** outlining recommended systemic changes to address findings. **Saved CBE $2+ million**, allowing expansion of under-funded programs.

- **United with other Computer Audit Specialty Team members** to review/evaluate complex client EDP systems and controls. Completed special training in advanced computer audit techniques, which sanctioned qualification **to train Arthur Andersen and client personnel** through **presentation of eight seminars** on various topics in areas of accounting, auditing and PC software.

EDUCATION

KRANNERT GRADUATE SCHOOL OF MANAGEMENT
PURDUE UNIVERSITY – West Lafayette, Indiana
Master of Science in Management (1983)
Concentration in **Finance** and **Accounting**

UNIVERSITY OF ILLINOIS AT URBANA-CHAMPAIGN
Bachelor of Arts in Finance (1981)

Victor Coppolini

266 Masters Avenue
Staten Island, NY 10314

Residence: (718) 448-0219
E-mail: vcopolini@aeol.com

Profile

Senior Executive of United States Immigrations Investigations with an extensive background in government operations. History of top performance in diversified challenging assignments. Combines cross-functional performance in operations analysis, recruitment and restructuring staffing patterns to ensure the ultimate success with regard to time and cost-efficient operations.

Summary of Qualifications

Strong resource allocation, communication and negotiation skills. Comprehensive experience in project planning, management, criminal and civil fraud investigations. Fluent in Italian.

Highlight of Qualifications

- Capacity Planning & Optimization.
- Import / Export Laws & Regulations.
- Project Planning, Estimating & Control

- Successful Policy Revision
- Budget & Utilization Review
- Leadership and Mentoring

Education and Training

MA, International Law, Harvard University, Cambridge, MA
BA, Psychology, City College, New York, NY

Professional Experience

United States Immigration Investigations, New York City, NY   1995 – Present
Special Agent in Charge

Principal advisor for covert operations in the Greater New York area. Manage external relations between law entities and logistics. Direct criminal investigations of 231 employees.

- Establish strategic direction of investigative operations for the Northeastern District.
- Monitor budgets and procedures of special operations on a monthly basis.
- Enhance qualitative and quantitative statistics by improving overall agent performance.

United States Immigration Headquarters, Washington, DC   1992 – 1995
Area Director for Europe and Africa

Scope of responsibilities included monitoring operational budget of $275 million for 5,500 employees and special investigations. Evaluated firearms training and performance appraisals for large multi-task force agency.

- Developed and mentored 45 employees engaged in Intelligence Operations.
- Directed operations and significantly increased efficiency at minimum cost.
- Supervised recruitment, staffing and training for 25 foreign offices worldwide.

United States International Operations, Rome, Italy   1988 – 1992
Assistant Attaché

Established every phase of start-up office in Naples. Put into action complex program to ensure the prompt extradition of international offenders of the IEEPA Act to the U.S. Directed investigations within the jurisdiction of the Attaché office for Italy and North Africa.

- Organized and trained international task force to ensure cooperation with covert operations.
- Held training seminars on International Law Enforcement Techniques.
- Monitored work performance for 11 special agents and 7 intelligence analysts.

United States Immigration and Naturalization, New York, NY   1985 – 1988
Supervisor, Violations in Intelligence Investigations   1987 – 1988
Organized investigations for New York and New Jersey seaports. Managed teams of special agents, Immigration Patrol Officers and intelligence analysts.
- Initiated narcotics investigations group with operatives integrated from several divisions.
- Consolidated data for law enforcement intelligence.

Criminal Investigator for Immigration and Naturalization   1985 – 1987
Conducted investigations for Immigration, which resulted in numerous arrests and convictions. Planned and led numerous investigations relative to the enforcement of Immigration laws.
- Consolidated data for law enforcement intelligence.
- Achieved practical knowledge of U.S. and international law.

Honors and Awards

"Mallet Award" for redesign and efficiency of operations, 1999
"Commissioners Unit Citation," presented by the Commissioner, 1997

Affiliations

International Chiefs of Police Association.
New York Police Benefits Association.

Richard F. Atkinson

555 Lindberry Street, London England S17 3NJ
E-Mail: Richard.Atkinson@adelpheea.net

Office: 44-555-555-4200
Residence: 44-555-555-6223

PERSONAL PROFILE

Director of IT Operations for one of the world's largest global banks. Proven management and technical expertise spanning technology infrastructures in the UK, Europe, and US financial services industry, as well as in US engineering and manufacturing environments. Assertive, decisive, profit-oriented executive; recognized as a "change agent" adept at delivering "bottom line" benefits in challenging technological environments. Areas of accomplishment include:

- Large-Scale Data Center Operations
- Voice and Data Telecommunications
- Internet Technology Infrastructures
- Systems Programming/Technical Support

- Office and Call Center Automation
- Information Technology Security
- Application Systems Development
- Information Technology Auditing

PROFESSIONAL EXPERIENCE

METROPOLITAN BANK, London, England   1996 - Present

Director of IT Operations

Transferred from the US to identify and implement the people, policy, and process changes necessary to improve the performance and cost effectiveness of a 1,200 person, $350 million IT infrastructure organization within this recently acquired 1,700-branch UK bank.

- Transformed core technology units into a performance-driven team. Achieved substantial business unit cost reductions and enhanced revenue generation opportunities through technology-based centralization strategies and CRM-driven empowerment of personnel.

- Drove continuous, year-on-year improvement in availability and reliability of centralized processing infrastructure across eight different technology platforms. In 2000, achieved record availability on every single platform, with overall availability consistently well above 99.9%, the best performance in the entire global corporation.

- While improving availability, implemented significant changes in core processing technology architecture to handle a near 500% growth in online processing over five years, with volume forecasted to exceed one billion transactions per month in 2001.

- Established a fully resilient and contingent Internet processing infrastructure encompassing intrusion detection, security firewalls, load balancing, web servers, and ISP connectivity/ performance monitoring.

- Served as Global IT Operations representative on corporate Internet Strategy Task Force.

- Replaced capacity-stressed, obsolete network to 2000+ locations, enabling browser-based services and improving network availability to 99.94%.

- Established financial control disciplines across disparate technology units, reducing year-to-date budget/reforecast variances from 20% to 1%.

- Revitalized IT Security function by upgrading subject matter competencies, staff reorganization, and management restructuring.

- Selected to lead bankwide, global study of IT Operations' organizational alternatives that would achieve global corporate objectives without sacrificing support of local business unit initiatives.

PROFESSIONAL EXPERIENCE (Continued)

REGIONAL BANK, Pittsburgh, Pennsylvania   1982 - 1996

Senior Vice President, Systems Development (1993 - 1996)

Directed a staff of 100 with responsibility for the design, implementation and support of the bank's consumer lending applications.

- Proposed and implemented a consolidation of diverse product-based customer call centers into a centralized organization for improved customer service and cost reductions.

- Implemented Computer Telephony Integration (CTI), Interactive Voice Response (IVR), and Outbound Power-Dialing technologies for call center, marketing, and bad debt collection units.

- Instituted a new mortgage processing system to facilitate integration of recently acquired mortgage origination and servicing businesses into the core bank organization.

Senior Vice President, Information Technology Operations (1990 - 1993)

Responsible for centralized computer operations, voice and data communications, office automation, infrastructure software services, information security, and quality assurance, with a staff of 240 and an annual budget of $55 million. Principal interface to technology vendors and service providers.

- "Right-sized" the organization, eliminating several management levels and reducing staff count from 365 to 240 to improve cost effectiveness.

- Directed the redesign of a 400+ location branch/ATM network utilizing digital technology, resulting in improved availability/reliability and an annual operating cost reduction of $1.5 million.

- Reengineered office automation platform standards and processes for more cost effective utilization of a $30 million, 12,000+ device investment, saving $1 million annually.

Department Executive, Network Services (1986 - 1990)
Department Executive, Corporate Applications Development (1982 - 1986)

GENERAL MANUFACTURING COMPANY, Pittsburgh, Pennsylvania   1980 - 1982

Group Manager, Corporate Systems

KESSLER MINING CORPORATION, Cleveland, Ohio   1974 - 1980

Supervising EDP Auditor

EDUCATION AND PROFESSIONAL CERTIFICATIONS

UNIVERSITY OF PITTSBURGH, Pittsburgh, Pennsylvania

BSc. Engineering

OHIO STATE UNIVERSITY, Columbus, Ohio

Post Graduate Studies in Business

Certificate in Data Processing (CDP)
Certified Information Systems Auditor (CISA)

Holt Lansing

261 North Reagan Avenue • Redland, CO 80007
Phone (555) 555-1234 • htq_lansing@aol.com

INTERNATIONAL BUSINESS DEVELOPMENT MANAGER

Fifteen-year career building national and worldwide marketing and business development programs for computer platforms. Expert marketing strategist and tactician with a solid technical background and excellent negotiation skills. Results-driven performer and quick decision maker who reacts well under pressure. Strong background in building partner relationships and international customer contact. In-depth knowledge of mechanical design markets and practical application of the Internet in supply chain management. Effectively manages intra- and inter-company endeavors. Expertise includes:

Business Development	Emerging Markets
Competitive Market Intelligence	Strategic Market Planning
Consultative Sales	Tactical Market Plans
Customer Satisfaction	Supply Chain Management

Career Accomplishments

- Expanded worldwide channel fulfillment resulting in shorter delivery time and increased sales.
- Achieved highest reseller satisfaction in history of product line.
- Developed marketing programs that penetrated breakthrough accounts in U.S., Europe, and Asia.
- Spearheaded CWI's entry into mainframe alternative marketplace in Asia.

Computer Workstation, Inc.

Expansion Manager, Channel Fulfillment Programs   1998 – present
Drive cross-functional implementation of channel fulfillment programs for Europe and Asia. Define channel strategy, locate alternative resource sources, select partners, manage business event information, and localize program tools.

Accomplishments:
- Developed worldwide expansion plan including resources requirements and budgets.
- Drove allocation of resources for European expansion.
- Identified and recruited 12 European and 6 Asian distributors for program membership.
- Built formal documentation suite and presentation materials for Channel Fulfillment Programs.
- Increased sales by 50% with Pilot Partners Program.
- Achieved highest reseller satisfaction in history of product line.

Automotive/Heavy Equipment Industries Manager   1996 – 1997
Investigated, analyzed, and recommended new business opportunities in marketplace, while continuing efforts in known opportunities. Worked with worldwide regional marketing centers to build marketing plan based on complete value chain approach. Implemented, delivered, and promoted program in each region.

Accomplishments:
- Selected Knowledge-Based Engineering (KBE) as an emerging opportunity.
- Recruited and empowered KBE consultants for China Auto Show '97.
- Led participation in multi-company supply chain management project to build customer awareness, knowledge and preference for CWI expertise with collaborative tools in extranets.
- Achieved breakthrough sales at major automotive account by creatively transitioning a dependent third-party product into the product line and establishing an internal support team.

Market Development Manager, Technical Mainframe Alternative Program   **1995 - 1996**
Developed and refined target account profiles in automotive, aerospace, and heavy equipment markets. Built the entire marketing infrastructure. Created sales training program, sales guide, and customer collateral, as well as support sales teams in efforts to further penetrate accounts.

Accomplishments:
- Developed and delivered worldwide sales training.
- Created sales and customer collateral including case study, sales strategy white paper, trade press articles for each major account sale, customer brochure, interoperability guide, program newsletter, and program literature platform.
- Built relationships with key targeted accounts: Nissan Motors, Mitsubishi Truck, Hyundai Truck, IPTN Aerospace, Chinese Aerospace Ministry, Mercedes-Benz, Porsche, and Westland Helicopter.

Asia Pacific Marketing Center, 1992 - 1995

Regional Technical Mainframe Alternative Program Manager   **1994 - 1995**
Adapted U.S. and European programs for the Asian market. Prepared and delivered program information to national sales and marketing teams. Publicized regional sales. Supported local targeted account sales teams. Led efforts to localize dependent third party products.

Accomplishments:
- Penetrated 6 new accounts by replacing mainframe seats with workstations and alternative applications.
- Successfully promoted program through region tour.
- Prompted creation of a Kanji version of third-party emulator to satisfy customer needs.

Technical Client/Server Computing Program Manager   **1992 - 1994**
Generated sales with awareness. Led generation activities and managed sales force training.

Accomplishments:
- Closed complex cluster sales in Japan, Korea, and Australia.
- Established working relationship with the technical server sales force.
- Improved working relationships with analysis software vendors.

Market Segment Development Manager   **1989 - 1992**
Managed mathematical/statistical Independent Software Vendors and porting house relationships, including coordination of resources in porting projects.

Accomplishments:
- Delivered Novell's "Portable NetWare for the CWI9000."
- Trained the Novell sales force on product and cooperative selling with CWI.

Member of Marketing Staff, CWI Technical Software Center   **1986 - 1989**
Stores Supervisor, CWI   **1984 - 1986**

Education

M.B.A., University of Michigan, Graduate School of Business Administration, May 1983.
B.A., University of Chicago, Economics, January 1970

MAURICIO ENZIO
enzioenterprises@enzioenterprises.com

8700 Rock Lake Drive
Tucson, Arizona 85750

Residence (520) 625-2955
Mobile (805) 529-6647

INTERNATIONAL MANUFACTURING EXECUTIVE
New Business & Global Market Development □ Operations & Production Management

Lived and worked in China and Scotland with extensive business dealings and government relationships in Europe, Japan, Korea, Israel, Egypt, Brazil and Argentina. Foreign and/or US foreign corporate negotiations have included Motorola, IBM, Alcatel and Fujitsu. MBA Degree.

High Tech Manufacturing	Start-Ups & Turnarounds	Resource Optimization	Capacity Planning
Commercial & Military	JV & Strategic Partnering	Manufacturing Processes	Integration
Profit & Loss	Strategic Business Planning	Process Reengineering	Quality Control

Product Expansion & Channel Management

❑ Launched a redefinition strategy in Scotland for Global Electronics UK Connector Operations. Executed capability plan and successfully expanded product lines, implemented a comprehensive global sales and distribution channel management program, and penetrated the European telecom market. Strategies repositioned the business unit from a stalled start-up to 100% revenue growth by year-end 2001.

Strategic Business Planning & Program Implementation

❑ Integral part of the executive management turnaround team chartered to restructure and revitalize -- manufacturing operations, program management, contract negotiations, client relationship management, quality control and marketing communications -- for Global Electronics Access Systems. Recommendations included plant consolidations, liquidation of surplus inventory, installation of new online marketing plan and aggressive global market positioning. Combined improvements won 3-year, $3 million contract with Egyptian government, increased margins 25% and saved $2 million in operating costs.

Multinational Joint Ventures, Initial Capitalization & Organizational Development

❑ Developed business plan for US Electronics and negotiated a $10 million JV to facilitate new market entry strategies into China. Sourced and secured $4 million investment funding and led team through all phases of start-up operations, from implementation of the organizational infrastructure and senior-level staffing to installation of a vertically integrated production system.

PROFESSIONAL EXPERIENCE

Global Electronics Industries; Chicago, IL   1996 – 2001
                                                                                and 1986 – 1988

Global Electronics Connector, UK Operations; Scotland
General Manager (1999-2001)
Highest-ranking country executive retained to design and execute an accelerated growth strategy, broaden the target market, and direct a highly focused sales and distribution channel management strategy. Assumed full budgetary, P&L and capital expenditure authority. Collaborated with country leadership teams in the US, Italy, Germany, Australia and offices throughout Europe.

  ❑ Penetrated the telecom market and increased manufacturing cells from 3 to 5. Transferred a product line from the US to Scotland and won renewal of $2 million customer contract by meeting customer's need for local sourcing. Successful retooling and reengineering of the production process resulted in 25% fewer workers and 40% reduced material cost.

PAGE TWO

CONTINUED...

Global Electronics Connector, UK Operations; Scotland
General Manager (1999-2001)

- ❏ Introduced new forecasting process which substantially improved revenue predictability and doubled size of sales funnel. Combined improvements including upgraded equipment, ISO 9002 certification, newly penetrated markets and expanded product line. Delivered a 50% sales increase per employee, a 40% growth in employee base and recovery from a stalled start-up to 100% growth within 18 months.

Global Electronics Network Access Systems; Richmond, VA
Vice President Business Operations (1997-1999)

Initially rehired by Global Electronics Industries as Contracts Manager (1996-1997) and promoted to VP to lead 6 senior reports and 100 employees – in operations, quality control, contract management and program management -- through dramatic turnaround of $15 million business unit.

- ❏ Negotiated $3 million foreign military funding (FMF) contract with the Egyptian Armament Authority for tactical fiber optic communications devices. Program revitalized a dying product line and transitioned line from a harvest status to a growth product. Captured opportunity to globalize recovered line and earned an additional $5 million in European market sales.

Minton Electronics Company; Wilmette, NJ   1984 – 1997

US-Zhenjiang Electronics; PR of China
General Manager (1994-1996)
Director International Marketing (1989-1993)
Director of Contracts (1984-1988)

Promoted specifically to develop the business plan for a $10 million JV investment and secure initial working capital for start-up operations in China. Negotiated $6 million in equipment purchases and directed transfer of capital assets from division in Germany as well as product line transfers from two outside sources in Japan and China.

- ❏ Designed and implemented the factory production system on a continuous flow basis for a full vertically integrated operation including metal stamping, plastic molding, gold plating of contacts, testing and shipping. Developed the organizational infrastructure, hired senior staff, and assisted HR in creating policy, procedures and operational/manufacturing standards.

EDUCATION & PROFESSIONAL TRAINING

University Of Illinois; Chicago, IL
MBA – Organizational Management, 1996

University of New Hampshire; Durham, NH
Bachelor of Science – Finance, 1984

University of Pennsylvania, Wharton Executive Education Program
Financial Management, 2000

Additional Corporate Training Programs:
International Negotiation; International Offset; Mequiladora Operations; EDI Management;
Commerce Department Export Regulations; Chester Karass; and Stephen Covey Leadership Program

Jordan Carlos

85 Leewood Drive
Eastchester, NY 10707

(914) 961-3928
J_Carlos@yuhoo.com

International MIS Manager

- **6+ years' experience providing technical, training, and support solutions in an international arena.**
- Simultaneously held roles of technical/account manager and trainer for 5 years. Attribute success to strong blend of technical, interpersonal, and business skills.
- In-depth knowledge of current information systems technologies.
- Recognized for developing and delivering effective applications training. Skilled at working with diverse people and facilitating understanding of technical terms and concepts.
- Earned increased responsibilities through demonstrated competencies in:

Systems Planning & Implementation	**Training**
Troubleshooting & Problem Solving	**Management**
Oral & Written Communication	**Research**
Data Analysis & Report Design	**Analytical Thinking**

Technical Skills

Applications	Euronet; Magic Support; Microsoft Word, Excel, PowerPoint, Access, Project, Outlook
Communication Packages	Citrix, Cisco VPN, Procom
Operating Systems	Windows 98/NT, Unix
Hardware	Intel-based PC's, Printers, Modems
Networking	LAN/WAN, Novell

Professional Experience

EuroRail International, Inc., Elmsford (N.A. Headquarters), NY   1994-Present
Global leader in European travel-related products with 1000 employees in North America.

Account Manager (1998-Present)
Trainer (1996-Present)
Technical Support Manager/Analyst (1995-1997)
Marketing Research Analyst (1994-1995)

Key member of Computer Services Division charged with development, support, and training for an online proprietary reservation system (Euronet) to travel in 26 European countries. Rapidly became company's Euronet subject matter expert and was promoted to manage accounts and training. Managed, trained, and reviewed five support desk staff. Determined technological directions and made informed decisions based on research and analysis. Delivered training for internal and external Euronet clients in corporate headquarters and onsite at large, international accounts.

Achievements: TECHNICAL SUPPORT/ACCOUNT MANAGEMENT

- Managed 24/7 operation to support Euronet users on four continents.
- Improved procedures and managed priorities which increased end-user satisfaction. Recommended hiring additional tech support staff based on a Gartner Group study.
- Managed a database of 400+ North American accounts and system subscribers to effectively monitor and document high-volume of customer service calls.
- Impacted sales and ensured client retention by troubleshooting most challenging issues that were passed on from call centers.
- Communicated closely with area sales managers to expedite problem solving for key accounts.
- Provided feedback to programmers to develop the Java-based version of Euronet.

Continued ... Achievements: TECHNICAL SUPPORT/ACCOUNT MANAGEMENT

- Wrote weekly status report to track progress of IT department projects.
- Fostered client communication by uploading information to bulletin boards using Unix Vi editing.
- Interacted with vendors and internal clients to evaluate new database technology to replace Magic Support application.
- Oversaw new user setups including creation of Citrix logins and user profiles.

Achievements: TRAINING

- Designed and delivered a comprehensive Euronet training program for clients throughout North America, Latin America, and Australasia. Incorporated ongoing application changes into curriculum and responded to evolving user needs.
- Increased profit by providing effective training in fewer days.
- Co-authored Euronet system user manual for corporate clients.
- Completed training, on-time and within budget, of 150 Manual Sales Outlets that were converting to online booking capabilities.
- Trained personnel in an acquired Portland call center and prepared headquarters staff for increased referred support issues.
- Initiated project to move toward online training (WebEx) that would dramatically reduce expenses and enable more clients to participate.
- Provided in-house training on Microsoft applications including Outlook, Excel, and Word.

United Nations, New York, NY   1981-1993
Economic Affairs Officer/Advisor

- Directed research and analysis of international economic issues and proposed alternatives and policy positions.
- Assessed impact of transnational corporations and the emergence of trading blocs (EEC, NAFTA) on international trade and GATT.
- Developed comparative analysis of major indebted countries and recommended policy positions for member states on financing by multilateral institutions.
- Performed an econometric analysis of the OPEC oil price structure and its implications on industrialized and developing countries.
- Initiated a study correlating the impact of exchange rate volatility, international debt, and protectionism on the world economy.
- Participated in the United Nations preparatory committee meetings that led to the adoption of the International Convention on Environment and Development in Rio de Janeiro in 1992.

Education

Master of Arts, International Economics   1986
New York University, Graduate School of Arts and Sciences, New York, NY

Bachelor of Arts, Economics and Mathematics   1981
University of Michigan, Ann Arbor, MI

RICHARD B. LACKERMAN

P.O. Box 13042
Gardiner, Maine 04345 - USA
Telephone: (207) 555-5555

Cell: (207) 234-5678

Fax: (207) 432-8765

CAREER PROFILE:

Fifteen plus years of experience providing development and technical support to shoe manufacturers all over the world. Possess strong overall technical skills with the ability to assess problems in all construction areas for specific shoe groups (including materials used, design problems, product wearing issues, and/or components).

QUALIFICATIONS:

Hands-on knowledge of shoe making --- Foreman in shoe manufacturing starting with leather cutting and lasting through packing. Extensive experience gained through working for the R.J. Boss Co., Harrington Shoe Co. (DESCO), and Weinburg Shoe Co.

Construction knowledge in shoe making — Worked with cements (Casual Construction), direct injection molding, welt process, vulcanized footwear, and the California process.

Extensive knowledge of varied shoe manufacturing companies and their processes – Currently work with the following on a regular basis: Crest Shoe Co. (Iron Age), New Balance, Dexter, Eastland, San Diego Shoe (SDS), Sebago, LL Bean, Timberland, Cole-Haan, Colby, Ballet Makers, Allen-Edmonds, and Saucony Shoe Co.

Work related travel (and language) experience — Speak German as a second language; presently travel throughout the U.S. (New England States as well as Texas), Caribbean, Dominican Republic, and Mexico. Other work-related travel has included Mainland China, Thailand, Korea, and Taiwan.

ACCOMPLISHMENTS:

Lowered returns by 80% (in 3-year period) -- Set up audits of returned shoes at various shoe shops; assessed problems with manufacturing processes, components, and design; made recommendations to resolve problems.

Assisted in start-up of a Washable Shoe Program (leather to rubber) in China (1990).

Involved in the development of first waterproof golf shoe at Falcon Shoe Co., Footrest, and Explore.

Involved in the manufacturing of the first footwear made in high-oil content leather with several major shoe manufacturing factories.

WORK HISTORY:

Technical Sales	(Baldwin Industries, Berlin, NH, USA)	1974-Present
Sales	(Hiram Shoe Machine, Brooklyn, NY, USA)	1971-1974
Foreman, Lasting & Making Rooms	(Hallowell Shoe Co., Hallowell, ME, USA)	1972-1974
Foreman, Cutting Room	(R.J. Boss Co., Bowdoinham, ME, USA)	1970-1972

EDUCATION:

University of Southern Maine, Augusta, ME, USA	One Year of Computer Training
Gardiner High School, Gardiner, ME, USA	Diploma

References & Portfolio
Available Upon Request

Elaine Schlossburger   (771) 544 – 7169

7903 – P North Flowers Drive   Health - Excellent
Atlanta, Georgia 30143   U. S. Citizen

CAREER OBJECTIVE	A challenging management position where my ability to communicate, make decisions and motivate performance will make a significant contribution to a more efficient and profitable operation.
SUMMARY of QUALIFICATIONS	Over 14 years of diversified practical experience in marketing, retail and administrative management in European and Middle Eastern markets. High-quality interpersonal skills, attention to detail and loyalty to organization, as well as an innovative cost-conscious approach to operations.
MARKETING MANAGEMENT	**Marketing Representative** for a rapidly growing entrepreneurial firm providing diagnostic imaging service throughout Europe and Middle East. Responsible for developing and implementing marketing and promotion programs, defining service areas and target markets, and expeditiously closing sales.

> Developed local physician, paramedical and community support resulting in a dramatic increase in sales and a solid referral base for the imaging centers in France and England.

> Prepared and professionally presented corporate exhibits to medical association conventions and meetings throughout Europe.

> Determined market environmental factors such as demographic and geographic trends, analyzed the data and recommended realignment of marketing areas to capitalize on these trends.

> Initiated, developed and implemented new marketing strategies resulting in optimal marketing campaigns for European markets.

GENERAL MANAGEMENT	Responsible for management of several diverse organizations in Europe. Positions involved planning, coordinating and implementing programs producing cost-effective services and operations.

> **Assistant Director of Radiology** for a large regional hospital in London. Supervised 23 subordinates with diverse technical backgrounds. Directed department operations, determined priorities, scheduled and assigned tasks, guided subordinates and orchestrated throughput. Served as Interim Director for a three-month period.

> **Assistant Chief of Radiology** for a large regional hospital in Germany. Supervised 15 subordinates in the performance of Computerized Tomography, Ultrasound, special procedures and all diagnostic radiology. Applied computer systems extensively to improve information flow and decision making. Initiated, refined and successfully implemented a more efficient patient flow resulting in a significant increase in revenue.

EDUCATION	Bachelor Degree in Medical Science, Emory University, USA
REFERENCES	Excellent professional and character references available upon request.

TROY R. MASON

4024 South Madison Avenue, Schenectady, NY 12306 • Email: mastroy@mindsprung.net
Mobile: 518-322-5982 • Home: 518-295-7479 • Pager: 518-295-6532

EXECUTIVE MANAGEMENT – PUBLIC RELATIONS
INTERNATIONAL LIAISON, PROJECT DIRECTOR, HUMAN RESOURCES, SALES
GLOBAL COMMUNICATIONS STRATEGIST
Focus on Spanish Interpretation / International Communications / Business Affairs

RESULTS-ORIENTED PROFESSIONAL with unique broad-spectrum experience utilizing skills in Crisis Resolution, Troubleshooting and Project Management. Highly intelligent and astute to grasp new concepts and ideas, generating innovative solutions to problems. Superior capacity to thrive under pressure in fast-paced environments while managing and directing multiple projects from conception to fruition. Equally adept at working individually or leading productive teams.

12 years' experience in Spanish translation with **extensive global travel including Australia, Mexico, Spain, Portugal, Canada and Chile**. Master communication and interpersonal skills. Compelling capacity to work well with diverse individuals from all cultures and backgrounds; **emphasis on Mexican and Spanish cultures**. Highly charismatic with superior powers of persuasion.

Collaboration with attorneys, courtroom and government officials combined with widespread expertise encircling all levels of law enforcement including FBI, DEA, CIA; extensive knowledge of court and penal systems from an attorney's perspective including US Customs, and US Immigration. Adept at leading and planning state of affairs analysis to effect decisive and immediate action in the face of chaotic or "hostile" environments.

Fluent comprehension of written and oral Spanish coupled with an eloquent ability to convey information through the written word; basic Italian language skills.

Seeking relocation to Latin America or frequent business travel.

CROSS-FUNCTIONAL COMPETENCIES

• *Project Planning & Management*	• *Crisis Resolution*	• *Strategic Planning*
• *Regulatory & Government Affairs*	• *International Communication*	• *Issues Management*
• *Tactical Assessment / Planning*	• *Sales / Marketing*	• *Business Consulting*

VALUE OFFERED

Leadership: Conceive, develop and implement strategic plans of action to surpass objectives.

Operations: Decisive, organized problem analysis and highly effective execution of solutions. Adept at structuring tasks, plans and objectives to establish and meet goals.

Marketing: Develop and execute business planning and strategies to generate substantial revenue streams.

(Professional Experience – At-Your-Service Interpreters continued)

PROFESSIONAL EXPERIENCE

At-Your-Service Interpreters, Albany, NY   1989 – present
— *Conceived and launched business strategies, directing all marketing efforts to establish clientele.*

CEO / PRESIDENT (Facilitate Spanish Interpretation)
Unique fast-tracked position **managing and directing communications for international events** encompassing federal, state and local government, and all aspects of judicial proceedings, including **international investigations.** Liaison between Spanish-speaking and American communities.

CAREER HIGHLIGHTS

- **Challenged to direct large-scale investigation in Spain.** Collaborated with team of federal investigators to apprehend criminal suspect. Succeeded in locating missing person within only three days with initial background information limited to name and city. Commended by investigators for remarkable performance.

- Recruited to remote mountain region of Mexico to track down witness. Successfully located witness and interpreted intact interview for investigators.

- **Spearheaded Federal Investigation in Mexico** for US defense attorney to uncover due process of Mexican legal system, substantially impacting investigation for US.

EDUCATION

Bachelor of Arts, Spanish Language and Culture, Union College - Schenectady, New York – 1994
Minor: Sociology   GPA: 3.5
Lifetime Member, National Honor Roll Society since 1992

Superior Spanish Certificate, University of Lisbon - Lisbon, Spain – 1989

OTHER INTERNATIONAL EXPERIENCE

Studied and traveled extensively in Chile from 1985-1987. Comprehensive training for over two years in Communication, Teamwork, Sales Techniques, and Goal Setting. Intense training in Spanish language.

PROFESSIONAL AFFILIATIONS

Member, American Translators Association – 1990-present
Member, National Association of Judiciary Interpreters and Translators – 1994-present

VOLUNTEER CONTRIBUTIONS

Ongoing *"pro-bono"* work among the Hispanic community, providing crisis intervention as necessary.

Otto H. Obermann

318 Curtis Crossroads
Hendersonville, TN 37075

Home: (615) 822-6734
Fax: (615) 822-9442

INTERNATIONAL SALES MANAGER

In-depth knowledge of international markets, business practices, and compliance with trade regulations for distributor and manufacturing environments. Strong background in sales and account management, marketing, and staff development and training. Highly-skilled negotiator, communicating ideas clearly and effectively to "close the deal." Speak and write fluent German (native language), English, and Italian, plus conversational French. Widely traveled throughout Europe, Asia, Central America, South America, and the US. Solid computer background in a variety of software applications.

CAREER HISTORY AND ACCOMPLISHMENTS

ERICKSON, INC. – Toledo, Ohio.. 1993 to Present
A manufacturer/distributor of electrical, utility, and fastening products for utilities, contractors, industry, and government agencies.

International Sales Manager (1998 to Present)
Driving force of multi-million dollar market development and strategic international alliances in the Caribbean, Central America, Venezuela, and Columbia. Build business relationships with key executives, government officials, and industry leaders to establish and expand sales goals. Personally involved in every aspect of each deal, from the negotiation of terms and competitive price structures to the timely delivery of product.
- Exceeded first-year sales goals 45% and increased second year sales 100%.
- Consistently achieve the highest gross profit margins within the company.

Regional Sales Manager (1995 to 1998)
Promoted to direct the US Central Region consisting of 24 independent sales agencies. Managed account development activities and significantly improved sales and profitability (1997 annual sales in excess of $3 million).
- Increased prices by 7.5% within the region while maintaining required level of sales volume.

International Sales Representative (1993 to 1995)
Provided on-site customer support to 50+ accounts throughout Europe.

SISAL DISTRIBUTORS, INC. – Vienna, Austria / Memphis, TN .... 1987 to 1993
An international distributor of padding products for mattress manufacturers.

National Accounts Manager / District Director (1990 to 1993)
Created sales and marketing plans, managed promotional programs, and monitored inventory levels.
- In 1993, assumed additional role of Sales Trainer for European sales representatives.

Product Manager (1987 to 1990)
Negotiated with suppliers worldwide regarding product quality and pricing. Worked closely with custom brokers and transport companies (land and sea).
- Studied ever-changing market demands and successfully reintroduced products to US market, resulting in more than $2 million in sales in a 12-month period.

EDUCATION

International Marketing and Management – 1985 to 1987
University of Vermont – Montpelier, Vermont

Appendices

Appendix A

Keywords for International Jobs and Careers

THE BEST INTERNATIONAL RESUMES AND CVs INCLUDE KEYWORDS that speak the language of employers. The following keywords frequently appear on resumes and in letters of international job seekers as they describe their experience and capabilities and articulate their goals. They also become important topics during interviews and salary negotiations. For a more extensive examination of this subject, including examples of resumes incorporating hundreds of keywords, see Wendy S. Enelow's *1500+ Keywords for $100,000+ Jobs* (Impact Publications).

Bilingual Communications
Cross-Border Transactions
Cross-Cultural Business Practices
Cross-Cultural Communications
Cultural Diversity
Diplomatic Protocol
Diplomatic Relations
Emerging Markets Development
Expatriate Compensation
Expatriate Recruitment
Export Operations
Foreign Banking & Lending

Foreign Currency Conversion
Foreign Government Affairs
Foreign Investment
Foreign Language Translation
Foreign Nationals
Foreign Trade
Global Business Management
Global Market Expansion
Global Marketing
Global Sales
Import Operations
In-Country Recruitment & Staffing

International Business Management
International Customs
International Financing
International Liaison Affairs
International Marketing
International Mergers & Acquisitions
International Negotiations
International Project Management
International Sales
International Trade Agreements
International Travel
Multicultural Business Relations
Multilingual Communications
Multinational Business Operations
Multinational Workforce Management
Offshore Operations
Worldwide Expansion
Worldwide Operations
Worldwide P&L Responsibility

Appendix B

Resume Preparation Forms

USE THE FOLLOWING FORMS TO HELP IDENTIFY YOUR CORE SKILLS, knowledge and achievements, and then link them to your career objectives. This information will serve as the foundation for your entire resume presentation. It will clearly outline the specific skills, qualifications, experiences, and accomplishments that you offer that tie directly to the positions(s) you are seeking. When you begin to write your resume (particularly your Objective, Career Summary, and Professional Experience), remember these are the most important things to highlight in order to communicate that you have the "right stuff." These forms should also serve you well in preparation for the job interview. The information you generate here should help focus your job search around what is really important to both you and the prospective employer.

Activity #1

Identify Your Skills & Knowledge

Make a complete list of the things that you do well. This list should include both professional functions (e.g., sales, product design, joint venture negotiations, technology implementation, strategic planning, budgeting) as well as more "general" skills (e.g., organization, project management, interpersonal relations, team building/leadership, oral and written communications, problem solving, decision making).

_____

_____

_____

_____

_____

_____

_____

_____

_____

_____

_____

_____

_____

Activity #2

Identify Your Career Achievements

Make a comprehensive list of the notable achievements, successes, project highlights, honors and awards of your career, with a focus on the past 10 years of employment. Whenever possible, use numbers or percentages to quantify results and substantiate your performance.

_____

_____

_____

_____

_____

_____

_____

_____

_____

_____

_____

_____

_____

_____

Activity #3

Identify Your Career Objectives

List the industries and positions in which you are interested in career opportunities.

_____

_____

_____

_____

_____

Activity #4

Link Your Skills & Achievements With Your Objectives

Using your responses to Activity #3 (Career Objectives), select skills and accomplishments from your responses to Activity #1 and Activity #2 that relate to your objective(s). In doing so, you're making a connection between what you have to offer and what type of position you are interested in. For example, if your objective is a position in Technology Sales & Marketing Management, the fact that you have strong plastic products assembly skills is probably not relevant and therefore not necessary to include. However, the fact that you have excellent negotiation and account management skills is critical and should be at the forefront of your resume. The strategy is to select items from #1 and #2 that support #3.

OBJECTIVE #1: _____

RELATED SKILLS:

_____

_____

_____

RELATED ACCOMPLISHMENTS:

_____

_____

_____

OBJECTIVE #2: _____

RELATED SKILLS:

_____

_____

_____

RELATED ACCOMPLISHMENTS:

_____

_____

_____

OBJECTIVE #3: _____

RELATED SKILLS:

_____

_____

_____

RELATED ACCOMPLISHMENTS:

_____

_____

_____

The information above will now serve as the foundation for your resume. You have clearly outlined the specific skills, qualifications, experiences and accomplishments that you offer that tie directly to the position(s) you are seeking. When you begin to write your resume (particularly your Objective, Career Summary and Professional Experience), remember these are the most important things to highlight in order to communicate that you have the "right stuff."

Resume Experts and Contributors

THE FOLLOWING PROFESSIONAL RESUME WRITERS PROVIDED EXAMples of the best international resumes from their client files. Their work is found in Chapters 4 and 5. Representing a network of exceptionally talented career professionals, these 55 individuals can assist you at various steps in your job search. Don't be "penny wise but pound foolish" by trying to write your own resume if you know writing such an important document, which can literally change your life, is not one of your major strengths. Indeed, there is a time and place to seek professional assistance. Writing a job-winning resume, which emphasizes patterns of accomplishments, often requires the assistance of a career professional. When it comes time to write your job-winning resume, we recommend that you consider contacting the following career professionals who have a track record of success.

Lynn Andenoro, CCM, CPRW, JCTC
My Career Resource, LLC
264 White Pine
Kalispell, MT 59901
(406) 257-4035
ljande@centurytel.net
www.MyCareerResource.com

Carolyn Braden, CPRW
Braden Resume Solutions
108 La Plaza Drive
Hendersonville, TN 37075
(615) 822-3317
bradenresume@comcast.net

Alice Braxton, CPRW, CEIP
Accutype Resume & Secretarial Service
635-C Chapel Hill Road
Burlington, NC 27215
(336) 227-9091
accutype@netpath.net

Martin Buckland, CPRW, JCTC, CEIP, CJST
Elite Resumes
1428 Stationmaster Lane
Oakville, Ontario, Canada L6M 3A7
(905) 825-0490
martin@AnEliteResume.com
www.AnEliteResume.com

Diane Burns, CPRW, CCM, IJCTC, CEIP
Career Marketing Techniques
5219 Thunder Hill Road
Columbia, MD 21045
(410) 884-0213
dianecprw@aol.com
www.polishedresumes.com

Annemarie Cross
A.E.C. Office Services
PO Box 91
Hallam, Victoria, Australia 3803
011-613-9796-4464
aec_office@alphalink.com.au
aec-office.alphalink.com.au/ResumeWriters.htm

Jean Cummings, M.A.T., CPRW
A RESUME FOR TODAY
123 Minot Road
Concord, MA 01742
(978) 371-9266
jc@AResumeForToday.com
www.AResumeForToday.com

Jewel Bracy DeMaio, CPRW, CEIP
A Perfect Resume.com
419 Valley Road
Elkins Park, PA 19027
(800) 227-5131
mail@aperfectresume.com
www.aperfectresume.com

Kirsten Dixson, JCTC, CPRW, CEIP
New Leaf Career Solutions
PO Box 991
Bronxville, NY 10708
(866) 639-5323
kdixson@newleafcareer.com
www.newleafcareer.com

George Dutch, Ph.D., JCTC, CCM
George Dutch Career Consulting
Suite 750 - 130 Slater Street
Ottawa, Ontario, Canada K1P 6E2
(800) 798-2696
george@jobjoy.com
www.jobjoy.com

Nina Ebert, CPRW
A Word's Worth
25 Oakwood Drive
New Egypt, NJ 08533

(609) 758-7799
keytosuccess@magpage.com
www.keytosuccessresumes.com

Debbie Ellis, CPRW
The Phoenix Career Group/Career Concepts
103 Patrick Henry Court
Danville, KY 40422
(859) 236-4001
debbie@PhoenixCareerGroup.com
www.PhoenixCareerGroup.com

Joyce Fortier, MBA, CPRW, JCTC, CCM
Create Your Career
23871 W. Lebost
Novi, MI 48375
(248) 478-5662
careerist@aol.com
www.careerist.com

Art Frank, MBA
Resumes "R" Us
1991 Diamond Court
Oldsmar, FL 34677
(727) 787-6885
AF1134@aol.com
powerresumesandcoaching.com

Louise Garver, MA, JCTC, CMP, CPRW
Career Directions, LLC
P.O. Box 587
Broad Brook, CT 06016
(860) 623-9476
TheCareerPro@aol.com
www.resumeimpact.com

Roberta Gamza, JCTC, CEIP, CJST
Career Ink
211 Springs Drive
Louisville, CO 80027
(303) 955-3065
rgamza@earthlink.net
www.careerink.com

Susan Guarneri, M.S., CCM, NCC,
   NCCC, LPC, CCMC, CPRW,
   IJCTC, CEIP
Guarneri Associates/Resumagic
1101 Lawrence Road
Lawrenceville, NJ 08648
(609) 771-1669

Resumagic@aol.com
www.Resume-Magic.com

Elona Harkins
Absolute Jobsearch Services
P.O. Box 2776
Westfield, NJ 07091
(866) 233-8910
wehark@att.net
www.absolutejobsearch.com

Beverly Harvey, CPRW, JCTC, CCM
Beverly Harvey Resume & Career Service
P.O. Box 750
Pierson, FL 32180
(386) 749-3111
beverly@harveycareers.com
www.harveycareers.com

Suzanne Helm
Career Resource Center
11553 S. Gold Dust
South Jordan, UT 84095
801-446-4000
lhelm@coastlink.com

Gayle Howard, CPRW, CRW, CCM
Top Margin Resumes Online
P.O. Box 74
Chirnside Park
Melbourne, Australia 3116
011-61-3-9726-6694
gayle@topmarginonline.com
www.topmargin.com

Leatha Jones
Write Connection Career Services
PO Box 351
Vallejo, CA 94590
707-649-1400
Leatha@write.connection.net
www.writeconnection.net

Nancy Karvonen, CPRW, CCM, JCTC, CEIP, CJST
A Better Word & Resume
4490 County Road HH
Orland, CA 95963
(530) 865-2781
careers@aresumecoach.com
www.aresumecoach.com

William Kinser, CPRW, JCTC
To The Point Resume Writing Service
4117 Kentmere Square
Fairfax, VA 22030
(703) 352-8969
resumes@tothepointresumes.com
www.tothepointresumes.com

Ann Klint, NCRW, CPRW
Ann's Professional Resume Service
2130 Kennebunk Lane
Tyler, TX 75703
(903) 509-8333
Resumes-Ann@tyler.net

Myriam-Rose Kohn, CPRW, JCTC, CCM, CEIP
JEDA Enterprises
27201 Tourney Road, Suite 201M
Valencia, CA 91355
(661) 253-0801
myriam-rose@jedaenterprises.com
www.jedaenterprises.com

Joanne Kowlowitz
PO Box 4194
St. Johnsbury, VT 05819
(802) 684-3803
writejob1@aol.com

Cindy Kraft, CCMC, CCM, CPRW, JCTC
Executive Essentials
P.O. Box 336
Valrico, FL 33595
(813) 655-0658
careermaster@exec-essentials.com
www.exec-essentials.com

Louise Kursmark, CPRW, JCTC, CCM, CEIP
Best Impression Career Services, Inc.
9847 Catalpa Woods Court
Cincinnati, OH 45242
(513) 792-0030
LK@yourbestimpression.com
www.yourbestimpression.com

Rolande LaPointe, CPC, CIPC, CPRW, IJCTC, CCM
RO-LAN Associates, Inc.
725 Sabattus Street

Lewiston, ME 04240
(207) 784-1010
RLapointe@aol.com

Lorie Lebert, CPRW, JCTC
Resumes For Results, LLC
PO Box 267
Novi, MI 48376
(800) 870-9059
Lorie@DoMyResume.com
www.DoMyResume.com

Diana LeGere
Executive Final Copy
PO Box 171311
Salt Lake City, UT 84117
(866) 754-5465
execfinalcopy@email.msn.com
www.executivefinalcopy.com

**Nick Marino, MA, CPRW, CEIP,
  USN-Ret.**
Outcome Resumes & Career Service
710 Aurora Drive
Bishop, TX 78343
(361) 584-3121
outcomerez@earthlink.net
www.outcomeresumes.com

Linda Matias, JCTC, CEIP
CareerStrides
34 E. Main Street #276
Smithtown, NY 11787
(631) 382-2425
careerstrides@bigfoot.com
www.careerstrides.com

Sharon McCormick
111 2nd Avenue NE #915
St. Petersburg, FL 33701
(727) 824-7805
career1@ij.net

Nicole Miller, IJCTC
Mil-Roy Consultants
1729 Hunter's Run Drive
Orleans, Ontario, Canada K1C 6W2
(613) 834-4031
resumesbymilroy@hotmail.com

**Meg Montford, Certified Career Coach,
  CCM, CPRW**
Abilities Enhanced
PO Box 9667
Kansas City, MO 64134
(816) 767-1196
meg@abilitiesenhanced.com
www.abilitiesenhanced.com

Sherri Morgan
Career Resumes
1311 Keats Street
Inverness, FL 34450
(352) 637-3150
sa.morgan@att.net

Doug Morrison, CPRW
Career Planners
2915 Providence Road, Suite 250-B
Charlotte, NC 28211
(704) 365-0773
dmpwresume@aol.com
www.careerpowerresume.com

Sally Morrison
LDS Employment Resource Services
54 S. Evergreen
Addison, IL 60601
(630) 901-6012
sasbsdm@aol.com

John O'Connor, MFA, CPRW
CareerPro Resumes
3301 Womans Club Dr. #125
Raleigh, NC 27612
(919) 787-2400
john@careerproresumes.com
www.careerproresumes.com

Don Orlando, MBA, CPRW, JCTC, CCM
The McLean Group
640 South McDonough Street
Montgomery, AL 36104
(334) 264-2020
yourcareercoach@aol.com

Jean Oscarson
3610 Plymouth Place
Lynchburg, VA 24503
(434) 384-7488
JeanO@aol.com

Marilyn Perlin, M.A.
Secretary a la carte
5627 Green Circle Drive #312
Minnetonka, MN 55343
(952) 938-4202
marilynp6@aol.com

Barbara Poole, CPRW
Hire Imaging
1812 Red Fox Road
St. Cloud, MN 56301
(320) 253-0975
eink@astound.net

Rosie St. Julian, CPRW
Aicron Career & Resume Services
PO Box 184
Cypress, TX 77410
(281) 351-7950
rstjulian@aicron.com
www.aicrcon.com

Janice Shepherd CPRW, JCTC, CEIP
Write On Career Keys
2628 East Crestline Drive
Bellingham, WA 98226
(360) 738-7958
janice@writeoncareerkeys.com
www.writeoncareerkeys.com

Don Skipper, M.S., M.M.A.S., CCM
Career Research International
PO Box 870941
Stone Mountain, CA 30387-0024
(770)465-4480
dskipper@careerresearchinternational.com
www.careerresearchinternational.com

Beth Stefani, Ed.M., MBA, JCTC, CPRW
Orison Professional Services
265 Union Street, Suites 101-102
Hamburg, NY 14075
(716) 649-0094
info@orisonservices.com
www.orisonservices.com

Billie Sucher, MS
Billie Ruth Sucher & Associates
7177 Hickman Road #10
Urbandale, IA 50322
(515) 276-0061
betwnjobs@aol.com

Gina Taylor, CPRW
Gina Taylor & Associates, Inc.
1111 W. 77th Terrace
Kansas City, MO 64114
(816) 523-9100
GinaResume@sbcglobal.net
www.GinaTaylor.com

Julie Walraven
Design Resumes
1202 Elm Street
Wausau, WI 54401
(715) 845-5664
design@dwave.net
www.designresumes.com

Jean West, CPRW, JCTC
Impact Resume & Career Services
207 10th Avenue
Indian Rocks Beach, FL 33785
(727)596-2534
resumes@tampabay.rr.com
www.impactresumes.com

Deborah Wile Dib, CCM, NCRW, CPRW, CEIP, JCTC, CCMC
Advantage Resumes of New York
77 Buffalo Avenue
Medford, NY 11763
(631) 758-6435
deborah.dib@advantageresumes.com
www.advantageresumes.com

Linda Wunner, CPRW, CEIP, JCTC
A+ Career & Resume Design
4516 Midway Road
Duluth, MN 55811
(218)729-4551
linda@successfulresumes.com
www.successfulresumes.com

Index

Authors

RONALD L. KRANNICH, Ph.D., is one of America's leading career and travel specialists. He is the principal author of more than 60 books, including such noted career titles as *High Impact Resumes and Letters*, *Dynamite Resumes*, *Dynamite Cover Letters*, *Discover the Best Jobs for You*, *The Savvy Networker*, *Dynamite Salary Negotiations*, *America's Top Internet Job Sites*, and *Change Your Job, Change Your Life*. He also has written several international career and travel guides, including the popular *The Directory of Websites for International Jobs*, *International Jobs Directory*, and *Jobs for People Who Love to Travel*. In the field of travel, he is author of *Travel Planning on the Internet* and 18 volumes in the unique "Impact Guides" travel-shopping series. His work is well represented on several websites: www.impactpublications.com, www.winningthejob.com, www.contentforcareers.com, www.ishoparoundtheworld.com, and www.contentfortravel.com. Ron is president of Development Concepts Incorporated, a training, consulting, and publishing firm in Virginia. A former Peace Corps Volunteer, high school teacher, university professor, and Fulbright Scholar, he received his Ph.D. in Political Science from Northern Illinois University. He has lived and worked abroad for several years. He can be contacted through the publisher: krannich@impactpublications.com.

WENDY S. ENELOW, CPRW, JCTC, CCM, is a recognized leader in the executive job search, career coaching and resume writing industries. In private practice for 20 years, she assisted thousands of senior-level job search candidates through successful career transition. She is now the Founder and President of the Career Masters Institute, an exclusive training and development association for career professionals worldwide. Wendy is the author of 12 books including the top-selling *Best Resumes for $100,000+ Jobs* and *Best Cover Letters for $100,000+ Jobs* (Impact Publications) and the recently released *101 Ways to Recession-Proof Your Career* (McGraw-Hill). A graduate of the University of Maryland, Wendy has earned several distinguished professional credentials – Certified Professional Resume Writer, Job & Career Transition Coach, and Credentialed Career Master. Wendy can be contacted at wendyenelow@cminstitute.com.

Career Resources

T HE FOLLOWING CAREER RESOURCES ARE AVAILABLE DIRECTLY FROM Impact Publications. Full descriptions of each title can be found on Impact Publication's website: www.impactpublications.com. Books by the authors of this book are highlighted in bold. Complete the following form or list the titles, include postage (see formula at the end), enclose payment, and send your order to:

IMPACT PUBLICATIONS
9104 Manassas Drive, Suite N
Manassas Park, VA 20111-5211 USA
1-800-361-1055 (orders only)
Tel. 703-361-7300 or Fax 703-335-9486
Email address: info@impactpublications.com
Quick & easy online ordering: www.impactpublications.com

Orders from individuals must be prepaid by check, moneyorder, Visa, MasterCard, or American Express. We accept telephone, fax, and email orders.

Qty.	TITLES	Price	TOTAL
Featured Title			
_____	Best Resumes and CVs for International Jobs (Krannich/Enelow)	24.95	_____
International and Travel Jobs			
_____	Back Door Guide to Short-Term Job Adventures	19.95	_____
_____	Careers in International Affairs	19.95	_____
_____	Careers in Travel, Tourism, and Hospitality	17.95	_____
_____	Career Opportunities in Travel and Tourism	18.95	_____
_____	**Complete Guide to International Jobs and Careers (Krannich)**	24.95	_____
_____	Directory of International Internships	25.00	_____
_____	**Directory of Websites for International Jobs (Krannich)**	19.95	_____
_____	Flight Attendant Job Finder and Career Guide	16.95	_____

_____	Global Resume and CV Guide	17.95 _____
_____	How to Get a Job in Europe	21.95 _____
_____	How to Get a Job on a Cruise Line	20.95 _____
_____	How to Live Your Dream of Volunteering Overseas	17.00 _____
_____	Inside Secrets to Finding a Career in Travel	14.95 _____
_____	International Jobs	18.00 _____
_____	**International Jobs Directory (Krannich)**	19.95 _____
_____	International Job Finder	19.95 _____
_____	**Jobs for People Who Love to Travel (Krannich)**	19.95 _____
_____	Kennedy's Directory of International Recruiters	149.95 _____
_____	Teaching English Abroad	15.95 _____
_____	Work Abroad	15.95 _____
_____	Work Worldwide	14.95 _____
_____	Work Your Way Around the World	17.95 _____

Customs, Culture, and Etiquette

_____	Art of Crossing Cultures	16.95 _____
_____	Breaking Through Culture Shock	18.95 _____
_____	Culture Shock! Secrets to Maximize Business Series (8 books)	107.95 _____
_____	Culture Shock! Series (56 books)	749.95 _____
_____	Culture Shock! Successful Living Abroad Series (7 books)	94.95 _____
_____	Do's and Taboos Around the World	15.95 _____
_____	Do's and Taboos of Humor Around the World	15.95 _____
_____	Do's and Taboos of Using English Around the World	14.95 _____
_____	Figuring Foreigners Out	21.95 _____
_____	Gestures: Do's and Taboos of Body Language Around the World	16.95 _____
_____	Global Etiquette Guide to Asia	17.95 _____
_____	Global Etiquette Guide to Europe	17.95 _____
_____	Global Smarts: The Art of Communicating and Deal Making	27.95 _____
_____	International Business Etiquette: Asia and the Pacific Rim	14.99 _____
_____	International Business Etiquette: Europe	14.99 _____
_____	International Business Etiquette: Latin America	14.99 _____
_____	Multicultural Manners	16.95 _____
_____	Survival Kit for Overseas Living	15.00 _____
_____	The Ugly American	13.95 _____
_____	When Cultures Collide	19.95 _____

Resumes and Letters

_____	101 Best .Com Resumes and Letters	11.95 _____
_____	101 Best Cover Letters	11.95 _____
_____	101 Best Resumes	10.95 _____
_____	101 Great Resumes	9.99 _____
_____	101 More Best Resumes	11.95 _____
_____	101 Great Tips for a Dynamite Resume	13.95 _____
_____	175 Best Cover Letters	14.95 _____
_____	**201 Dynamite Job Search Letters (Krannich)**	19.95 _____
_____	201 Killer Cover Letters	16.95 _____
_____	**1500+ KeyWords for $100,000+ Jobs (Enelow)**	14.95 _____
_____	$100,000 Resumes	16.95 _____
_____	Adams Resume Almanac, with Disk	19.95 _____
_____	America's Top Resumes for America's Top Jobs	19.95 _____
_____	Asher's Bible of Executive Resumes	29.95 _____
_____	**Best Resumes and CVs for International Jobs (Krannich/Enelow)**	24.95 _____
_____	**Best Resumes for $100,000+ Jobs (Enelow)**	24.95 _____

_____ Best Resumes for $75,000+ Executive Jobs	15.95	_____
_____ **Best Cover Letters for $100,000+ Jobs (Enelow)**	24.95	_____
_____ Building a Great Resume	15.00	_____
_____ Building Your Career Portfolio	13.99	_____
_____ **Cover Letter Magic (Enelow)**	16.95	_____
_____ Cover Letters for Dummies	16.99	_____
_____ Cover Letters That Knock 'Em Dead	10.95	_____
_____ Cyberspace Resume Kit	18.95	_____
_____ **Dynamite Cover Letters (Krannich)**	14.95	_____
_____ **Dynamite Resumes (Krannich)**	14.95	_____
_____ e-Resumes	14.95	_____
_____ The Edge Resume and Job Search Strategy	23.95	_____
_____ Electronic Resumes and Online Networking	13.99	_____
_____ The Everything Cover Letter Book	12.95	_____
_____ The Everything Resume Book	12.95	_____
_____ **Expert Resumes for Computer and Web Jobs (Enelow)**	16.95	_____
_____ Federal Resume Guidebook	21.95	_____
_____ Gallery of Best Cover Letters	18.95	_____
_____ Gallery of Best Resumes	18.95	_____
_____ Gallery of Best Resumes for 2-Year Degree Graduates	18.95	_____
_____ Global Resume and CV Guide	17.95	_____
_____ Haldane's Best Cover Letters for Professionals	15.95	_____
_____ Haldane's Best Resumes for Professionals	15.95	_____
_____ **High Impact Resumes and Letters (Krannich)**	19.95	_____
_____ **Military Resumes and Cover Letters (Krannich)**	19.95	_____
_____ Overnight Resume	12.95	_____
_____ Power Resumes	12.95	_____
_____ Professional Resumes for Executives, Managers, & Other Administrators	19.95	_____
_____ Professional Resumes for Accounting, Tax, Finance, and Law	19.95	_____
_____ Proven Resumes	19.95	_____
_____ Resume Catalog	15.95	_____
_____ Resume Magic	18.95	_____
_____ Resume Shortcuts	14.95	_____
_____ Resumes for Dummies	16.99	_____
_____ Resumes for the Health Care Professional	14.95	_____
_____ Resumes in Cyberspace	14.95	_____
_____ Resumes That Knock 'Em Dead	12.95	_____
_____ Sales and Marketing Resumes for $100,000 Careers	19.95	_____
_____ **The Savvy Resume Writer (Krannich)**	12.95	_____
_____ Sure-Hire Resumes	14.95	_____
_____ Top Secret Executive Resumes	14.99	_____

Testing and Assessment

_____ Career Tests	12.95	_____
_____ **Discover the Best Jobs for You (Krannich)**	15.95	_____
_____ Discover What You're Best At	14.00	_____
_____ Do What You Are	18.95	_____
_____ Finding Your Perfect Work	16.95	_____
_____ Gifts Differing	16.95	_____
_____ I Could Do Anything If Only I Knew What It Was	13.95	_____
_____ I'm Not Crazy, I'm Just Not You	16.95	_____
_____ Making Vocational Choices	29.95	_____
_____ Now, Discover Your Strengths	26.00	_____
_____ Pathfinder	14.00	_____
_____ Please Understand Me II	15.95	_____

_____	Self Matters	25.00 _____
_____	What Type Am I?	14.95 _____
_____	What's Your Type of Career?	17.95 _____
_____	Who Moved My Cheese?	19.95 _____

Attitude and Motivation

_____	100 Ways to Motivate Yourself	18.99 _____
_____	Change Your Attitude	15.99 _____
_____	Reinventing Yourself	18.99 _____

Inspiration and Empowerment

_____	Do What You Love for the Rest of Your Life	24.95 _____
_____	Do What You Love, the Money Will Follow	13.95 _____
_____	Doing Work You Love	14.95 _____
_____	Personal Job Power	12.95 _____
_____	Power of Purpose	20.00 _____
_____	Seven Habits of Highly Effective People	14.00 _____

Career Exploration and Job Strategies

_____	25 Jobs That Have It All	12.95 _____
_____	50 Cutting Edge Jobs	15.95 _____
_____	100 Great Jobs and How to Get Them	17.95 _____
_____	**101 Ways to Recession-Proof Your Career (Enelow)**	14.95 _____
_____	Adams Jobs Almanac	16.95 _____
_____	American Almanac of Jobs and Salaries	20.00 _____
_____	Back Door Guide to Short-Term Job Opportunities	19.95 _____
_____	**Best Jobs for the 21st Century (Krannich)**	19.95 _____
_____	Break the Rules	15.00 _____
_____	Career Change	14.95 _____
_____	**Change Your Job, Change Your Life (Krannich)**	17.95 _____
_____	Complete Guide to Occupational Exploration	39.95 _____
_____	Cool Careers for Dummies	19.95 _____
_____	Directory of Executive Recruiters	47.95 _____
_____	Enhanced Guide for Occupational Exploration	34.95 _____
_____	Enhanced Occupational Outlook Handbook	37.95 _____
_____	High-Tech Careers for Low-Tech People	14.95 _____
_____	How to Be a Permanent Temp	12.95 _____
_____	Is It Too Late to Run Away and Join the Circus?	14.95 _____
_____	**Job Hunting Guide (Campus*Career*Center's) (Krannich)**	14.95 _____
_____	Job Smarts	16.95 _____
_____	Knock 'Em Dead	12.95 _____
_____	**No One Will Hire Me! (Krannich)**	13.95 _____
_____	Occupational Outlook Handbook	16.95 _____
_____	O*NET Dictionary of Occupational Titles	49.95 _____
_____	Quit Your Job and Grow Some Hair	14.95 _____
_____	Rites of Passage at $100,000 to $1 Million+	29.95 _____
_____	Switching Careers	17.95 _____
_____	What Color Is Your Parachute?	16.95 _____

Internet Job Search

_____	100 Top Internet Job Sites	12.95 _____
_____	Adams Internet Job Search Almanac	10.95 _____

_____	**America's Top Internet Job Sites (Krannich)**	19.95 _____
_____	CareerXroads (annual)	26.95 _____
_____	Career Exploration On the Internet	24.95 _____
_____	Cyberspace Job Search Kit	18.95 _____
_____	**Directory of Websites for International Jobs (Krannich)**	19.95 _____
_____	e-Resumes	11.95 _____
_____	Electronic Resumes and Online Networking	13.99 _____
_____	Everything Online Job Search Book	12.95 _____
_____	Guide to Internet Job Searching	14.95 _____
_____	Haldane's Best Employment Websites for Professionals	15.95 _____
_____	Job-Hunting On the Internet	9.95 _____
_____	Job Search Online for Dummies (with CD-ROM)	24.99 _____
_____	Sams Teach Yourself e-Job Hunting	17.99 _____

Dress, Image, and Etiquette

_____	First Five Minutes	14.95 _____
_____	John Molloy's Dress for Success	13.99 _____
_____	New Professional Image	12.95 _____
_____	New Women's Dress for Success	13.99 _____
_____	Power Etiquette	14.95 _____

Networking

_____	**Dynamite Telesearch (Krannich)**	12.95 _____
_____	A Foot in the Door	14.95 _____
_____	Golden Rule of Schmoozing	12.95 _____
_____	Great Connections	11.95 _____
_____	How to Work a Room	14.00 _____
_____	Masters of Networking	16.95 _____
_____	Power Networking	14.95 _____
_____	Power Schmoozing	12.95 _____
_____	Power to Get In	14.95 _____
_____	**The Savvy Networker (Krannich)**	13.95 _____

Interviews

_____	**101 Dynamite Answers to Interview Questions (Krannich)**	12.95 _____
_____	101 Dynamite Questions to Ask At Your Job Interview	13.95 _____
_____	250 Job Interview Questions You'll Most Likely Be Asked	9.95 _____
_____	Behavior-Based Interviewing	12.95 _____
_____	Dancing Naked	14.95 _____
_____	Games Companies Play	24.95 _____
_____	Great Interview	12.95 _____
_____	Haldane's Best Answers to Tough Interview Questions	15.95 _____
_____	**Interview for Success (Krannich)**	15.95 _____
_____	Interview Rehearsal Book	12.00 _____
_____	Job Interviews for Dummies	16.99 _____
_____	**The Savvy Interviewer (Krannich)**	10.95 _____
_____	Sweaty Palms	11.95 _____
_____	**Winning Interviews for $100,000+ Jobs (Enelow)**	17.95 _____

Salary Negotiations

_____	Better Than Money	18.95 _____
_____	**Dynamite Salary Negotiations (Krannich)**	15.95 _____

_____	**Get a Raise in 7 Days (Krannich)**	14.95	_____
_____	Get More Money On Your Next Job	14.95	_____
_____	Get Paid More and Promoted Faster	19.95	_____
_____	Haldane's Best Salary Tips for Professionals	15.95	_____

Travel Guides and Companions

_____	Air Traveler's Survival Guide: The Plane Truth from 35,000 Feet	14.95	_____
_____	Penny Pincher's Passport to Luxury Travel	13.95	_____
_____	**Travel Planning on the Internet (Krannich)**	19.95	_____
_____	The Traveling Woman: Great Tips for Safe and Health Trips	14.95	_____
_____	**The Treasures and Pleasures of . . . Best of the Best**		
	in Travel and Shopping (19 books) (Krannich)	269.95	_____
_____	The World's Most Dangerous Places	21.95	_____

SUBTOTAL _____

Virginia residents add 4½% sales tax _____

POSTAGE/HANDLING ($5 for first
product and 8% of SUBTOTAL) $5.00

8% of SUBTOTAL -- _____

TOTAL ENCLOSED --- _____

SHIP TO:

NAME _____

ADDRESS _____

_____

_____

PAYMENT METHOD:

❏ I enclose check/moneyorder for $ _____ made payable to
IMPACT PUBLICATIONS.

❏ Please charge $ _____ to my credit card:
❏ Visa   ❏ MasterCard   ❏ American Express   ❏ Discover

Card # _____ Expiration date: ____/_____

Signature _____

IMPACT PUBLICATIONS
The Global Career Resource Center